Governance, Development, and Social Inclusion in Latin America

Series Editors
Rebecka Villanueva Ulfgard
International Studies
Instituto Mora
Mexico City, Mexico

César Villanueva
Department of International Studies
Universidad Iberoamericana
Mexico City, Mexico

This series seeks to go beyond a traditional focus on the virtues of intra-regional and inter-regional trade agreements, liberal economic policies, and a narrow security agenda in Latin America. Instead, titles deal with a broad range of topics related to international cooperation, global and regional governance, sustainable development and environmental cooperation, internal displacement, and social inclusion in the context of the Post-2015 Development Agenda – as well as their repercussions for public policy across the region. Moreover, the series principally focuses on new international cooperation dynamics such as South-South and triangular cooperation, knowledge sharing as a current practice, and the role of the private sector in financing international cooperation and development in Latin America. The series also includes topics that fall outside the traditional scope of studying cooperation and development, in this case, (in)security and forced internal displacement, cultural cooperation, and *Buen Vivir* among indigenous peoples and farmers in Latin America. Finally, this series welcomes titles which explore the tensions and dialogue around how to manage the imbalance between state, markets, and society with a view to re-articulating cooperation and governance dynamics in the 21st century.

More information about this series at
http://www.palgrave.com/gp/series/15135

María Eugenia Rausky • Mariana Chaves
Editors

Living and Working in Poverty in Latin America

Trajectories of Children, Youth, and Adults

palgrave
macmillan

Editors
María Eugenia Rausky
CONICET, Facultad de Humanidades
y Ciencias de la Educación
Universidad Nacional de La Plata
La Plata, Buenos Aires, Argentina

Mariana Chaves
CONICET, Facultad de Trabajo Social
Universidad Nacional de La Plata
La Plata, Buenos Aires, Argentina

Governance, Development, and Social Inclusion in Latin America
ISBN 978-3-030-00900-7   ISBN 978-3-030-00901-4 (eBook)
https://doi.org/10.1007/978-3-030-00901-4

Library of Congress Control Number: 2018960400

Cover image © lutty moreira / Alamy Stock Photo
Cover design: Oscar Spigolon

This Palgrave Macmillan imprint is published by the registered company Springer Nature Switzerland AG
The registered company address is: Gewerbestrasse 11, 6330 Cham, Switzerland

Series Editors' Preface

Since the heydays of the structural adjustment programs between the 1980s and 1990s, improving the macro-economic outlook of Latin American economies while sending large groups of people into a permanent state of socio-economic deprivation has been the economic credo of many nations in the region. As a reaction to these policies, the continent has been swept by both progressive and conservative waves. First, the victory of Luiz Inácio Lula da Silva (Lula) in 2002 and new anti-poverty programs brought improvements to many of Brazil's poor. Also, the "pink tide" in the late 1990s and 2000s saw leaders like Hugo Chávez, Rafael Correa, Fernando Lugo, Luiz I. Lula, and Evo Morales put forward a stronger social agenda during their mandates, aided by the revenues generated from the "extractives boom". Then, the pendulum swung again to the right: Michelle Bachelet was replaced with Sebastián Piñera, the Kirschner era was substituted by rightist Mauricio Macri, and Brazil experienced turbulent political conflict after the ousting of Dilma Rousseff and the takeover by conservative Michel Temer. Simultaneously, the decreasing demand of China, in particular, for primary resources from the "Southern Cone" triggered economic slowdown. Many of Latin America's economies have limited capacity to find a new competitive role in the global supply chains since they are dominated by manufacturing industries and service sectors, but short of innovations and technically intensive production processes. Consequently, spending on social policies and welfare provisions was cut back, and public money invested in boosting the private sector as generator of growth. Nothing new, then, under the Latin American sun.

Throughout this period, organizations like the United Nations Economic Committee for Latin America and the Caribbean (ECLAC), the United Nations Development Programme (UNDP), Oxfam, Save the Children, and many other NGOs presented reports and documents revealing increasing poverty and socio-economic inequality in the wider continent.[1] Year after year following the same trend, over elections and across the political spectrum, cemented the precariousness experienced by large groups of people, both in formal and in informal work. The recipe was always the same everywhere; less government spending, more liberalization and deregulation, and more fiscal discipline. The Washington Consensus at its best. However, the results of many of these policies have left millions of people without real opportunities to improve their material conditions in order to escape poverty. Social conflict is on the rise and new possibilities to bring about social change are nowhere to be found. It is worth noticing that the Organisation for Economic Co-operation and Development (OECD), in June this year, published a report on the risks with "sticky ceiling" (wealth accumulation, inherited favorable life conditions) and conversely, "sticky floor" (inherited vulnerable life conditions, low upward mobility), and expressed recommendations for how to promote more social mobility in the OECD countries.[2]

For long, Brazil and Mexico, together with Chile, have stood out in statistics as Latin America's most unequal countries (as measured by the Gini Index). More than 15 years since Lula came to power, on July 1, 2018, Mexican voters decided they had had enough of corruption, insecurity, and false promises to curb poverty and inequality, and voted massively in favor of the leftist candidate, Andrés Manuel López Obrador. Known for using pro-poor rhetoric all along his political life, during his first speech on the night of the election, the incoming president said: "Para el bien de todos, los pobres primero" ("For the good of all, the poor people first"). This credo is actually reflected in the political program; more public money will be invested in improving the living conditions of more than half of Mexico's population, who are poor and extremely poor citizens. Is this a real move to tackle poverty, or just a political posture to gain power? It is hard to know if we compare different experiences in the region.

Evidently, political-economic contexts and successive governments' management of the poverty/inequality dilemma have produced different impacts on the lives of those individuals coming forward in this volume, *Living and Working in Poverty: Trajectories of Children, Youth and Adults in Latin America*, edited by María Eugenia Rausky and Mariana Chaves.

In this original, comparative volume, whose contributing authors have several years of experience researching these topics, a set of well-known relevant variables such as age, income, and gender are fundamental when studying poverty, extreme poverty, and socio-economic inequalities set in different social contexts and geographical locations across four countries: Argentina, Brazil, Cuba, and Mexico. However, if one intends to comprehend the life dilemmas and the existential vulnerabilities, then the interviews which draw from life experiences of girls, boys, adolescents, and adult women in their childhood, adolescence and adult life, make all the difference. It is a unique collection of testimonies and analyses of life trajectories shared by many people in Latin America's deeply unequal societies.

A significant characteristic of this volume is the common methodological-conceptual framework drawing on the life course approach, developed by Glen H. Elder since the 1970s. Chapter authors analyze different stages in the lives of individuals approached and their insertion into social structures like the family, community, and wider society. Some of the authors combine a quantitative and qualitative methodology, using statistical data from Permanent Household Surveys and comparing these results with smaller surveys and in-depth interviews to get a more nuanced picture. Overall, this volume is characterized by its strong commitment to anthropological and sociological research methodologies such as in-depth interviews, participant observation, reconstruction of biographies, and discourse analysis.

Facing disadvantages and vulnerability is part of a cumulative process, as the editors capture succinctly in their "Introduction". These accumulated disadvantages may appear individual but in reality they transcend both family and class, since they are conditioned by both regional and local economic-social policies of wealth redistribution; moreover, they fundamentally limit the horizon of expectations and future plans of the voices heard throughout this volume. It becomes clear from reading the individual chapters that children born in poor or even extremely poor families facing initial disadvantages in childhood—coupled with deficient support from publicly funded programs/activities targeting education and social mobility, or absence of such measures—continue leading their lives in precariousness. This is, starting life with bad odds becomes interwoven with other disadvantages that together make up vulnerable life courses.[3] In other words, to speak with the recent OECD report, many people in Latin America are stepping on a "sticky floor" in terms of persistent poverty, marginalization, and lack of social mobility. Children are particularly vulnerable and are less captured by public poverty reduction efforts than adults. Moreover, women seem to be stuck in poverty more easily than men. In particular, girls are exposed to "double inequality" because of their age and because of their sex (indeed, the city can be conceived as an "adult, masculinized space", as argued in the first chapter).[4] The gender variable plays a crucial role for determining social and work-related roles: many of the women interviewed entered motherhood at an early age, a factor often leading to school dropout. To subsist, they became domestic workers facing job uncertainty, low payment, no social protection or health protection schemes, exposed to psychological or physical abuses. The few initiatives there are to organize female domestic workers in specialized syndicates, for example in Argentina and Mexico, should be multiplied and their existence facilitated by governments, we contend.

Just as any sound volume that takes social research seriously, the concept of "work" is central for this book: the reader will encounter children working in the streets, young people being "entrepreneurs" (term here not used with euphemistic connotation), struggling to reconcile work and schooling/studying, coping with broken dreams of becoming something... For many families, putting their children to work is not really about choices or options but pure necessity to subsist. Therefore, the editors argue, the debate around child labor has to be context-sensitive, a claim to be taken seriously. Moreover, many of the interviewees started working as children, so the problem does not really rest with absence of work, "but rather the type of work and the material and symbolic rewards obtained from it", as the editors point out in their "Introduction". Importantly, "the life experiences represented here show that their efforts to survive were often invisibilized and/or characterized by denigration as they were stigmatized and blamed for the positions they occupied in society". Seen in this light, the claim that the solution to poverty is "work" becomes ambiguous, also when taking into consideration that the informal economy makes up a large share in many Latin American countries.

Some of the chapters point to the gap between the rather ambitious visions surrounding children's rights and child labor, women's rights and vulnerable groups in society (ethnic minorities, disabled persons, and elderly people) embedded in the United Nations Sustainable Development Goals towards 2030, endorsed by many Latin American governments, and the bleak prospects facing the men and women coming forward in this volume to have their life courses substantially transformed for the better.

Leading a life exposed to health and security risks in marginalized urban environments, facing class segregation and discrimination, runs like a red thread throughout the chapters. Further research could focus on how governments in the region are addressing work-related stigmatization and social exclusion, to respond to one of the key pledges in the 2030 Agenda for Development, "leaving no-one behind", and enable people to lead their life with dignity.

Lastly, we believe that those patterns of vulnerability, insecurity, and exploitation appearing in this volume are shared by many children, adolescents, women, and men in Africa, Asia, and the Middle East. This volume is a much needed contribution from Latin America to the ongoing debate about living and working in poverty at the downside of political, economic, and cultural globalization, and it occupies a special place in this series on *Governance, Development and Social Inclusion in Latin America*.

Mexico City, Mexico
July 10, 2018

Rebecka Villanueva Ulfgard
César Villanueva

Notes

1. United Nations. Economic Commission for Latin America and the Caribbean. Verónica Amarante. Income Inequality in Latin America. Data challenges and availability from a comparative perspective. Social Policy Series, 185. October 2013. United Nations, Santiago, Chile; United Nations. Economic Commission for Latin America and the Caribbean. Social Panorama of Latin America 2016; Naciones Unidas. Comisión Económica para América Latina y el Caribe (CEPAL). Bernardo Atuesta Montes, Xavier Mancero, Varinia Tromben Rojas. Herramientas para el análisis de las desigualdades y del efecto redistributivo de las políticas públicas. Junio 2018. Naciones Unidas, Santiago, Chile; United Nations Development Programme. Regional Human Development Report for Latin America and the Caribbean: Multidimensional progress: well-being beyond income. UNDP, New York, United States, 2016.
2. OECD (2018), A Broken Social Elevator? How to Promote Social Mobility, OECD Publishing, Paris. https://doi.org/10.1787/9789264301085-en.
3. Amartya Sen (1992) *Inequality Reexamined*. New York: Oxford University Press.
4. Martha Nussbaum (1999) *Sex & Social Justice*. New York: Oxford University Press.

Contents

Notes on Contributors

Gonzalo Assusa holds a PhD in Anthropological Sciences and is researcher at the National Scientific and Technical Research Council (CONICET) based at the National University of Córdoba (UNC). He is a postdoctoral fellow at the Humanities Institute. He researches about the symbolic dimension of class inequalities in relation to work and consumption in Cordoba families. He is a member of the Research Program on Social Reproduction in Great Córdoba. He has publications in the field of sociology of youth, work, public policies, and inequalities.

Ana Karina Brenner holds a PhD in Education Studies and is a professor of the School of Education and the Post-Graduate Program in Education (ProPEd) at the State University of Rio de Janeiro. She is a researcher at the Observatório Jovem do Rio de Janeiro and a member of the group of studies and researches "Learning Throughout Life." Her research topics are about youth sociology and youth and adult education, with emphasis on youth relations, political activism, and educational processes.

Paulo Carrano holds a PhD in Education and is a professor of the School of Education and Post-Graduate Programs in Education and obtained his master's degree in "Culture and Territorialities" at the Federal Fluminense University. He coordinates with the Young Observatory of Rio de Janeiro, a research group. He is a researcher and holds a "Young Scientist of our State" from the Research Foundation of the State of Rio de Janeiro (FAPERJ). His research is in the field of sociology of youth with emphasis on young people, schools, and public spaces.

Mariana Chaves holds a PhD in Natural Sciences and is an anthropologist at the National University of La Plata (UNLP). She is a professor at UNLP, Argentina. She is a researcher affiliated with the National Scientific and Technical Research Council (Consejo Nacional de Investigaciones Científicas y Técnicas (CONICET)). She is Director of the Laboratory of Social and Cultural Studies, Faculty of Social Work, UNLP. She is also a researcher at the Center for Urban Social Research Policies and National University of Tres de Febrero. She is a member of the social organization Work of Father Cajade, in the day center Young House BA. She is involved in different research projects related to youth, public policy, inequality, and urban space. She has publications in the area of youth, inequality and daily life, cultural practices, social programs, popular sectors, ethnographies, and social intervention.

Débora Gorbán is a researcher at National Scientific and Technical Research Council (CONICET) and the National University of General Sarmiento (UNGS), Buenos Aires, Argentina. In 2009, she obtained her PhD in Social Sciences at the Universidad de Buenos Aires and her PhD in Sociology at the Ecole des Hautes Etudes en Sciences Sociales in Paris. She is involved in different research projects related to women's work, informal labor, representations of work, and inequality. Her research topics are related to labor transformations and their consequences on the experiences of the popular sectors, ethnographies of labor, interclass social boundaries, and conflicts around inequality.

Begoña Leyra Fatou holds a PhD in Social Anthropology at Complutense University of Madrid (UCM) (Spain). She obtained her master's degree in Gender and Development at Complutense Institute for International Studies (ICEI). She obtained her bachelor's degree in Social and Cultural Anthropology and degree in Social Work at UCM. She works as a full-time Professor in the Social Work and Social Services Department at UCM (Faculty of Social Work), and she is also Director of Gender Area and Academic Secretary at ICEI.

María Eugenia Rausky holds a PhD in Social Sciences at the University of Buenos Aires. She obtained her master's degree in Methodology of Social Sciences (National University of Tres de Febrero and University of Bologna). She is a sociologist. She is a professor at the National University of La Plata, Argentina. She is a researcher affiliated with the National Scientific and Technical Research Council. She is a co-director of the

Center for Interdisciplinary Methodology of Social Sciences at the Institute of Research of Humanities and Social Sciences (Faculty of Humanities and Educational Sciences). Her publications are in the area of poverty, childhood, child labor, and methodology.

Magela Romero Almodovar is an Auxiliar Professor and a researcher in the Department of Sociology at the University of Havana since 2005. She holds a PhD in Sociological Sciences from the University of Havana. She obtained her master's degree in Gender Studies in 2009 and in Sociology in 2010. She graduated in Sociology in 2005 and Law in 2010. Her research is about gender, social inequalities, and paid domestic work.

Ania Tizziani graduated with a degree in Sociology from the National University of Buenos Aires and then holds a PhD in Sociology from the Université Paris I Panthéon-Sorbonne. Since 2009 she has worked as a researcher at National Scientific and Technical Research Council (CONICET), based at the National University of General Sarmiento. Her research topics are oriented toward women's work, including unpaid, precarious, and informal domestic work, and inequality.

List of Tables

CHAPTER 1

Introduction

María Eugenia Rausky and Mariana Chaves

The life stories we tell in this book, the social conditions we interpret and the trajectories we analyze occur in territories of Latin America. According to various studies, this is the most unequal region in the world. Notwithstanding occasional periods of economic growth, inequality persists and is reproduced over time, causing serious problems and obstacles for the achievement of the United Nations Sustainable Development Goals looking toward 2030. Governments, political movements, civil organizations and individuals have all sought to combat and bring an end to poverty in a myriad of ways through programs, plans and unequal investment. However, despite these efforts, poverty persists throughout Latin America. Poverty is reproduced as wealth is reproduced. While not unique to Latin America, the ongoing mechanisms that generate poverty and wealth are entrenched in the region's economic, productive and social regimes and their systems of wealth accumulation.

M. E. Rausky (✉)
CONICET, Facultad de Humanidades y Ciencias de la Educación,
Universidad Nacional de La Plata, La Plata, Buenos Aires, Argentina
e-mail: erausky@fahce.unlp.edu.ar

M. Chaves (✉)
CONICET, Facultad de Trabajo Social, Universidad Nacional de La Plata,
La Plata, Buenos Aires, Argentina
e-mail: mchaves@fcnym.unlp.edu.ar

M. E. Rausky, M. Chaves (eds.), *Living and Working in Poverty in Latin America*, Governance, Development, and Social Inclusion in Latin America, https://doi.org/10.1007/978-3-030-00901-4_1

The chapters in this volume reconstruct an image of what it is like to live and work in poverty at different stages of life in four different countries: Argentina, Brazil, Cuba and Mexico—during the same time frame. This shared period of time does not imply shared ideologies, public policies or a similar management of poverty in these countries.

This chapter first traces a brief overview of the Latin American scene to show structural features of social inequality and poverty. Second, it shares the conceptual tools used in the research. Third, and finally, it outlines the structure of this book.

Socio-economic Context

Latin America, on a continental and historical level, has experimented with numerous colonial and developmental models, mostly viewed today as ranging along the neoliberal, neodevelopmental and post-neoliberal spectrum. However, it should be remembered that each country has been through cycles with specific local processes linked to political traditions, social policy development and different relationships to the global market and world geopolitics. Sometimes these processes have more or less in common with other countries in the region.

According to the Economic Commission for Latin America and the Caribbean (CEPAL, 2016), inequality is mainly caused by the heterogeneous structure of the economic and productive systems, whereby sectors of high productivity coexist with sectors of low productivity, often in huge metropolitan centers (Chavez Molina, 2015). CEPAL (2016) claims that "The link which connects this heterogeneous productive system and its inherent inequality in terms of access and quality of employment to the acute inequality of household income is the labor market. Data on structural heterogeneity reveal that a high percentage of jobs (43% in 2013) are concentrated in sectors of low productivity."

These lower sectors generally do not demand much from workers in terms of technical skills and offer jobs which can be characterized as informal, low paid and with little or no access to social security protections. According to Bárcena and Prado (2016), inequalities caused and reproduced by the productive structure overflow from this sphere, extend into labor and social spheres and are interwoven with inequalities of gender, ethnicity, race and age. Hence, there is a notably higher percentage of young people, women and nondominant ethnic groups in conditions of poverty.

Although poverty and inequality have persisted in structural terms in our societies, several indicators show that the evolution of recent decades has not occurred uniformly. Subsequent to the well-known "structural adjustment" suffered by Latin American economies throughout the neoliberal agenda of the 1990s, the early 2000s saw a post-neoliberal turnaround in some countries of the region. This occurred in both Argentina and Brazil, where widespread measures were undertaken to combat poverty and inequality (Pérez Sáinz, 2014). Other countries such as Mexico, on the other hand, have remained faithful to the dominant neoliberal agenda.

The early 2000s saw notable economic changes throughout the world, and although Latin America and the Caribbean retained their standing as the most unequal region, the Gini[1] index showed some gains compared to the previous decade. Improved distribution of wealth was registered in 15 of the 17 Latin American countries with the exception of Costa Rica and the Dominican Republic. This trend took place within a context of sustained economic growth and the reduction of poverty in the region (Jiménez, 2015). It is worth noting, however, that these statistics allow for a homogenized overview which does not reveal the specific reality of each country and certain internal populations which have continued to remain in poverty.

One of the most evident expressions of inequality, as shown by CEPAL (2018), is the income gap found at the extremes of wealth distribution. According to data from a survey of households in 2016, the richest quintile received 45% of income wealth, while the average income of the lowest quintile received only 6% of income wealth. Moreover, the income of the richest 10% is approximately equivalent to the lower three quintiles which make up 60% of the population. The same source also demonstrates that the income gap between the groups of highest and lowest incomes has been reduced since the beginning of the early 2000s. Between 2000 and 2012, the income of the first quintile went from 4.8% to 6.2% while that of the fifth quintile decreased from 50.7% to 45.0%. This trend toward lowering inequality continued from 2012 to 2016 but, to a lesser degree, causing some analysts to refer to a standstill in the process of the reduction of income inequality.

Another interesting finding from the Gini index[2] is that Latin America showed an average value of 0.467 in 2016; however, when we compare three of the countries under study, Brazil and Mexico are found to have values over 0.500, while Argentina shows values less than 0.400 (CEPAL, 2018).

The reduction in Gini values was accompanied by a decrease in poverty, notably in urban areas, from 2002 to 2008. Economic expansion resulted in an increase in employment together with a moderate increase in real incomes for households. This together with a series of social policy measures brought down the figures for poverty by 25% and extreme poverty[3] by 33%. The global economic crisis of 2008–2009 affected economic growth, but measures for protecting wages and jobs, together with a speedy recovery in growth, meant that poverty did not increase and continued to decline in the first decade of the twenty-first century (Fuentes Knight, 2014). Data show 45.9% of the Latin American population in poverty in 2002 and 12.4% in extreme poverty, with figures reaching their lowest point in 2014 showing 28.5% and 8.2%, respectively. However, this promising trend began to slow down and even show a reversal in later years. In 2015 the figures rose to 29.8% and 9% and then again in 2016 and 2017 with 30.7% of the population in poverty and 10% in extreme poverty (CEPAL, 2018).

Age and gender are key factors in the incidence of poverty and extreme poverty, as revealed in our interviews with girls, boys, adolescents and adult women. In Latin America, children 0–14 years make up the largest category of persons in conditions of poverty, reaching a figure of 60% (almost double that of person of 60 years or older). Children are also 50% more likely to suffer extreme poverty than the rest of the population. The reduction in the poverty rate during the period 2002–2006 did not affect all age groups in the same way. For children it was reduced by little more than a fifth, while for most adults of working age, there was almost a 50% reduction. Therefore, as of 2016, 47 out of 100 children under 15 continue to live in conditions of poverty and 17 out of 100 continue to live in conditions of extreme poverty (CEPAL, 2018).

As regards gender variables, the CEPAL data on poverty and extreme poverty did not show a substantial difference in aggregated rates: 31.3% of women compared to 30.1% of men were in poverty, while the extreme poverty rates were 10.2% and 9.8%, respectively. However, there are notable differences when certain life stages are studied; a higher rate of poverty was found in women 15–29 and 30–59 years (CEPAL, 2018).

As mentioned above, the labor market functions as a space where the major effects of structural inequality are found, where the rewards of productivity are distributed, where employment and wages are stratified and where there is access or obstacles to social security (Bárcena and Prado, 2016). The period 2002–2013 saw a notable reduction in unemployment (2.8%) across the region, with women and young people, who had systematically suffered higher than average unemployment, benefiting from this trend. However, the current recession in some parts of the region and low growth in others has effected a reversal of this trend, with a slight increase in unemployment for the first time since 2009 (the second since 2002). The decrease in urban employment by 0.3% has led to more self-generated work which often means a worsening in working conditions and access to benefits (CEPAL, 2016).

This brief overview of some key indicators for the Latin American scene aims to give the reader an idea of the structural context within which the life trajectories of this book are set. The girls and boys, youth and adult women whose lives are represented here occupy the most disadvantaged positions in the social structure, working from an early age in activities with low income and low skill. They are the most vulnerable, a sector of the population which have barely benefitted from regional economic improvements.

Methodological Tools

A qualitative approach was used in the research compiled for this volume. This serves, on one hand, to provide a perspective from the point of view of the individual concerning his or her own trajectory and conditions of life and, on the other hand, to appreciate each particular case within its own location. Interviews were the main tool for data collection, although some researchers also used participant observation and mixed methods, combined with quantitative statistical sources. Types of analysis also vary and include discourse analysis and statistical analysis. However, the central thread of the compilation is the focus on life course and the interpretation of trajectories concerning work and poverty.

The life course approach is a theoretical and methodological perspective which recognizes the importance of different stages in the lives of agents and their insertion in specific historical contexts and emphasizes the interdependency of individuals and the important role of the family as the space where a person first interprets the social world. The key principles of this approach are (1) socio-historical and geographical location, (2) timing of lives, (3) heterogeneity or variability, (4) "linked lives" and social ties to others, (5) human agency and personal control and (6) how the past shapes the future (Elder, 1994, 1998; Elder, Kirkpatrick Johnson, & Crosnoe, 2003).

The approach is not new but has gained increasing vitality in recent years, particularly in Latin America where several authors have studied trajectories in relation to inequalities (Bayon, 2015; Mora Salas & de Oliveira, 2014; Saraví, 2009, 2015). Other authors who have revitalized the sociological debate on inequality in relational rather than asymmetrical terms are Dubet (2015), Goldthorpe (2012), Reygadas (2004), Therborn (2015) and Tilly (2000).

The chapters of this book comprise studies which use this general methodological framework, and while not all the elements of the original approach are used by every writer, all of them analyze life trajectories within their different socio-historical contexts and geographical locations. Each chapter outlines the specific context of each country where the social interactions take place, and positions are represented both as perceived and as occupied. The study of Argentina over three chapters analyzes different stages in the life course: childhood, youth and adulthood. Childhood trajectories were studied in Mexico, youth in Brazil and adulthood in Cuba, allowing a level of comparison between the different realities of poverty and work in the different socio-political contexts and an understanding of the multiple ways in which poverty is reproduced.

Researchers in many countries in Latin America are faced with the methodological difficulty of limited written records related to individuals in their different life stages; therefore the reconstruction of trajectories, through biographical narratives and interviews, provides an extremely valuable tool for gaining knowledge about the reality of life in poverty. In this vein, we are aware that the use of only women's trajectories in the chapter on adulthood could be seen as limiting and that the life stage of old age is absent from this study. However, we hope to provide an insight into diverse realities of poverty in different life stages and to show how disadvantage is a cumulative process which severely affects any future plans of the subjects. Both the adult women studied in Cuba and the young people studied in Argentina had been living in poverty as children and adolescents. In our commitment to social change, we sincerely hope that the children living in poverty who participated in this research will be able to tell us at a future date that their life conditions of adolescence and adulthood have been favorably transformed.

The life course approaches in this compilation confirm the hypothesis that life in poverty is frequently socially influenced by a series of accumulated disadvantages which may appear individual, but which transcend family and class, are conditioned by both regional and local social policies of wealth redistribution and are determined in many ways by the position of each country within the global economy. This body of work also disputes the idea that the solution to poverty is "work." The problem is not the lack of work itself, since the subjects have worked since they were children, but rather the type of work and the material and symbolic rewards obtained from it. The life experiences represented here show that their efforts to survive were often invisibilized and/or characterized by denigration as they were stigmatized and blamed for the positions they occupied in society.

Outline of the Book

In Chap. 2, Begoña Leyra Fatou presents a study on child labor in Mexico The main objective of this chapter is to analyze the limits established between the city as an adult, masculinized space and the girls who work in the streets of Mexico City. By means of an ethnographic approach, this study deals with three aspects that are essential to an understanding of this phenomenon. First, the spaces of girls' work will be analyzed, visibilizing the double inequalities to which they are exposed because of their age and because of their sex. Second, gender differences in working conditions comparatively with a group of boys. Finally, based on the analysis of these inequalities, it is necessary to review the discourses and programs of social attention to childhood derived from the 2030 Global Agenda on Sustainable Development.

In Chap. 3, María Eugenia Rausky shares the results of a mixed methods research project developed between 2014 and 2016 in the urban area of the city of La Plata (Buenos Aires, Argentina), with children who work in the streets. Through the analysis of the life stories of these workers, this research aims to reveal the heterogeneous ways in which the new generations inhabit a part of their life course: childhood and youth. The reconstruction of the trajectories allows showing the different risks to which these children are exposed throughout childhood, as well as the different ways in which integration into the social fabric can be blocked.

In Chap. 4, Gonzalo Assusa and Mariana Chaves analyze how people between 15 and 24 years old work and live in poverty. These young people have several years of working experience, since most of them began working during childhood or adolescence and are part of families—both nuclear and extended—with low incomes. Methodologically, the text has been based on the complement of field work by the two authors. Chaves's field work was located in a suburban neighborhood of the city of La Plata (Province of Buenos Aires), and Assusa's field work was located in different neighborhoods of the city of Córdoba (Province of Córdoba). Both made interviews and kept records of participant observation. Population analysis through Permanent Household Survey (PHS) processing is also provided, contributing elements for an initial characterization of the situation of working and poor youth in Argentina, which also allows us to make diachronic (change in time) and synchronic (differences and inequalities among social classes) comparisons that make possible for readers from other regions to understand the strong trends in social conditions in Argentina. The richness of combining both data records and the complement of quantitative and qualitative results provide a much wider interpretation framework for the analyzed phenomenon.

In Chap. 5, Ana Karina Brenner and Paulo Carrano focus on the processes of poor young people going into adult life taking the relationship between school and work as the main vector. The empirical basis of the discussion comes from quantitative and qualitative data obtained through the study "Jovens Fora de Série" (outstanding holdbacks) about young high-school students in the city of Rio de Janeiro between 2013 and 2015.

In Chap. 6, Débora Gorbán and Ania Tizziani focus on the labor trajectories of a group of women who enter the labor market mainly through paid domestic work. The study of these trajectories will enable us to see how the characteristics of the ways that they enter the market considerably limit their occupational mobility. For this reason, the form of labor mobility observed among domestic workers is strictly horizontal. In cases when workers do find a way out of domestic employment, it is into other occupations with similar characteristics. Based on a qualitative study that have been carrying out in Buenos Aires since 2009, the chapter examines these forms of mobility so as to account for the dynamics of inequality that limit the horizon of opportunities for women from popular sectors in the world of work.

In Chap. 7, Magela Romero Almodovar, based on a qualitative study, proposes a reading of the configuration and reconfiguration processes experienced by domestic workers and paid domestic work in the informal space after the labor restructuring process, who has been implementing since 2008 in Cuba. There are problems associated with this type of work, which reappear and worsen in the current context and could be pointing to possible setbacks in terms of social equity and gender. In this sense, it is interesting to understand how these women have reached this situation, what and how their labor trajectories have been, how social inequalities in this sector are (re) configured within the current context, which persist in relation to previous periods and what factors have contributed to reproduce them over time.

Finally, the Conclusion reflects on the main results from each chapter and points to future research in the main areas of study.

Notes

1. The Gini coefficient measures the empirical difference between persons or households relative to what would be a line of perfect equality. Values from 0 to 1 calculate the absolute difference in the average incomes of two persons selected randomly from the population compared to the overall average income in that society.

2. The work by Gasparini, Bracco, Galeano and Pistorio (2018) on inequality in developing countries categorizes a country as one of very high inequality if it has a Gini value 50 or above, high for a coefficient between 40 and 50, medium for between 30 and 40 and low inequality if the value is below 30.
3. In Latin America, the measurement of poverty is made through the use of a "poverty line" based on estimating the income that a household, according to its composition, requires to satisfy its basic food and non-food needs. For it: (1) the income that households receive is calculated, and (2) the value of the Total Basic Basket (CBT) is calculated, which determines the poverty line. Households with incomes lower than the CBT are poor, and those who do not reach to cover the Basic Food Basket (CBA) live in extreme poverty. In developed countries there is a tendency to use a "relative" criterion, which sets the poverty line in relation to the average income of a country. In this way, poverty is considered a situation of "relative deprivation," in which an individual is more or less poor according to how much others have.

Bibliography

Bárcena, A., & Prado, A. (2016). *El imperativo de la igualdad. Por un desarrollo sostenible en América Latina y El Caribe*. Buenos Aires, Argentina: Siglo XXI.

Bayón, M. C. (2015). *La Integración Excluyente*. Mexico City, México: Bonilla Artigas/IISUNAM.

CEPAL. (2016). *Estudio Económico de América Latina y el Caribe. La Agenda 2030 para el desarrollo sostenible y los desafíos del financiamiento para el desarrollo*. Santiago de Chile, Chile: UN-CEPAL.

CEPAL. (2018). *Panorama Social de América Latina 2017*. Santiago de Chile, Chile: UN-CEPAL.

Chavez Molina, E. (2015). Desigualdad y movilidad social en un contexto de heterogeneidad estructural: notas preliminares. In E. Chaves Molina (Ed.), *Desigualdad y movilidad social en el mundo contemporáneo. Aportes empíricos y conceptuales. Argentina, China, España y Francia* (pp. 117–138). Buenos Aires, Argentina: Imago Mundi.

Dubet, F. (2015). *Por qué preferimos la desigualdad*. Buenos Aires, Argentina: Siglo XXI.

Elder, G. (1994). Time, Human Agency, and Social Change: Perspectives on the Life Course. *Social Psychology Quarterly, 57*(1), 4–15.

Elder, G. (1998). The Life Course as Developmental Theory. *Child Development, 69*(1), 1–12.

Elder, G., Kirkpatrick Johnson, M., & Crosnoe, R. (2003). The Emergence and Development of Life Course Theory. In J. T. Mortimer & M. J. Shanahan (Eds.), *Handbook of the Life Course* (pp. 3–19). New York, NY: Kluwer.

Fuentes Knight, J. A. (2014). *Inestabilidad y desigualdad: la vulnerabilidad del crecimiento en América Latina y el Caribe, Libros de la CEPAL, 128*. Santiago de Chile, Chile: CEPAL.

Gasparini, L., Bracco, J., Galeano, L., & Pistorio, M. (2018). *Desigualdad en países en desarrollo ¿ajustando las expectativas?* Documentos de Trabajo CEDLAS.

Goldthorpe, J. (2012). De vuela a la clase y el estatus: por qué debe reivindicarse una perspectiva sociológica de la desigualdad social. *Reis, 137*, 43–58.

Jiménez, J. P. (Ed.). (2015). *Desigualdad, concentración del ingreso y tributación sobre las altas rentas en América Latina, Libros de la CEPAL, 134*. Santiago de Chile, Chile: CEPAL.

Mora, M., & de Oliveira, O. (2014). ¿Ruptura o reproducción de las desventajas sociales heredadas? Relatos de vida de jóvenes que han vivido situaciones de pobreza. In M. Mora & O. De Oliveira (coord.), *Desafíos y Paradojas. Los Jóvenes frente a las Desigualdades Sociales* (pp. 245–312), Ciudad de México, México: Colmex.

Pérez Sáinz, J. P. (2014). *El tercer momento rousseauniano de América Latina. Posneoliberalismo y desigualdades sociales* (Working Paper Series 72). Berlin: desigualdades.

Reygadas, L. (2004). Las redes de la desigualdad: un enfoque multidimensional. *Política y cultura, 22*, 7–25.

Saraví, G. (2009). *Transiciones vulnerables: Juventud, desigualdad y exclusión en México*. Mexico City, México: CIESAS.

Saraví, G. (2015). *Juventudes Fragmentadas: Socialización, Clase y Cultura en la Construcción de la Desigualdad*. Mexico City, México: FLACSO.

Therborn, G. (2015). *Los campos de exterminio de la desigualdad*. Buenos Aires, Argentina: Fondo de Cultura Económica.

Tilly, C. (2000). *La desigualdad persistente*. Buenos Aires, Argentina: Manantial.

PART I

Childhood, Poverty and Child Labor

CHAPTER 2

Resizing Children's Work: Anthropological Notes on Mexican Girls

Begoña Leyra Fatou

Introduction

Mexico City is one of the most populous cities in the world, presenting a cultural mosaic of opportunities, bursting with social and historic references. While I walked through its streets, squares, and boulevards, I encountered an apparently diverse or pluralistic population that has made the street its own habitat of subsistence, with markets, *tianguis*,[1] street peddling, improvised stalls, and so on. This is a way of life in which the separation of the formal sphere from the informal, and the private sphere from the public one, is notably difficult to define.

Among this diversity of working people, I frequently found girls in different urban activities: working at stalls selling food, vegetables, and other articles; peddling at traffic lights, in the subway, on the *micros*[2]; performing these jobs within the family sphere or through a contractual relationship (implicit or explicit).

B. Leyra Fatou (✉)
Complutense University of Madrid (UCM), Madrid, España
e-mail: mbleyra@ucm.es

M. E. Rausky, M. Chaves (eds.), *Living and Working in Poverty in Latin America*, Governance, Development, and Social Inclusion in Latin America, https://doi.org/10.1007/978-3-030-00901-4_2

The ages of the girls varied, as well as the type and significance of the tasks performed, and each girl's own perception of the concept of work. According to information on the phenomenon of children's work, there are more boys than girls working outside their homes in Mexico and girls are more often relegated to domestic tasks (INEGI, 2015; STPS, 2014). Girls are to be seen selling products in different areas of the city, as singers, musicians, clowns, *pepenadoras*, window cleaners, baggers in supermarkets: girls' labor takes many forms and warrants adequate analysis.

The origins of children's work in Mexico are complex and multifaceted (UNICEF, 1999). On one hand, some types are driven by development, in the form of regional imbalances, unequal distribution of incomes, explosive urban growth, and the dispersion and isolation of the rural population. The process known as megalopolization (Luna & Gómez, 1992) also plays a part, as well as the migratory influxes experienced by Mexico City in different decades of the twentieth century, especially from 1980 to the present. On the other hand, new social processes have also contributed to this phenomenon: migratory currents incorporating increasingly large populations of minors and women, as well as family disintegration and the increase in single-parent homes (mainly headed by women), leading to changes in cultural norms and values (Estrada, 1999a).

Current economic policy has also encouraged the creation of family-run businesses that require a specific kind of work force. These businesses have resorted to networks of relatives to sustain themselves. As a consequence of these combined circumstances, one out of every five families does not obtain sufficient income for food, while one out of every two people who live in the country and one out of every nine of those in the city live in conditions of extreme poverty (ILO, 2016; UNICEF-CONEVAL, 2013).

In this context, this study's aim was to discover the particularities of working girls compared to working boys and the girls' differentiated processes of socialization, leading to inequalities and fewer social rights. I also wanted to review how studies on childhood can help to avoid these injustices.

Writing about girls means writing about women: from childhood to adulthood, the historical succession of discrimination and marginalization exercises significant influence on how their life stories play out. For adult women, this disadvantageous situation has created an enormous parallel response in theoretical and scientific production, rebellion, and vindication, mainly through the feminist movement. However, writing about girls implies additional challenges due to the lack of specific information included about them in childhood studies. They are lost in the gap between studies of women and studies of "children," where boys, whose situation does not always reflect that of girls, predominate as subjects. Therefore, this study attempts to unite two theoretical spheres that have traditionally been differentiated: women and childhood. My objective is to cast a ray of light on working children, from the particular experience of girls.

Based on assumptions of urban anthropology, gender, and work and understanding childhood as a crucial period in our lifetime that determines possibilities and leaves lasting impressions (Saraví, 2015), in this chapter I intend to analyze the limits established between the city as a masculine, adult space and the girls working in the streets of Mexico City. I will also explore some of the strategies they have created for cushioning the challenges presented by work and living environments, finding ways to reconstruct their perception of the city and create less harmful spaces within it, despite the structural complexity that surrounds them.

By viewing these girls through this particular lens, I intend to demonstrate how gender, class, and ethnic inequalities that are influenced by context and formed throughout childhood have a direct impact on their adult lives. Likewise, this chapter reveals how a gender-based analysis of these studies constitutes a fundamental tool for analyzing how inequalities and differences in life experience in the urban area are expressed and how the area contributes to reproducing gender relationships within each specific geographic, social, and time context (Ciocoletto, 2004; Chant, 2013; Durán, 2008; Falú, 2002; Falú & Segovia, 2007).

From the feminist studies perspective, an attempt has been made to address these inequalities, advocating for intersectional approaches that explain the persistent poverty, discrimination, and exclusion of millions of human beings, and how these inequalities are formed and reinforced from birth. Gender inequality is not a women's issue, but rather a social issue since it affects the overall process of growth and development. When we discuss the significance of gender, inequality is a crucial factor, whether it is related to power, access to resources, or the ability to make decisions. The rules, values, and norms that control the sexual division of work and the distribution of resources, wealth, responsibilities, power, and so on are the critical elements that comprise the nature of gender inequality in different spaces and societies (Carballo & Leyra, 2017). Gender inequality varies depending on time and space, which gives rise to what is known as the geography of gender (Kabeer, 2015). This geography of gender helps us explain the differences in institutions, repeating patterns in homes, and gender divisions associated with resources and responsibilities that occur in different regions of the planet. Similarly, this chapter also focuses on distinctions between productive and reproductive, paid and unpaid, and domestic and public. Lastly, this study and approach toward Mexican girls also aims to contribute some ideas for consideration regarding the challenges presented by the 2030 Agenda for Sustainable Development, which recognizes the interconnection between gender inequalities, the deficient fulfillment of the rights of women and girls, and the issues presented by the current inequitable and unsustainable economic governance.

Methodology

This chapter is but a limited selection of observations and a reflection of the data obtained during ethnographic fieldwork performed in longitudinal sequence from September 2002 to September 2005 (in two phases of work for a total of 21 months) with working girls and their family environments in Mexico City. This research was carried out using the characteristic techniques of social and cultural anthropology (classic or holistic ethnography) (Bernard, 2002; Hammersley & Atkinson, 1994; Reeves, Kuper, & Hodges, 2008) and the qualitative techniques of the social sciences in general (Denzin & Lincoln, 1994; García Ferrando, Alvira, Alonso, & Escobar, 2015; Strauss & Corbin, 1990). The techniques used were (i) individual (semi-structured) in-depth interviews; (ii) informal (unstructured) interviews; (iii) participant observation of the boys and girls in various common areas, as well as observations of their families and communities, accompaniment in their work routines, help with homework, and accompaniment in play activities; (iv) life stories from the girls considering the theoretical and methodological hypotheses of the life course perspective (Elder, 1998) and work genealogies of their families; (v) review of bibliographic, journalistic, and documentary sources; (vi) consultation of statistical sources and social indicators; (vii) analysis of drawings (combined with the interviews with the youngest boys and girls), undertaken with the aim of searching for aspects of the socialization surrounding children's work.

Scientific work on childhood ethnography is not highly developed, and this caused some difficulty at first, as other strategies were needed to approach the subject, working girls, adapting the ethnographic techniques to the different conditions of each case. For example, I combined interview techniques with drawings, which provided a great deal of information and were a way of overcoming the monotony of a regular interview for a nine-year-old girl.

The interviews came after a long period of other approaches, after playing games, helping with homework, and, always, working previously with the family. Similarly, participant observation was crucial for my work, providing more data than the interviews themselves. As such, a qualitative approach was essential to this work on childhood, given that quantitative data alone would have made it impossible to reach deeper into the issue. Boys and girls are social subjects with rights, and the holistic vision offered by ethnographic research helps to understand this complexity. A number of important international studies on childhood also support the importance of going back to ethnography with boys and girls in order to understand the different phenomena and contexts that surround them (Atkin, 2016; Boyden & Ennew, 1997; Brannen & O'Brian, 1995; Christensen & James, 2000; De Leeuw, Borgers, & Strijbos-Sits, 2002; Holzscheiter, 2016; Liebel, Overwien, & Recknagel, 2001; Mayall, 2002; Myers, 1999; Schlemmer, 2000).

I chose seven observation sites for my fieldwork: the neighborhood of Tepito, Colonia Morelos, the Central Supply Station of Mexico City, Colonia Santa María La Ribera, Sonora Market, La Merced Market, and the Chimalhuacán garbage dump. These sites held a vast representation of types of children's work, as well as being areas of importance for trade activity in Mexico City. I chose 29 girls (and their respective households) according to variables such as the type of work carried out by the girls, the type of household to which they belonged—taking into consideration residence and relationship criteria—the place of work, and their ages. These girls were between 4 and 15 years of age (in Mexico the celebration of the 15th birthday, "the *quinceañera*," is a ritual which marks the transition from childhood to adolescence), and they worked *on* the street[3] and in public areas (alone or accompanied) within the urban area (specifically in the Mexico City Metropolitan Area). I included the working girls and their families, as well as some working boys, within the scope of observation and analysis, which enabled me to analyze gender differences. I carried out a total of 81 in-depth interviews.

Regarding the contents of the interviews, I structured the interview designs for adults, boys, and girls in four main blocks: sociodemographic data, socialization and family/domestic unit, work, and ideological aspects. These four blocks are fundamental to fully understanding the meaning of children's work; they unfailingly complement one another in understanding the complexity of this phenomenon.

The criteria for selecting the domestic units, starting with the girls as the point of reference (this being the reason that all ethnographic quotes and references to kinship are in relation to the girl who is *Ego*), were determined according to certain variables such as the kind of work the girl did, the kind of household to which she belonged (taking criteria of residence and kinship into account), the place of work, and age. The girls belonged to households with the following structure: 12 extended households (4 of them were *reconstructed* households[4]), 11 nuclear households (7 of which were reconstructed), 5 monoparental nuclear families (headed by women), and 1 extended monoparental family (headed by a woman).

When I analyzed these domestic units, I broke them down by the number of members, age, job typology, work space, and other data that could be relevant to the study (such as the dynamics of production, reproduction, and consumption)—understanding the complexities of the families helps to understand the reality that surrounds the working girls and the particular details of their life and work.

The jobs girls do (job typologies) that were finally selected were:

- peddling (in open areas or inside the indoor market)
- sales at a *chácharo*[5] stall
- stall assistant at an indoor market
- collection and sale of cardboard
- salesperson in the *abarrotes*[6] shop
- sales in a permanent street stall
- *lava trastes*[7]
- salesperson at a shoe stall
- cooking assistant
- *maquila doméstica*[8] or home production worker
- *pepenadora*[9] in an open-air garbage dump and *pepenadora* in a closed market container
- clown and outdoor artistic activities
- *cerillita*[10]
- food server
- beggar[11]

It is also important to highlight the fact that many of the girls combined different tasks and activities. The simultaneous combination of activities depended on other momentary, family, and economic factors, as will be shown in the analytical section of this chapter.

The City and the Girls: Incompatible Spheres? Social Control and Use of Space

From a theoretical approach, we can see how people in charge of urban planning usually work with abstract categories such as "population," "homes," and "families"; consequently, the answers they give on these matters do not consider the diversity of needs in the social universe, nor do they contribute to reducing gender discrimination (Falú, 2002). Studies for which the *Urban Habitat* is understood as a historical-social construction have necessarily led to intersections between different disciplines and fields of knowledge. In these studies, gender analysis constitutes a basic tool for analyzing how inequalities and differences in life experience in an urban space are expressed and how this space contributes to reproducing gender relationships in each specific geographic, social, and time context (Ciocoletto, 2004; Chant, 2013; Durán, 2008; Falú, 2002; Falú & Segovia, 2007).

Traditionally, the abovementioned studies and the actual social configuration and construction of men and women and boys and girls have relegated women to the private sphere, considering the public and productive sphere to be for men. For several decades, the feminist movement[12] has tried (with partial success) to demolish these exclusionary dichotomies by promoting equality between men and women and otherwise rethinking ways to approach gendered power relationships. Major demands arising through different waves of feminism include ending the patriarchy, vindicating the public significance of the personal sphere, denouncing oppression against women, advocating for sexual and reproductive rights as well as voluntary abortion, and seeking equality in the professional and/or educational fields. Currently, regardless of great progress, these demands are still a key feature of political agendas focused on women and girls.

Critical contributions by feminists call into question the universal principles of the studies, with the aim of overcoming women's invisibility. This invisibility is especially remarkable in the urban field. Studies of generalized paradigms often consider "masculine" as a universal trait and "feminine" as a particular one, falling once more into dangerous dichotomies built around the relationships between genders.[13] In the case of the girls in this study, the same thing happens as with studies about women: they are encompassed within a masculine space, while their specific experiences of the phenomenon and situations studied are largely ignored, silenced, and considered too obvious to mention. However, these other studies (e.g. Anker, 2000; Bar-Din, 1995; Bey, 2003; Cunningham & Viazzo, 1996) leave aside anthropological reflections and social interventions such as the participation of girls in public spheres; work as an element of socialization and as part of family relationships; the use of time, space, and money; and the different proportions of social control for girls and boys. They fail to take into consideration the differences in gender, thus perpetuating the legitimacy of inequalities due to the weight of tradition and culture.

Being a girl and a woman in Mexico (as in many other parts of the world) carries a complex moral burden, as the market and the streets where they work are a common area, where everything is known, and they must look after their image, watch what they do and with whom. Following the dichotomies of the male-centered model, boys are considered "by nature" to be more rebellious, more independent and autonomous, and therefore lower levels of demand and control are directed toward them than toward girls and women.

The following anecdotes provide a sense of women's own perception of the dangers inherent in their lives:

> *Well, you already know it is more dangerous for a woman than for a man and truthfully, well yes, I say to women: "such-and-such a time" and at such-and-such a time they have to be here, I worry more about the girls than the men.* ***(Mother of a 15-year-old working girl)***

> *When we have permission to go out, I feel as if [my brother] has more because he is a man, and when I want to go out, my mother only says "who are you going with, and I want you here at such-and-such a time", or she even waits for me until I come back.* ***(14-year-old working girl)***

Female presence depends on the environments and on the different jobs performed in them: for example, women's visibility is greater in areas like kitchens, meal preparation, or the sale of food products, due to "women's domestic role" being extended to the public sphere.

When asked what work women and men and boys and girls do, the majority answered that women work in meals and food and that men do not (when one actually sees many men working in food-related jobs). They also stated that girls looked after younger brothers and sisters, while their brothers worked outside the home.

> *Women work in kitchens, they prepare food, make tortillas, wash the dishes (...) there are hardly any men...well, there are but they work in different things such as the tortilleria, selling keys, coffee.* ***(Brother of 13-year-old working girl)***

> *Other girls also stay home looking after their younger brothers and sisters while their brothers work outside the house.* ***(9-year-old working girl)***

In other areas, we see how discourse and practice continuously contradict one another as women realize that they work more hours than many men. This is demonstrated through income differences, despite the continuing expectation that men should assume the family's "expenses." The image of the man as "head of the family" persists, and it is interesting to see how in homes led by women, the absence of men makes women more strict when controlling their children, especially their girls, as there is certain fear of harassment for "looking" vulnerable, without a male figure to "protect" them. This vulnerability that is assumed in girls is gradually assimilated by them and turns into a greater dependence on men (who may be their fathers, brothers, friends, partners, or boyfriends). This also encourages them to develop worse future prospects. Many subjects either had not even thought about their future or already assumed it would involve tasks of assistance and care.

One example of this situation is the interesting response by the mother of a 15-year-old girl, a discourse that captures all the weight of "how things should be." Her daughter's future (at least on the level of discourse) is conceived according to the man she will marry, reflected particularly in the phrase "she will leave me." Her son's future, due to patrilocal residence, will remain within the organization and decisions of the family.

> *If she did not get married, as long as she is with me, I plan to send her to school; she should keep studying, finish that degree and go on to another. And if she gets married, she won't be able to, because if her husband lets her, I could help with the expenses so that she can keep studying, I would talk to him and tell him, let her finish studying this, even if I have to pay the expenses, well, yes, because I would really like her to finish studying this degree. If, once she finishes she doesn't get married, I already told my son, too, son, keep studying, but it's easier for him, you go to school, keep studying, if you end up getting married and you're living with your wife, I can help you, don't worry about that, even though you're grown up, keep studying (...) if you get married or get together with someone and you want to finish the degree you're doing, or you want to continue, you can, because, imagine, if he is going to school and his wife is at home, I can take*

> *care of the expenses, that's my idea, help his wife and he can continue studying. For her (her daughter), this is harder, she will go away from me, maybe my son will live with me, I can't know that, and she is my daughter, I'm not going to say then go away, she needs to find a house. I have also thought about if she gets married and things don't go well, I'd bring her back to my house or go get her and help her to see where she could go and live with him, if I see that they both get along, well, I'd help them, but if I see that he isn't getting along with her, well, then I'd talk to my daughter, see what you should do. But as for studying, I can't, because that depends on him, on her husband, no matter how much I would talk to him, but if he doesn't want her to, I can't make him.* ***(Mother of a 15-year-old working girl)***

Then there is the case of another girl who, despite the importance her mother places on marriage and on the attention that she should give to her husband, still wants to join the army in the future:

> *No, I don't want to be a teacher any more, I want to go into the army, because I like it, but my mother says she doesn't want me to go into the army, because she says if I end up getting married, I'll devote myself more to the army than if I get married and have my children.* ***(12-year-old working girl)***

However, reality often weighs more than any hint of change, so girls' expectations are lower and their plans are limited.

> *The future…well, I have never had plans for the future, I'm not one of those people who makes plans, because I feel like I make plans and then everything falls apart, so whatever comes will come and, if things go well for me, that's good, and if things go badly, well there's nothing to do about it… I think that I'll work until I meet someone who loves me and marries me, I don't know, because I'm not going to quit this job.* ***(13-year-old working girl)***

Working Conditions from a Gender Perspective: Job Routines and Tasks Assigned

As with other events that involve women and girls, and especially girls, work has been considered in scientific studies as a generalized whole, without considering the specific elements faced by women and girls as a group, as distinct from those of men and boys.[14] Likewise, the definition of work has included numerous meanings with a certain amount of overlap and ambiguity between them. Neither have the important contributions of women's work to societies (not only within the family in the strict sense and/or in the reproductive sphere) always been considered worthy of analysis.[15]

From a feminist point of view, if we are to develop a more realistic perspective of social analysis, we should include the different activities people carry out to satisfy their subsistence needs. Thus, we can observe how our industrialized societies work and subsist by means of processes we could call "production and reproduction." Goods, people, and relationships are produced and reproduced. All of these processes are completely related and interconnected and inseparable. Human participation in these processes is usually called work, employment, or activity, and the definitions and limits of each—perhaps with the exception of employment—are unclear. Among these "jobs or activities," three can be pointed out as the most relevant, both for their magnitude and for their meaning: employment (or self-employment), housework for the family, and citizen engagement. The first, employment, is socially assigned to men. Unlike other forms of work, employment is remunerated and is therefore the only one that the economy considers legitimate "work." The second, housework, has traditionally been carried out by women with the objective of caring for human life. The third, also known as volunteer work, includes a large variety of activities carried out in different social spaces and plays a significant role in what we could call social cohesion (Carrasco, 2004, 2013; Pérez Orozco, 2006, 2015).

There has been criticism from different disciplines regarding the ambiguity or lack of precision given to the concept of "work," especially when the term is applied to the activities carried out by women and girls. This criticism argues that this category is biased in nature, emphasizing the need to analyze different forms of work activity, both remunerated and unremunerated. This is particularly true when comparing the terms "work" and "employment": traditionally, the term "work" was used in a wider sense (covering remunerated and unremunerated work), while the term "employment" refers specifically to remunerated commercial work (Benería, 2005; Benería, May, & Strassmann, 2011; Carrasco, 2004, 2013; Elson, 1979; Elson, Fukuda-Parr, & Vizard, 2012).

According to the United Nations Children's Fund (UNICEF), the concept of children's work may be considered at different levels (Alarcón, 1994: 135). The *first level* considers children's work to be any activity carried out by boys and girls in the productive field, trade, and services, including all occupations performed in the informal sector, in formal companies, and on farms, as well as housework and prostitution. According to this approach, begging and robbery, despite being subsistence behaviors, are separate from the economic system and can be categorized as "marginal activities."

A *second level*, more restricted in nature, defines children's work as any legal activity performed by children that has the following characteristics:

- Children participate directly in production processes, trade, and provision of services.
- The goods or services must be consumed mainly outside the boy's or girl's home.
- Children may or may not receive a salary, which does not necessarily have to be money, for these activities.
- Participation means temporal regularity, certain hours of the day or days of the week.

In general, UNICEF[16] (1997: 32–45) considers there to be many forms of children's work throughout the world, although these activities may be grouped into seven main types: (i) housework/domestic labor, (ii) menial or forced work, (iii) sexual exploitation with commercial purposes, (iv) industry and plantation work, (v) work on the streets, (vi) work for the family, and (vii) girl's work (considered a specific type of work, as it is a sector of the population with added problems ranging from sexual harassment to exclusion from education).

Nevertheless, there are other theoretical approaches (Cussianovich & Márquez, 2002; Liebel, 2003, 2013; Liebel & Martínez, 2009) that prefer not to limit the definition to statistical aspects, moral judgments, or economic terms or to equate the term with specific activities. These approaches do not even qualify children's work as something about which there is a "common understanding," as there is no common understanding on a worldwide level. Rather, these theories favor a definition that takes into consideration the specific circumstances of each culture. They have a broad understanding of the great number of activities that are objectively and/or subjectively promote the individual or social reproduction, and they consider a wide spectrum of work forms. Although this definition may seem excessively broad, it serves to differentiate children's work from other children's activities, without obviating the broad spectrum of culturally characterized work forms, including subjective judgments and assignments of meaning. As Hungerland and colleagues explain, "The search for causes proceeds from a view of child work that sees it exclusively as a social or economic problem, but not as an open field marked by widely differing forms and conditions, and which involves multifarious experiences for the children" (Hungerland, Liebel, Milne, & Wihstutz, 2007: 10).

In all the areas where I did my fieldwork, I searched for different types of children's work; although my objective was to understand the working lives of girls, I could not leave boys out, as numerically there are many more boys than girls, according to census data. Boys and girls perform similar tasks, except in specific types of employment such as *diableros*—I did not find girls pushing a *diablo*[17] and I did not see boys washing clothes; this may be the most evident difference, while boys and girls alike were found performing the other tasks in similar numbers.

As for family ties, tasks are generally related to the professional activity performed by the adults of the home unit—for example, if the mother and the father have a fruit stand, both boys and girls will work at the stand. The gender differences manifest themselves in different ways: not in the performance of the duty in itself, but rather in the forms of payment, in the capacity to decide whether to work in other places or not, and in the use of leisure time with male and female friends.

For example, gender differences are highly visible regarding control over activities and the use of free time. Boys are allowed greater mobility than girls and it is easier for them to have relationships with both men and women, while adults tend to exert control over who girls can be friends with and how these friendships work. Gender differences are also visible in the way tasks are assigned, to whom they are assigned, and in the value given to the activities assigned to boys and girls. The same thing happens in the adult world: housework and care-giving work are undervalued compared to physical activities, contact activities, and competitive activities; these last kinds of activities are reflected particularly in games and group dynamics.

> *[My brother] has been working with my father, and I stay at home taking care of my brothers, because I am a woman.* ***(12-year-old working girl)***

> *[The girl] stays with her dad selling things, [the boy] goes out by himself. It's more dangerous for a woman to go out on the street alone, a boy isn't the same as a woman, if he wants to go to work he can go alone, but his father says: "I'm in charge here and if [the girls] want to go out they need to go out with their father."* ***(Mother of an 11-year-old working girl)***

Q: Who washes the clothes? *A: My mother and we girls, we're the women…we wash other big things, each one of us washes our clothes, the clothes that are there. And my mother washes, we wash some of each of my brothers' clothes, and my mother washes my little brothers' clothes, and some of the jackets and coats.* Q: Do the men wash clothes? *A: No.* Q: And who cooks? *A: My mother cooks and we help her.* ***(10-year-old working girl)***

Similarly, in many rural and urban families, the assignment of different tasks seems to be the center of boys' and girls' socialization. This double standard for boys and girls also finds its way into other areas beyond the differentiated assignment of tasks. According to Córdova (1996: 23), "male children are expected to be moving around all the time, bothering people, demanding things, while little girls should be docile, quiet, and obedient."

Table 2.1 lists some of the most common activities and tasks that are carried out throughout the day (both inside and outside the home), based on observations and reports obtained during fieldwork. The table shows mainly the activities that both boys and girls do—in other words, activities that are socially assigned to both boys and girls.

Table 2.1 Distribution of activities and tasks by sex

Distribution of activities and tasks	*Girls*	*Boys*
Work (according to the typologies)	Yes	Yes
Washing cooking utensils (outside of the home)	Yes	Yes
Washing cooking utensils at home	Yes	No
Sweeping shops or work stalls	Yes	Yes
Sweeping and picking up at home (*desescombrar*)	Yes	No
Caring for younger brothers and sisters	Yes	No
Washing the family car or truck	No	Yes
Doing errands (during work hours)	Yes	Yes
Doing errands (near home)	No	Yes
Taking the *diablo* and loading merchandise	No	Yes
Making beds (*levantar-tender camas*)	Yes	No
Preparing food at home	Yes	No
Washing clothes	Yes	No
Totals Yes-No	**10 of 3**	**7 of 6**

Source: Original data (from author's investigation carried out between 2002 and 2005)

The quantitative results show that girls carry out 77% of the activities listed compared to boys, who carry out 54% of these activities. In addition, the repercussions of different tasks must be analyzed from a qualitative point of view, including their socially assigned value and the time that it takes to do them. The activities carried out by girls are nearly equally divided between activities in the home and outside of the home (60% at home and 40% away from home) and they take more time, taking up more of their day and thus causing them to have less free time and fewer chances for leisure activities. Boys' activities are mostly carried out in the public sphere (10% at home and 90% away from home), generating more freedom of movement for them, as well as more time for other leisure and relational activities.

Evidently, washing the car does not take the same amount of time as washing the clothes, nor are the effort and temporal framework the same. Caring for younger siblings requires a different level of attention and dedication from doing errands when one comes home, even though, in the father's and mother's eyes, both boys and girls "apparently" collaborate in the work routines and in the family obligations.

Contributions and Reflections on the 2030 Agenda for Sustainable Development and the Sustainable Development Goals

Since 1989, when the United Nations Convention on the Rights of the Child (CRC) laid the foundation for considering children as individuals with rights, studies addressing phenomena affecting childhood have provided a significant and binding referential framework, as well as conceptual models for most of the activities and policies currently focused on childhood. Without a doubt, the CRC has led to a new way of understanding childhood. The CRC's most basic concept (Gaitán & Liebel, 2011; Liebel, 2006) is known as the "best interest of the child" and views children not only as being in need of protection and aid measures but also as individuals who possess their own rights and are responsible for their own life and growth. As such, they are viewed as being able to take part in decisions that concern them.

Taking into account the challenges posed by child labor in the last few decades (ILO, 2015),[18] multilateral institutions have developed a series of regulations and approaches[19] aimed at providing answers to this complex reality.[20] For example, the 2030 Agenda for Sustainable Development (henceforth "2030 Agenda") problematizes certain aspect of the working world, specifically child work. The importance of decent work for creating sustainable development is presented in Goal 8, whose objective is to "promote sustained, inclusive and sustainable economic growth, full and productive employment and decent work for all."[21] Likewise, the 2030 Agenda addresses child labor with Goal 8.7[22] in which it exhorts governments to:

> *Take immediate and effective measures to eradicate forced labour, end modern slavery and human trafficking and secure the prohibition and elimination of the worst forms of child labour, including recruitment and use of child soldiers, and by 2025 end child labour in all its forms.*

In the 2030 Agenda (UNICEF, 2014, 2015), we see undeniable progress in the efforts to overcome child labor, exploitation, and forced labor; however, sometimes the confusion over terms describing child work, the homogenized vision of the phenomenon, and the exclusion of contextualized analyses lead to the desired results actually undermining children's ability to make decisions, determine their own lives, and place value in their personal and vital processes that are promoted and defended by the CRC. Child work is part of family dynamics, routines, and habits and, in many instances, is normalized and internalized in daily dynamics:

> *I get up at 8 o'clock, I eat breakfast, I bathe and then I'm off to work, I help my mom, err…sell, arrange things, until a quarter past two, I eat lunch in the stand or sometimes I go to school and eat there, until six, then my mom comes and picks me up and then I play, do my homework, watch T.V. and after that I go to sleep.* ***(11-year-old working girl)***

Moreover, UNICEF (1997: 24) recognizes the existence of a large variety of activities that, when performed, do not imply a negative effect on boys' and girls' development. Children's work becomes *exploitation* when working conditions restrict children's access to school, involve danger, or are in any way harmful to their physical, mental, moral, or social well-being. UNICEF explains that for children's work to be considered exploitation, one or more of the following characteristics must occur:

- Full-time work at an excessively early age
- Prolonged work hours
- Jobs that cause improper tensions of a physical, social, or psychological nature

- Work and life on the street in bad conditions
- Inadequate remuneration
- Excess of responsibility
- Jobs that hinder access to education
- Jobs that undermine the children's dignity and self-esteem, such as slavery or menial work and sexual exploitation
- Jobs that are prejudicial to full social and physiological development

However, in order to avoid confusion between the identification of child work and the exploitation of child work, we must review the different variables that make it a complex phenomenon that goes beyond the economic aspect and forms part of cultural knowledge and the life experience of successive generations. Child work is integrated into family dynamics and must therefore be analyzed as a multidimensional phenomenon (Bourdillon & Boyden, 2014; Estrada, 1999b; Nieuwenhuys, 1996). In Mexico, we find this same complexity in the spaces where girls work, in the duties they perform, and in the very concept of what is public and what is private. The street functions as the stage where cultural rules learnt are played out; it is presented as the workplace, the place for trade and recreation, the place of social practices, of journeys and movements. The street is an area of multiple interactions and it is polysemic, presenting itself simultaneously as what is ours and what belongs to others (González, 1999: 547–548). If we take a closer look at the reality lived by Mexican girls, the street becomes a second area of socialization outside the family environment, not as a neutral and asexual area, but contemplated in all its dimensions and magnitude, incorporating multiple elements with which working women and children start to shape and identify themselves.

For Manar Hammad (2006), it is important to analyze not only the functions of a public space but also the potential actions it makes available. For this reason, it is worth exploring how Mexican women and girls use and appropriate the work area and the living area, to avoid falling into conceptual distortions that will later have repercussions on the social assistance programs and the public policies created around them. Ethnographic discourse presents the workplace as one of the spaces where friendships are made, on the same level as school, and that work activity is also a focus of identification within a peer group:

> *The majority of friendships are from here in the market, they spend all day here, from school, too... but they spend more time with the people in the market, basically you are just never at home.* ***(Mother of a 9-year-old working girl)***

> *My friends are from the market, well, the ones I spend most time with are from the market (...) well, since my cousin and my brother are here, the kids get together here at my stall more.* ***(13-year-old working girl)***

Working infancy is a phenomenon that occurs throughout the world and has existed since ancient times, both in developing and developed countries. As proposed by Roger Hart:

> *The place of work in children's lives in the industrialized and developing countries is a complex subject which cannot simply be resolved only through single pieces of legislation which prohibit children from working or which require more schooling. Experience from the industrial nations should tell us that the solution for the developing nations is not just more and more schooling, for we are now seeing the effects of youth who have had no opportunities to discover the pleasures of meaningful work. Our solutions must therefore involve not only a recognition of the grim realities of exploitative labour balanced against the economic realities of a child's family and the need for income; we must also consider a child's desire to develop competence which is relevant to the kinds of work demanded of her, both now and in the future. We need more thoughtful development and evolution of a variety of solutions within each culture involving unique combinations of play, work, and school. From these different experiences, every child should be able to find a route to a meaningful role in his or her community and to discover both the rights and the responsibilities for participating with others in the development of this community.* (Hart, 1992: 21–23)

Working children's movements have jointly collaborated with states to bring dignity to their own work[23] and to monitor that their rights are respected, and although there has been some discourse concerning child participation in implementing the 2030 Agenda, it is not yet clear how this will be orchestrated in practice. Child participation in public policy-making and global agenda-setting is still a long way from being operational and applicable.

The victimized image cast by international institutions on child work often creates obstacles to differentiating working conditions or to understanding the role played by child work in the family context, because it eclipses the particularities of local contexts and the ways in which gender, ethnicity, and socioeconomic status combine to further the emergence and persistence of the phenomenon. In the case of Mexico, we have attempted to broaden our approach to this phenomenon because it is no use proposing global policies without taking cultural idiosyncrasies and particularities into account, the better to prepare for social intervention oriented by human rights and the empowerment of individuals. Just as Mark Goodale (2006: 492) suggests, "human rights can legitimately function as a local normative framework, but their legitimacy will be derived not from their universality—as is assumed by all of the major foundational instruments of international human rights—but from the conditions through which they emerge or are incorporated." This is an essential and decisive question for working Mexican girls.

Conclusions... Or How to Deconstruct Barriers

Often, girls' work takes place within the family network, and their tasks form part of a tradition; their jobs give them a place within this tradition, allowing them a sense of belonging and identifying with that place. This sense of belonging changes depending on people's age, the amount of time they have been there, and the dynamics in which they are involved—although undoubtedly, their workplace forms part of their identity and socialization. Despite multiple adaptations, work environments are undeniably complex, with four common elements standing out as inevitable parts of daily tasks: noise, garbage, insecurity, and harassment—aspects involving the potential for danger to children's physical and psychological safety.

Nevertheless, the perception of danger must be put into context to avoid the kinds of conclusions that are subsequently used for political and social programs and positioning that do little to address the underlying reality. Also, not all "dangers" carry equal weight; some are assumed characteristics of a particular space and, as such, are perceived to represent a greater risk to outsiders, while local social and family networks are structured around mitigating potential harm. This invisible protection from the "outside world" can be highly efficient, incorporating many symbols and practices that diminish risks and establish other elements of protection.

Also, as discussed above, women and girls are perceived to be more vulnerable due to their condition (according to the gender stereotypes that confer weakness, fragility, and vulnerability against men), and this perception is used to justify restrictions on freedom, autonomy, and the use of spaces. Women and girls will continue to experience limitations on the free exercise of their rights until these discriminatory factors are changed.

While it is true that the work areas analyzed (public markets, *tianguis*, dumps, public squares) are settings for certain situations of violence, prostitution, dirtiness, and harassment, both in discourse and in practice, the dangers are relativized and normalized, because these are the conditions in which people have to live. We must consider that in the end, the entire city is "dangerous" both for men and women (everybody is exposed to something happening to them) and that, depending on how we sense that danger, this will condition us more or less to carry out certain activities. Nevertheless, girls prove every day that they are capable of transforming their environments, making them closer, taking them over, and demystifying the prejudices, because life must go on.

"Protectionist" approaches that surreptitiously entail a deprivation of freedoms and limited access for women (from childhood to maturity) must be avoided when considering ways to improve living conditions in urban work environments, not only for women and girls but for everyone. Women and girls are capable of adapting and modifying their environment, and their voices must be heard before initiatives are taken that cause the gender gap to become even wider. Programs are needed that defend children's participation and human rights, rather than programs that predispose women and girls to situations of social disadvantage, resulting in their incapacitation, loss of potential, and limited possibilities for their individual and collective empowerment.

In this chapter, I have laid out an approach that serves as a starting point for the analysis and theoretical consideration of children's work, which must be redefined avoiding determinisms and vacuous categorizations that do not question the hierarchies of domination and the structures have long given short shrift to childhood issues. Ineffective approaches imagine girls as "individuals subject to intervention" in a greater measure than boys, without considering other conditioning elements that contribute to inequity. An approach is needed that works to eliminate inequalities, but which avoids suggesting vulnerability as a starting point.

The 2030 Agenda represents an opportunity to discuss different factors of development, re-politicize participation, and bring gender equality to the forefront of the conversation, putting special emphasis on poverty reduction and improved education, healthcare, and access to jobs while posing essential questions about environmental sustainability that will improve the well-being of humanity as a whole, but especially for children. At the same time, this new global agenda faces great challenges, such as designing coherent and comprehensive policies that unite economic, social, and environmental dimensions and the productive and reproductive spheres. We must also accept the challenge posed by the gap between policy declarations and the actual implementation and financing of those policies, especially the indicator and accountability challenges regarding the protection, provision, and participation of children as part of humanity, rather than a vulnerable, minority collective. State and public policies must constitute the backbone of protection and provision, but they must also establish channels of participation, and the approach toward girls must be one of development and valuation, at least under conditions equal to the rest of society.

The proposal is to continue to build citizenship without succumbing to exclusionary dichotomies while valuing capabilities and analyzing reality in all its complexity, both qualitatively and progressively. Only in this way will we contribute to a more fair and equitable society and achieve more habitable cities for everyone.

Notes

1. *Tianguis* is a Náhuatl word that means an open-air market. It can be temporary or permanent in certain urban areas, although they are usually mobile. Sometimes they are also called *markets on wheels*.
2. The *micros* are small private buses that provide public transport. They are also called *peseros* because in the past they use to cost one Mexican *peso* (currently the price ranges between four and six pesos).
3. By "minors *of* the streets" I mean boys and girls who have broken the family bond temporarily or permanently, who sleep on public streets and survive by performing marginal activities in the informal street economy, while "minors *on* the streets" refers to boys and girls who maintain their family bonds, usually are in school, and perform marginal activities in the street economy for their own subsistence or to help the family.
4. I use the concept *reconstructed* household to refer to second unions due to previous separations or widow/widowerhood.
5. *Cháchara* refers to second-hand articles that are sold at the open-air market.
6. Grocery store, food store.
7. Cooking pots and utensils.
8. *Maquila doméstica* refers to the small-scale production at home or in private buildings of certain products that are finished later in factories and industrial businesses.
9. Pepenadora is the person who search among dumps and waste for food or other articles that can subsequently be re-sold.
10. Girls who pack bags in supermarkets.
11. In typical definitions of children's work, this activity is not considered to be work but rather "a marginal income activity." I believe this is an error because this activity has the characteristics of other jobs such as temporal regularity, direct participation in the process, and retribution, monetary, or otherwise.

12. It is impossible to quote all the theoretical reflections and demands contributed by feminism. Some of the main references are the works by Beauvoir, Wollstonecraft, Friedan, and Pateman, among many others (see full references in the bibliography).
13. Regarding gender dichotomies, there is the male-centered model that presents men's roles as active, strong, and pragmatic and with a command of reason, while women occupy roles of passivity, weakness, kindness, and feeling. In contrast to this model, the classical contributions made by the anthropologist Michelle Z. Rosaldo are interesting (regarding the domestic and public dichotomy) and Sherry B. Ortner (on the nature and culture of dichotomy) in Harris and Young (1979).
14. Due to advances in gender studies, in recent years this issue has been gaining visibility. Many studies have begun incorporating the economic contributions of domestic work (mainly done by women) in their analyses while at the same time making progress in recognizing the care economy as part of the international agenda and public policy. For more information on the subject, see, among many others, some reference works such as Himmelweit (1995) or the Special Issue on Unpaid Household Work published by the journal *Feminist Economics* (1996). However, in the case of female child work, there are still many aspects that must be reflected upon and studied in more depth.
15. The anthropology of gender has analyzed this situation in depth with many theoretical contributions. One classic publication is the study by Martin and Voorhies (1978).
16. Each year, UNICEF publishes a Report on the Worldwide State of Childhood. In 1997, UNICEF prepared a monograph on Children's Work which is a classic reference for this subject.
17. Hand truck or dolly.
18. It is important to highlight that the current global number of children in a child labor situation has decreased by a third, from 246 million to 168 million, since the year 2000. About half, 85 million, are performing hazardous work (compared to 171 million in the year 2000) (SIMPOC, ILO-IPEC). For more information, see http://www.ilo.org/ipec/ChildlabourstatisticsSIMPOC/lang%2D%2Des/index.htm
19. As proof of this international progress, we can highlight certain conventions and protocols, such as the following:

    - Conventions and Recommendations on child labor (Convention no. 138 and Recommendation no. 146 (year 1973), Convention no. 182 and Recommendation no. 190 (year 1999)).
    - Conventions, Protocols, and Recommendations on forced labor (Convention no. 29 (year 1930) and its protocol from 2014, Recommendation no. 35 and no. 203, and Convention no. 105 (year 1957)).
    - Palermo Protocol (year 2000) to Prevent, Suppress and Punish Trafficking in Persons, Especially Women and Children.

20. Similarly, since 1997 countries from around the world have shared information on policy and "good practices" and have committed to eliminate child work during a series of global conferences on child work held in Norway (1997), the Netherlands (2010), and Brazil (2013). The last of these, the III Global Mundial, held in Brasilia in October 2013, approved the Brasilia Declaration on Child Labor. At the end of the conference, the Government of Argentina announced that, in collaboration with the ILO, it would host the IV Global Conference on the Sustained Eradication of Child Labor in 2017.
21. See http://www.un.org/sustainabledevelopment/
22. For more information regarding global progress on the fight against child labor, consult Alliance 8.7, available online at http://www.alliance87.org
23. Proof of this is their participation in the creation of ILO's C-182 (1999) and their proposals for the Kundapur 10 points (1996). For more information on child participation, see (among others) http://molacnats.org/; https://www.unicef.org/adolescence/cypguide/index_child_led.html

Bibliography

Alarcon, W. (1994). *Ser niño. Una nueva mirada de la infancia en el Perú*. Lima, Peru: UNICEF-IEP.

Anker, R. (2000). The Economics of Child Labour: A Framework for Measurement. *International Labour Review, 139*(3), 257–280.

Atkin, D. (2016). Endogenous Skill Acquisition and Export Manufacturing in Mexico. *American Economic Review, 106*(8), 2046–2085.

Bar-Din, A. (Comp.) (1995). *Los niños marginados en América Latina. Una antología de estudios psicosociales*. Mexico City, Mexico: Centro de Investigaciones Interdisciplinarias en Humanidades-UNAM.

Benería, L. (2005). *Género, desarrollo y globalización. Por una ciencia económica para todas las personas*. Barcelona, Spain: Hacer.

Benería, L., May, A. M., & Strassmann, D. L. (2011). *Feminist Economics*. Northampton and Cheltenham, UK: Edward Elgar.

Bernard, H. R. (2002). *Research Methods in Anthropology. Qualitative and Quantitative Approaches* (3rd ed.). Walnut Creek, CA: Altamira Press.

Bey, M. (2003). The Mexican Child. From Work with the Family to Paid Employment. *Childhood, 10*(3), 287–299.

Bourdillon, M., & Boyden, J. (Eds.). (2014). *Growing Up in Poverty: Findings from Young Lives*. New York, NY: Palgrave Macmillan.

Boyden, J., & Ennew, J. (Eds.). (1997). *Children in Focus: A Manual for Participatory Research with Children*. Stockholm, Sweden: Rädda Barnen.

Brannen, J., & O'Brien, J. (1995). Childhood and the Sociological Gaze: Paradigms and Paradoxes. *Sociology, 29*(4), 729–737.

Carballo, M., & Leyra, B. (2017). Consideraciones sobre la pobreza y las desigualdades de género. In M. Carballo (Coord.), *Género y Desarrollo: cuestiones clave*

desde una perspectiva feminista (p. 75–99). Madrid, Spain: Los libros de La Catarata-IUDC-ICEI.
Carrasco, C. (2004). *Trabajo con Mirada de Mujer. Propuesta de una encuesta de población activa no androcéntrica*. Madrid, Spain: Consejo Económico y Social. Colección Estudios 155.
Carrasco, C. (2013). El cuidado como eje vertebrador de una nueva economía. *Cuadernos de relaciones laborales, 31*(1), 39–56.
Chant, S. (2013). Cities Through a "Gender Lens": A Golden "Urban Age" for Women in the Global South? *Environment and Urbanization, 25*(1), 9–29.
Christensen, P., & James, A. (2000). *Research with Children: Perspectives and Practices*. London, UK: Falmer.
Ciocoletto, A. (2004). *Urbanismo para la vida cotidiana. Herramientas de análisis y evaluación urbana a escala de barrio desde la perspectiva de género*. Barcelona, Spain: Universidad Politécnica de Cataluña.
Córdova, R. (1996). Sexualidad y relaciones familiares en una comunidad veracruzana. In L. Bazán & A. Levi (Coords.), *Espacios Familiares: Ámbitos de Sobrevivencia y Solidaridad* (pp. 11–51). Mexico City, Mexico: Sistema Nacional DIF.
Cunningham, H., & Viazzo, P. P. (1996). *Child Labour in Historical Perspective 1800–1985: Case Studies from Europe, Japan and Columbia*. Florence, Italy: UNICEF.
Cussiánovich, A., & Márquez, A. M. (2002). *Hacia una participación protagónica de los niños, niñas y adolescentes*. Lima, Peru: Save the Children.
De Beauvoir, S. (1952). *The Second Sex*. New York, NY: Vintage Books.
De Leeuw, E., Borgers, N., & Strijbos-Sits, A. (2002). *Children as Respondents: Developing, Evaluating, and Testing Questionnaires for Children*. Presented at the International Conference on Questionnaire Development Evaluation and Testing Methods, Charleston, South Carolina.
Denzin, N. K., & Lincoln, Y. S. (Eds.). (1994). *Handbook of Qualitative Research*. Thousand Oaks, CA: Sage.
Durán, M. A. (2008). *La ciudad compartida. Conocimiento, afecto y uso*. Santiago de Chile, Chile: Ediciones Sur.
Elder, G. (1998). The Life Course as Developmental Theory. *Child Development, 69*(1), 1–12.
Elson, D. (1979). *Value: The Representation of Labour in Capitalism*. London, UK: Calvert's North Star Press.
Elson, D., Fukuda-Parr, S., & Vizard, P. (2012). *Human Rights and the Capabilities Approach: An Interdisciplinary Dialogue*. New York, NY: Routledge.
Estrada, M. (Ed.). (1999a). *1995. Familias en la crisis*. Mexico City, Mexico: CIESAS/ SEP-CONACYT.
Estrada, M. (1999b). Infancia y trabajo. La experiencia de los sectores populares urbanos. *Estudios Sociológicos, XVII*(49), 54–73.

Falú, A. (Ed.) (2002). *Ciudad y Vida Cotidiana. Asimetrías en el uso del tiempo y del espacio.* Córdoba, Argentina: Red Mujer y Hábitat de América Latina.

Falú, A., & Segovia, O. (2007). *Ciudades para convivir: sin violencias hacia las mujeres.* Santiago de Chile, Chile: Ediciones Sur.

Feminist Economics. (1996). *Special Issue on Unpaid Household Work* (in Honour of Margaret Reid), *2*(3).

Friedan, B. (1963). *The Feminine Mystique.* New York, NY: Norton.

Gaitán, L., & Liebel, M. (2011). *Ciudadanía y derechos de participación de los niños.* Madrid, Spain: Universidad Pontificia Comillas-Editorial Síntesis.

García Ferrando, M., Alvira, F., Alonso, L. E., & Escobar, M. (Eds.). (2015). *El análisis de la realidad social: métodos y técnicas de investigación.* Madrid, Spain: Alianza Editorial.

González, F. (1999). La casa, la calle y la escuela como instancias de socialización en dos comunidades étnicas mazahuas del Estado de México. In A. Civera (Ed.), *Experiencias educativas en el Estado de México. Un recorrido histórico* (pp. 514–541). Zinacantepec, Mexico: El Colegio Mexiquense.

Goodale, M. (2006). Toward a Critical Anthropology of Human Rights. *Current Anthropology, 47*(3), 485–511.

Hammad, M. (2006). *Lire l'espace, comprendre l'architecture.* Paris, France: Geuthner.

Hammersley, M., & Atkinson, P. (1994). *Etnografía. Métodos de Investigación.* Barcelona, Spain: Paidós.

Harris, O., & Young, K. (1979). *Antropología y feminismo.* Madrid, Spain: Anagrama.

Hart, R. (1992). *Children's Participation: From Tokenism to Citizenship.* Essays 4. Florence, Italy: Innocenti: UNICEF.

Himmelweit, S. (1995). The Discovery of "Unpaid Work". The Social Consequences of the Expansion of Work. *Feminist Economics, 1*(2), 1–20.

Holzscheiter, A. (2016). Representation as Power and Performative Practice: Global Civil Society Advocacy for Working Children. *Review of International Studies, 42*(2), 205–226.

Hungerland, B., Liebel, M., Milne, B., & Wihstutz, A. (Eds.). (2007). *Working to Be Someone. Child Focused Research and Practice with Working Children.* London, UK/Philadelphia, PA: Jessica Kingsley Publishers.

ILO. (2015). *World Report on Child Labour 2015: Paving the Way to Decent Work for Young People.* Geneva, Switzerland: ILO.

ILO. (2016). *Labour Overview 2016. Latin America and the Caribbean.* Lima, Peru: ILO-OIT. Oficina Regional para América Latina y el Caribe.

INEGI. (2015). *Encuesta Nacional de Ocupación y Empleo (ENOE). Módulo de Trabajo Infantil.* Mexico City, Mexico: INEGI.

Kabeer, N. (2015). Gender, Poverty, and Inequality: A Brief History of Feminist Contributions in the Field of International Development. *Gender and Development, 23*(2), 189–205.

Liebel, M. (2003). *Infancia y Trabajo.* Lima, Peru: IFEJANT.

Liebel, M. (2006). *Entre Protección y Emancipación. Derechos de la Infancia y Políticas Sociales.* Monografías del Experto en Políticas Sociales de Infancia. Serie Teoría N° 1. Madrid, Spain: Universidad Complutense de Madrid.

Liebel, M. (2013). *Niñez y Justicia Social. Repensando sus derechos.* Santiago de Chile, Chile: Pehuen.

Liebel, M., & Martínez, M., (Coords.) (2009). *Infancia y Derechos Humanos. Hacia una ciudadanía participante y protagónica.* Lima, Peru: IFEJANT.

Liebel, M., Overwien, B., & Recknagel, A. (Eds.). (2001). *Working Children's Protagonism. Social movements and empowerment in Latin America, Africa and India.* Frankfurt, Germany/London, UK: IKO.

Luna, M. A., & Gómez, R. (1992). Límites al crecimiento de la Zona Metropolitana de Ciudad de México. In *La zona metropolitana de la ciudad de México. Problemática actual y perspectivas demográficas y urbanas.* Mexico City, Mexico: Consejo Nacional de Población.

Martin, K., & Voorhies, B. (1978). *La Mujer: Un enfoque antropológico.* Barcelona, Spain: Anagrama.

Mayall, B. (2002). *Towards a Sociology for Childhood. Thinking from Children's Lives.* Buckingham, UK/Philadelphia, PA: Open University Press.

Myers, W. E. (1999). Considering Child Labour: Changing Terms, Issues and Actors at the International Level. *Childhood, 6*(1), 13–26.

Nieuwenhuys, O. (1996). The Paradox of Child Labour and Anthropology. *Annual Review of Anthropology, 25*, 237–251.

Pateman, C. (1988). *The Sexual Contract.* Palo Alto, CA: Stanford University Press.

Pérez Orozco, A. (2006). *Perspectivas feministas en torno a la economía: el caso de los cuidados.* Madrid, Spain: Consejo Económico y Social.

Pérez Orozco, A. (2015). Subversión feminista de la economía. *Sociología del trabajo, 83*, 7–15.

Reeves, S., Kuper, A., & Hodges, B. D. (2008). Qualitative Research Methodologies: Ethnography. *BMJ* (online), *337*(7668), a1020. doi: https://doi.org/10.1136/BMJ.A1020

Saraví, G. (2015). *Juventudes Fragmentadas. Socialización, clase y cultura en la construcción de la desigualdad.* Mexico City, Mexico: FLACSO.

Schlemmer, B. (Ed.). (2000). *The Exploited Child.* London, UK/New York, NY: Zed Books.

Strauss, A., & Corbin, J. M. (1990). *Basics of Qualitative Research: Grounded Theory Procedures and Techniques.* Thousand Oaks, CA: Sage.

STPS (Secretaría del Trabajo y Previsión Social). (2014). *El Trabajo Infantil en México: Avances y Desafíos.* Mexico City, Mexico: STPS-Gobierno de México.

UNICEF. (1997). *Estado Mundial de la Infancia. Tema: Trabajo Infantil.* New York, NY: UNICEF.

UNICEF. (1999). *Informe número 11 sobre Trabajo Infantil.* Mexico City, Mexico: UNICEF.

UNICEF. (2014). *Children of the Recession: The Impact of the Economic Crisis on Child Well-Being in Rich Countries.* Innocenti Report Card 12. Florence, Italy: UNICEF Office of Research.

UNICEF. (2015). *Progress for Children. Beyond Averages: Learning from the MDGs.* N° 11/2015. New York, NY: UNICEF.

UNICEF-CONEVAL. (2013). *Pobreza y derechos sociales de niñas, niños y adolescentes en México, 2008–2010.* Mexico City, Mexico: UNICEF-CONEVAL.

Wollstonecraft, M. (1792). *A Vindication of the Rights of Women.* New York, NY: Cosimo.

CHAPTER 3

From Childhood to Adolescence: Vulnerable Life Stories and Persistent Inequalities in Argentina Since Post-Convertibility (2003)

María Eugenia Rausky

Introduction

Over the past two decades, Latin American countries, with the support of international cooperation, have made progress on a series of aims and objectives to "eradicate" child labor. In fact, the International Labour Office (ILO) has committed itself as the agency of technical assistance in the advancement and achievement of the Sustainable Development Goals (SDGs), embedded in the 2030 Agenda for Sustainable Development, to

This chapter was elaborated in the context of the INCASI Network, a European project that has received funding from the European Union's Horizon 2020 research and innovation program under the Marie Skłodowska-Curie GA No 691004, coordinated by Dr. Pedro López-Roldán. This chapter reflects only the author's view, and the European Union's Horizon 2020 research and innovation program is not responsible for any use that may be made of the information it contains.

M. E. Rausky (✉)
CONICET, Facultad de Humanidades y Ciencias de la Educación, Universidad Nacional de La Plata, La Plata, Buenos Aires, Argentina
e-mail: erausky@fahce.unlp.edu.ar

M. E. Rausky, M. Chaves (eds.), *Living and Working in Poverty in Latin America*, Governance, Development, and Social Inclusion in Latin America, https://doi.org/10.1007/978-3-030-00901-4_3

promote global development cooperation toward the year 2030. The core of this commitment is expressed specifically in SDG #8 which refers to decent work, and particularly target 8.7:

> To adopt immediate and efficient measures to eradicate forced labour, bring about the end to all forms of modern slavery and the trade in human beings, ensure the prohibition and elimination of the worst forms of child labour, including the recruitment and use of child soldiers and in 2025 at the latest, to bring about the end of child labour in all its forms. (UN, 2015, p. 22)

Measures to achieve these aims have seen varying degrees of success, perhaps most importantly through the broadening of access to education and the expansion of social protections.[1] With regard to the latter, social security income has become one of the most important mechanisms to combat both poverty and child labor. Also, more effective workplace inspections combined with public service announcements and campaigns to increase awareness among the population, by offering a hotline for reporting "sweat shops," for instance, have all accompanied these measures.

There is no doubt that working during childhood feeds social inequality (as demonstrated by socioeconomic stratification)[2]; however, the underlying assumptions made by agents of international development cooperation in identifying causes, consequences, and proposals for intervention are often oversimplified, limiting the argument to possible "solutions." Perhaps one of the biggest weaknesses of the approach is that in the apparent haste to address the problem, specific and heterogeneous modes of the complex processes of child labor in different social contexts have been lost from view. As shown by Llobet (2012), the significance and consequences of child labor depend on the context in which it occurs, including social class, ethnic group, rural or urban environment, and so forth. Therefore, in order to better understand what is happening and how best to approach it, a close observation is needed of the social relationship networks in which the child labor takes place. Seeking to contribute to the debate, and recognizing that child labor allows us a clear view of how social inequalities are structured, linked, and reproduced from an early age, in this chapter I share the results of research undertaken between 2014 and 2016 in the urban area of the city of La Plata (Buenos Aires, Argentina), with children who work on the streets. By analyzing the life stories of these workers, this research aims to reveal the heterogeneous ways in which the new generations experience the foundational part of their life course: childhood and youth. One element that enables understanding of this heterogeneity is related to the development of labor practices. Here, we see not only the contrasts between different infant and youth experiences but are also made aware of the need to understand that different childhood experiences in their contexts are *questioned* by international aid agencies, among other actors.

It is worth remembering that for some time now, the social sciences have underlined the need to think about these phenomena in context—to see childhoods in a plural and not singular form, recognizing the heterogeneity of childhood experiences and the different ways in which children go through this stage of life (Sirota, 2001; James & Prout, 1990). In Argentina, some studies have contributed to the field by tracing a map of childhoods, seeking to question the interrelationship between diversity and social inequality, and concentrating on different topics related to childhood. Works such as Enriz (2014), Hetch and García (2010), Remorini (2015), and Szulc (2016) focus on indigenous childhood, while others such as Ortale (2015) and Colángelo (2014) focus on the ways children are brought up; some look at the processes of education and schooling (Santillán, 2006, 2007), at state measures to assist children (Llobet, 2006; Llobet & Litichever, 2010), at street children (Pojomovsky, 2008; Silva, 2014), at the access to and consumption of games and toys (Duek, 2014), and at child labor (Macri, Ford, Berliner, & Molteni, 2005; Noceti, 2006; Rausky, 2009, 2011, 2015). All these studies in one way or another show the heterogeneous nature of experiences for those who are going through the childhood stage of life. Often, though not always, this diversity is related and directly linked to the foundations of social inequality, perpetuating and consolidating disadvantage for a large part of the infant population, following and affecting them in successive stages of life.

As demonstrated by several researchers, economic and social hardship in childhood can have a long-lasting effect, making it very difficult for children who grow up in low-income homes to escape poverty in future life stages (Wagmiller Jr. & Adelman, 2009). My work focuses precisely on this phenomenon, for which a combination of life stories (Bertaux, 2005) is used to analyze the life courses of a group of children who have worked on the street since childhood and continue through adolescence. I aim to reveal common aspects as well as singularities between those who share the same life course and its disadvantages.

Two characteristics shared by the children are that they have occupied and continue to occupy subordinate positions in society (in conditions of poverty) and that they have worked on the streets throughout their childhood in the streets and continue to do so in their adolescence. I explore the life courses of these children, prioritizing the analysis of the labor dimension in relation to their worlds of family, school and daily social relationships, observing specific factors, interrelationships and convergences.

I have chosen a biographical studies approach due to its fundamental interest in the analysis of life courses and their effects; moreover, I acknowledge the interest in the diversity of life courses and effects of certain sociological studies (Casal, Garcia, Merino & Quesada, 2006). The strength of the biographical approach for this type of research lies in the fact that it allows us to draw a more complete map of the transition from childhood to youth, since it does not focus on one single moment in life, but on a longer period of time: the path from childhood to adolescence and its accompanying transformations. Childhood and adolescence are crucial periods in the course of a person's lifetime, in that they not only leave deep impressions for the future but also influence the range of opportunities available to the subjects (Saraví, 2015).

For Elder (1994), the life course paradigm refers to the interlacing of courses ordered by age, growth, and movement throughout a person's life, encompassing a variety of related areas such as school and work. The paradigm also refers to short-term transitions such as the phase in which a child abandons school or the phase when a person retires from the world of work. These transitions, defined as changes of state, indicate the assumption of new roles and are embedded into trajectories. These two concepts form the basis of the course of life model to which he adds a third: the concept of "turning point" that refers to non-predictable events provoking a discontinuity in the vital trajectories and, as such, entails strong modifications to the course of life (Blanco, 2011).

Elder goes on to define four fundamental axes to the paradigm: (1) the interrelationship between human lives and historical time; (2) the "timing" of an event—the same event can have very different consequences depending on whether it occurs at an earlier stage or at a later stage, according to the normative expectations and beliefs associated with age; (3) the notion of interconnected lives which allows us to analyze the interdependence of an individual's life course in the context of his or her relationship with other groups or individuals; and (4) the human being as an agent, highlighting the subject's active role in the definition of his or her life course, but without ignoring structural constraints.

To be more precise, I analyze the biographical itinerary of the young people interviewed, emphasizing their spheres of work and considering some of the elements of the theoretical model proposed by Mora Salas and Oliveira (2014). These authors look at how the life course can be analyzed by focusing on different analytical axes located at different moments in time—past, present, and future—but which are interrelated. While family origin is a key factor in understanding the weight of inherited inequalities, the authors give as much importance to the material conditions of existence as to the forms of socialization differentiated by gender, the position of the subject as regards other siblings, and the characteristics of a family living together. Although the subjects share inequalities of origin, the individual life course is retold as it goes from past to present, passing through different spheres. Finally, I look into the role of the future as a particular time frame. All of these factors are molded by a combination of external resources, such as opportunities offered by the labor market, networks, and institutional support, which all play an important role in the creation of possibilities and constraints within life itineraries.

The latter acquires even more relevance when considering the changes that have occurred in Argentina in modern times. Many previously published studies not only show different features related to the evolution of social structure but also how they have influenced the survival processes of childhood and youth. Argentina stands out from other Latin American countries in that a large part of the twentieth century was characterized by high levels of social integration as evidenced by average lower unemployment than Europe, higher salaries, significant rates of both inter- and intra-generational mobility, a more equal income distribution, and the most advanced social protection network in Latin America (Kessler & Espinoza, 2003). Carli (2005), in her research on the history of education, says that this period of the twentieth century was characterized by a unified vision of childhood, due to a highly homogenous society with a high level of social integration and an inclusive education system for all. This panorama, however, was to become severely altered. The last military dictatorship (1976–1983) followed in the 1990s by the impact of the various effects of emerging neoliberal economic and political globalization combined to cause a series of unprecedented changes that severely slowed down the characteristic upward mobility of Argentina's population.

The transition from a model of social integration at the beginning of the 1970s to a polarized and impoverished society at the end of the 1990s shows how childhood as a social construct assumes different types of experiences compared to previous generations and how new processes and modes of identity take shape (Carli, 2010). The children I studied lived part of their childhood through the devastating effects of what occurred during that period. However, they also spent part of their childhood and youth under three governments, from 2003 to 2015, with a mandate to promote a more inclusive model of society, applying a series of social and economic policies that allowed many Argentinians to rise above the deep crisis and alleviate some of the effects of neoliberal economic and political principles.

In this same period, other Latin American countries also introduced renewed social and economic policies, the so-called pink tide, which sought to change the direction, at least at the level of political discourse, away from the neoliberal model, appealing to the need for measures to redistribute wealth, eradicate poverty, and reduce or alleviate existing inequalities (Pautassi, 2007).

However, hidden behind this overhaul was the fundamental fact that stable and protected employment was and still is inaccessible for a large part of the lower income sector, an underlying cause of huge suffering. As pointed out by Kessler and Merklen (2013, p. 14):

> For vast sectors of the population their experience is structured (…) by the experience of several generations which never benefited from integration to a position with a stable wage. Much more extensively, for young people who aim to lead an autonomous life, start a family, raise children and enter into adult life and the world of work, the future horizon is one of massive instability.

These experiences form the basis of this chapter, recognizing that a comprehensive analysis of the problems of childhood poverty requires consideration of both its material and cultural dimensions. Regarding the latter dimension, I do not consider the subject as possessing a single culture, but that in different ways they use and create cultural symbols to bring sense to their lives. I emphasize "in different ways" because, although faced with identical structural constraints, these disadvantages can take on differences in significance and experience for each person. The analysis of poverty's cultural dimensions therefore allows us to identify heterogeneous responses and reveal how constructed meanings contribute to the reproduction of inequality (Bayón, 2013).

Children and Youth Who Work on the Street: A Mixed Method Study

Data used in this analysis draws from a study of children, adolescents, and young people who work on the street, carried out in the city of La Plata, Argentina, from 2014 to 2016.[3] The aims of the study were to map street work, to observe its dimensions and characteristics, and identify the life courses of the subjects involved in work activities.

My first objective was a general one, to allow us to draw a picture of the situation, asking questions like "how many," "what do they do," "what kind of work do they perform," and so forth. The second objective was to analyze the way in which different spheres of work such as family, education, and friendship interconnect and contribute to the early construction of different biographical itineraries that consequently shape different childhoods and adolescence. These fundamental questions are related to how inequalities are interlinked from an early age, what factors persist and interact, and the reason for this persistence.

Due to the specific objectives of the study, I used a mixed sequence design in two phases (Teddlie & Tashakori, 2006).[4] The tool must be applied in sequence, which means that the methodological procedures cannot occur simultaneously, but must take place consecutively in each separate phase. In this way, each subsequent phase emerges from the previous one and is fed by it. The two phases of the study are developed as follows: the first is quali-quantitative with the emphasis on qualitative (QUAL+/QUAN). The second is quanti-qualitative with the emphasis on qualitative (QUAN/QUAL+).

In the first phase, based on observations and a survey, I attempted an exhaustive sweep of public places in the city of La Plata where the work was taking place, then quantified the volume and the observable characteristics of the work of children and youth. The survey[5] detected a total of 449 workers who carried out a wide range of street work. Of these, 71% were male and 29% were female. Observing the composition of the two age categories under study—children and youth—the youth age group was notably larger at 74.2%, while the group of children made up 25.8%.

The second phase of the research was based on interviews and a short, structured questionnaire focused on life courses. However, I did not use the same units of analysis as those used in the census; instead, I chose a sample of young workers, taking into account the heterogeneous nature of profiles as revealed by the census information.[6] I interviewed 37 children[7] and adolescent workers. Sometimes, when I felt the need, the same person was interviewed twice with the aim of getting a deeper understanding of his/her life story. The interview with youth included questions about the following: work, school experience, family background, social relationships (family, friends, love), access to state programs, experience of street life, experience of incarceration in closed institutions, substance abuse, and the use of free time. All of the above considered a broad time axis, talking about the present as well as the past that was imprinted in childhood memories and asking about future plans. When studying a phenomenon over time, it is important to define whether the process under analysis is taken from its origin to the present (prospective studies) or from the present to the past (retrospective studies) (Muñiz Terra, 2012). In accordance with the aims of this study, the latter approach was chosen, with a focus on the analysis of a sub-group of young workers: those who have been involved in street work since childhood. Of the 15 people interviewed, 12 are male and 3 female, aged from 13 to 24 years.

Tracing Unequal Trajectories

A large number of studies analyzing groups of children and youth who are living and/or working on the streets use the perspective of social exclusion as a theoretical tool to show the processes of vulnerability and social fragility (Makowski, 2010). I share the view that social exclusion is the result of a process of cumulative disadvantage that leads to the undermining of the individual's relationship to society. As Saraví (2007, p. 30) pointed out:

> The central importance of the processes of disadvantage and vulnerability as key dimensions in the analysis of social exclusion establishes a direct and necessary connection with the perspectives of life course…If the central element discovered by the notion of social exclusion is the vulnerability of wide sectors of the population trapped in a spiral of disadvantage, what is needed is a methodological strategy that allows us to focus on the processes of concrete biographical experiences and at the same time evaluate factors and situations before they materialize.

This chapter takes a closer look at these processes. The lives of the young people I studied are far from following standard life course patterns: they work on the street from childhood and survive by self-employment, living in temporary homes, or escaping from family life and spending certain periods living on the streets or in institutions, abandoning basic education, and so forth.

Analyzing their biographies, I note how the initial disadvantage of living in poverty—in many cases extreme poverty—is linked and interwoven with other disadvantages that lead to vulnerable life trajectories.

However, I wish to emphasize that despite sharing such decisive features and faced with similar situations, subjects' responses to these challenges were diverse, shaping different life stories. Drawing on the responses, I outline three types of trajectories based on the analysis of particular cases: (1) controlled, (2) inert, and (3) limited, as explained below. The reconstruction of trajectories allows us to examine the different risks to which these children are exposed throughout childhood, as well as the different obstacles they face to integration into the fabric of society.

The above three possible directions for life itineraries draw attention to the key role of certain analytical elements (and I contend that it is crucial to elaborate models involving multiple factors): the different resources that the subjects bring into play and the different orientations that guide their actions, some with more control over their destiny than others.

I discuss the opportunities available to them to make decisions about their future lives and look at the biographical approach to the tension between the concepts of subject/structure and individual/society, which exist in constant interplay.[8] To quote Bayón (2013, p. 100):

> The stories people tell about their own lives reveal how individuals give meaning to their experiences, constraints and opportunities, showing the ways in which structures distribute power and disadvantage. It involves the identification of segments of social structure and culture that come into in play in individual life stories, moving continually between the worlds of individual lives and the social conditions which produce them and are reproduced by them.

The following reconstructions of itineraries and trajectories emphasize the work dimension and highlight turning points in life experiences—the events that, according to the subjective interpretation of the interviewees, produced substantial modification in their lives. Each type of itinerary is represented by a case study which exemplifies its characteristics. The classification of different trajectories into controlled, inert, and limited relates to the main factors driving the social actions of these young people. In some cases, there is a possibility of obtaining control and/or greater predictability over the course of the trajectories; these fit into the first category. In others, the logic of inertia prevails, where a limited range of choices converges with a disposition to reproduce or produce the same pattern; these belong in the second category. Finally, there are cases of permanent crisis where day-to-day living involves life itself being under constant threat—these fall into the third category.

Controlled Trajectories

Joaquin is 22 years of age. He sells flowers on a busy corner of the city. He lives in the town of Berazategui, about 35 km from La Plata, and began working at around 11 or 12 years old with his parents who sold flowers in La Plata, an activity he continues. At the time, his mother rented a stall on a street outside the city center, on a busy road which provided access to different key points of sale.

> "I came and helped her and sometimes I crossed the Street and helped by selling at the traffic lights …I always helped her in some way. And then as the people got to know me always being there, I started to come here alone…at first I helped my parents and then when I was about 16 I started to invest my own money…let's say I invested 200 pesos and this then grew…I invested in flowers, like I bought bunches of flowers, I sold them and then I had more money, I saved some, invested again and kept on like that… I went to school and my dad used to pick me up in the car and we used to come here, first I did my homework in the flower stall and then I helped them…anyway they never kept me short of anything…they always bought me stuff and I didn't have to ask them…well they were my parents! I helped them."

Joaquin's memories of his childhood are clearly shaped by his feeling of being protected by his family and a strong sense of emotional and material well-being—"I was never short of anything"—although, in Joaquin's own words, his father never had formal or stable employment and was always "looking out for work," selling cleaning products door-to-door. At some moment that Joaquin could not exactly identify, after selling door-to-door for years, his father began selling flowers, also on the street, slowly managing to expand the business and steadily increasing the number of customers. Then came the point when he stopped "working on the streets" to deliver flowers by car to different neighborhoods of La Plata, Berisso, and Ensenada (neighboring towns). In fact, it was his father who taught him the trade and who encouraged him to work for himself. At age 16, Joaquin became economically independent and recognizes what he sees as the first turning point in his life, an event carrying deep repercussions, since the condition of being a worker will follow him—he believes—for the rest of his life.

Helping his parents to sell flowers on a daily basis as a child did not hamper his ability to maintain friendships or to fulfill his other commitments. His education followed a "normal" path: he did not have learning difficulties, did not have to repeat any year, and were it not for failing exams in just three remaining subjects, he would have successfully finished high school. Rather than the experience of child labor, he recognized the decision to work for himself as the true turning point:

A: There are boys of my age who just mess round and don't do anything...you see them and like they don't care about anything, they are different, different...me, I grew up suddenly ...I don't know...I really grew up when I started to work on the street, when I started to work, like when I became independent and had my own money and stood on my own feet.

Q: So it was at 16 you felt you grew up?

A: From then on didn't ask my parents for money, I went and bought the flowers, went to work, made my money, bought stuff I wanted, ...or for my house...I had a room first...this room I gave to my sister who had a son and I went back to my parent's house. I left her the room and everything...but I built it myself, a room and a bathroom to live alone...and I think this makes you grow up a bit, it wasn't all that much money, I went out to dance and stuff, I spent money but not that much, I was careful, I always tried to be careful and this pays off, see? I saved money, at 17 I managed to buy my own motorbike, and I sold that and at 18 I got my first car, an old VW, one of those square ones. Well later I sold that one and I bought the one I've got now. Always working and saving and always tried to invest the money, otherwise you just waste it, buying a car you don't waste it you invest, you've got capital tomorrow, you sell and you've got it. I think that's when I grew up, when I started to manage on my own...."

Taking on the responsibility to work for himself set him clearly apart from other youngsters his age. His coming of age was taking the path of economic autonomy that allowed him not only to satisfy immediate necessary consumption (food, clothes, etc.) as do most of those who work on the street but also to plan and execute other types of long-term consumption: the construction of his own home and a vehicle. Whereas during his childhood work was just one among many daily activities, once he made the decision to become autonomous, work became the central focus in his life, having more weight in the shaping of his biographical trajectory than any other vital sphere.

Although he feels tired and understands that street work is "hard" and a "sacrifice," he prefers it to other opportunities that he has had: he enjoys his autonomy, and his earnings help to meet the needs of his family. Unlike the majority of youngsters interviewed, he was offered a number of diverse work opportunities which, while limited, included formal, more secure positions as well as informal, precarious ones. "They've offered me lots of jobs, people who know me offer them." Through family networks (his brothers, sisters, and his "in-laws" and their brothers and sisters), he has had the opportunity to enter different labor environments. One of his memories of such work was a brief period in the call center of a bank in 2013, through one of his sister's contacts. He decided to leave the job, not so much because of the pay but because of the social distance he felt between himself and his work mates.

> I didn't like the place, I didn't like the people, I didn't get on with them… there were all sorts there, lots of guys who just go because they go, they don't care about anything, lots of people, guys who study, I don't get on with them, I don't know… I'm a worker…and maybe I socialized with people who don't give a shit: if I go to work today I go, or I don't go, if they deduct it that's ok, know what I mean? I didn't like the place, I worked there three months and then I left.

These comments highlight the heavy weight of social fragmentation and the importance of the thesis of Saraví (2015) who claims that today, individuals face a fragmented society as an objective reality, and due to this perception of reality, they end up developing social experiences which produce and reproduce social fragmentation.

The best job-related experience Joaquin remembers was when (through his brother-in-law's contact) he worked for one year at an air conditioning company serving the City Government of Buenos Aires (CABA). Although he thought the pay was sufficient, he did not like having to be a self-employed contractor. In fact, he believes that not wanting to be "self-employed," preferring a formal job with social security, was one of the factors which caused his dismissal from the company, with no compensation whatsoever.

The networks he has formed on the street, both in the area where he lives and the area where he sells, have also been sources of potential employment, but the jobs offered are always informal and offer lower pay than what he earns on the street—indeed, this same problem has also led him to refuse work in the formal labor market.

Joaquin's satisfaction with his work comes not so much from the type of work, which is exhausting and subject to climatic and economic instability, but rather because it has provided him with a means of subsistence. Accordingly, I can deduce that his work has an instrumental[9] meaning since it was "chosen" above other work opportunities that he refused, or that he tried out and did not like because he felt out of place, or because the low pay made them unacceptable.

The second turning point, the moment when he feels that his life took a downward turn, is when his child was born. The pregnancy was planned with his partner (two years older), and they had decided to live together some time before the pregnancy.

> And well what made me grow up completely…was my son… it's like you throw in the towel and I was really young, 22 and I threw in the towel, it's very early, and well I know, someday I'll be better off and things won't be so hard, and then I might enjoy life a bit more, because me and him [his cousin who sells flowers] we work all day, we don't enjoy life much, I see my son and he sees his children for a while at night and then next day it's the same again. I mean it's no fun, you just work, work, work, you can't enjoy what you should enjoy and your life is passing you by…when you were younger you had some fun, but not for long and when you have to take on a lot of responsibilities at that age it like hits you…see we wanted to have kids but maybe we rushed it a bit because we were so young. I think this is carrying the weight of responsibility…or maybe you can do your best to make sure they are alright…but the weight is so heavy…it's really hard work and all this makes you really tired and you feel wrecked, well maybe not wrecked, but you don't feel like going out like before: 'come on let's go and dance', 'let's go to that place'…you don't care anymore.

In chronological terms, he realizes he is young; however, the life he leads has made him feel older, describing himself as "wrecked." These representations about himself and what youth means seem to show that social expectations about age are still very important for some young people who see their future in terms of some hegemonic patterns of reference.

As regards the future, he aspires to finish his high school studies and is working toward this through a state program called "Plan FinEs" and with the economic support of a "Beca Progresar."[10] His hope is to be able to get a job as a bus driver, or at least a job with certain guarantees of stability and salary, rather than subsistence. A stable job, with its guarantees and securities, neither disappears nor loses its significance as a symbolic traditional reference. As regards the future and his son, Joaquin is reaching for a horizon that would allow him to offer his son the type of opportunities he never had, such as a university education and freedom from the need to work at such an early age.

Viewing Joaquin's biographical trajectory through the lens of Mora Salas and Oliveira's work (2014), certain indicators of inherited inequality are visible that have played an important part in shaping his trajectory: being a male child (although his sisters are older, they did not work as early as he did) in a low-income family made for an early entrance to the world of work, setting the conditions of his itinerary, and charting the course of his life. However, the support of his parents and a warm family life constituted key factors contributing to his overall positive image, one that has allowed him to rationalize many of his actions and choices and to decide what he wants and what he does not want within a limited context.

Faced with these scarce opportunities, Joaquin appears to have control over his life: he chooses from different work options that appear; he evaluates and attempts to control the path he follows, showing organization and foresight: saving money, buying a car, building a small brick house on his parents' plot, choosing to start a family early, and so forth.

Compared to other trajectories that combine activity with inactivity, Joaquin works continuously, six days a week for a routine number of hours, and this holds significant weight in the shaping of his identity. At the same time, his is an almost normal educational trajectory in which he did not fall behind in the institutional school year. His working life was compatible with his school life. However, his working activity and his constructed future expectations show the weight of the intergenerational reproduction of vulnerability: he does the same job as his father, a significant reference in the construction of his subjectivity.

Inert Trajectories

Mauricio is 17 years old. He works minding cars on a block in the city center. He lives in the area of Olmos (La Plata), about 12 km from the center. Every day, he commutes by bus with his father, who is disabled and in a wheel chair, to the center of La Plata where they earn a living minding and washing cars. He started work at age 6 or 7, minding cars at night in the center with his sister, while his father sold popcorn at the entrance to a cinema while also minding cars with his sons.

> My dad was working there...he started...because my dad was selling popcorn. And the owner of the stand said 'Why don't you start minding cars here? Mind the cars and work the stand at the same time'. Because we were in the entrance of the mall. He said 'do both things: sell and mind cars', so he said 'well, ok.' So he did what the owner said, and did both things. And so through the owner he started minding cars in 50 street, when it [the parking] wasn't metered. And so my dad was there for 25 years minding cars.

His parents are together, he is one of three children. He is the eldest, followed by a sister and a baby of a few months, and they make up the nuclear family. He also has an older brother, from his father's first marriage, with whom he has a very good relationship. When telling stories of his childhood, he makes no mention of any unusual or traumatic experience, though he remembers he often missed school during the times he worked on the street and when he worked as helper on a building site. His survival activities on the street played a hugely important role in shaping his biographical trajectory. It was here that he built up a solidarity network of social relationships, to which he is closer than to that of his own neighborhood; this is a key space of sociability for many low-income youths.

> And here on the street I feel more comfortable than at home...I feel more relaxed. Because ...there's more...I feel that the street can teach me more, more than school let's say...it gives you friendship and all that. Friendship! You meet new people every day. Those kind of opportunities.

Although Mauricio highlights his positive experiences in the search for subjective mechanisms that value his work in public spaces—"you have friends," "you get to know people," "you don't have a boss," and "you can do what you like"—and although it was a family experience (since he is a boy is there and that's what his father has done for 25 years), the fact is that he did not choose to work on the street. He worked there because throughout his life he never had any other opportunities for survival. Also, if he had a choice, he would prefer construction work, where he has been gathering experiences since a young age through his neighborhood contacts.

> Neighbors came looking for me…because they've known me since I was young, they know I can do everything. They call me to shovel earth and to lay bricks. All this…if I had to choose, I prefer construction work. Because there I've got 300 for sure, now 350. And on the street it's hard. On the street there's some days you make money and some days you don't, you know?

According to Mauricio's story, the preference for one activity over another comes exclusively from the ability to obtain a regular income, rather than concern over working conditions or even pay. He places more importance on knowing how much money will be coming in—money that will not be spent on personal expenses, but will contribute to the family household. In his biographical story, something happened that marked his path and redirected his life: the decision to abandon school education and dedicate himself to full-time work.

A: I went up to second year of high school. I left because I had to repeat the year and…well I repeated and after that …well I repeated the second year twice and then I kind of got lazy…I went and slept in class, I went and messed around with my mates, we messed around with the boys in the other third year, because we messed around in every way. We'd go and then go outside, buy a soft drink, get something to drink. I just went to waste time…

Q: And after school you used to come here?

A: No, when I went to school I used to come here now and then, let's say. But then later on I lost interest in school and I liked working more than studying.

Considering the frustrations generated by school failure ("I'm lazy"), particularly in the context of an educational system in crisis due to fragmentation and segmentation processes, it is possible to understand how the choice to leave school early and the preference for work could have appeared to be a reasonable response to his situation. Nevertheless, he has not abandoned hope of concluding his school education at some point on his future horizon. Thinking about a possible future, Mauricio shows a desire to finish his studies and apply to enter the police force.

> I want to apply. Not for money but because I want to study, I want to finish [school] and then I want to join the police. I've got this idea, to finish school and become a police officer. I don't like it but …I tell everyone, It's not

> about being a cop it's for the money let's say. Because the police earn good money... I know that if I'm in the police I'll get by, I'll have things I need. And there'll be something for me. I know that in the future if I can't work as a policeman anymore, I know I'll be settled, and I know I'll have one day....I know I'll have a house, a bit of land, all mine. I'll know that it's mine.

As in the case of Joaquin, work has an instrumental significance, and at the same time, it organizes and marks the rhythm of his daily life. He leaves home every day at the same time and goes by bus with his father to work in the center for an average of eight hours per day. He also combines this activity with odd jobs in his neighborhood at the weekend. The fact that he has always worked with his father shows the key role of family support in this type of trajectory. In the construction of his biography, an amenable family atmosphere is clearly perceivable in the way he relates his life experience.

In contrast to Joaquin, the social relationships he was able to build on the street did not lead to doors opening to other, different work opportunities. He has continued to oscillate exclusively between street work and construction work. The possibilities of choice are much more limited in his case, showing a tendency, with certain inertia, to develop practices that reproduce his position.

As regards a probable future, his highest aspiration appears to be to conclude his schooling and enter a low-qualified job in the police force on the understanding that this job would give him stability and a reliable, sufficient income to improve his conditions and "get by."

Limited Trajectories

This type of biographical narrative is typical of most of the young people interviewed. They share experiences of suffering from an early age, conditions of misery and extreme poverty with an absent or dead parent or parents. Other recurring features of the itineraries of these young people are the consumption of different types of drugs from early in life, experiences of neglect and delinquency, times when living on the street was the only option, and long periods of absence from school (not secondary, but primary) and institutionalization (in macro institutes for minors, the penal system or closed institutions for drug rehabilitation). On numerous occasions, these factors have combined to put their very lives at risk. It is notable that there are not one or two, but numerous turning points in these itineraries that directed and redirected the life courses. In some cases, these experiences led to positive expectations for the future associated with a vague possibility of finishing primary school and going on to secondary and further education, thereby hoping to change things and improve their conditions of life.

Augusto is 18 years old, minds cars in the city center, and is about to become a father. His partner, a little older than himself, is also working on the street with her mother and sisters. He lives in a poor neighborhood on the outer edge of the city and started work aged 10. His first work activity was on the street doing a bit of everything: selling flowers, washing windscreens, minding cars—experiences that intermittently transformed the street into his home.

> From when I was little I wanted to have my own money but couldn't get a job anywhere…I found one here, on the street…I've been here a long time, I learnt the bad, the good and I'm still young but I know a lot.
>
> I've been in places you would never imagine!…I always used to hang out with people older than me…people who knew …what they used to call the 'law of the street', that was before, not like the 'gauchos' now with nothing in their heads, before you learnt to have some respect and you didn't rob an old lady or an old man. You robbed someone who you can see has got money and is doing well. But I've robbed a lot, I was in drug rehab a long time, about seven or eight months, I got into trouble with the police…I was like that then, …going around off my head…but I always knew, I don't know, I always knew what's wrong and right but I was into the wrong and I knew I shouldn't do it…there are things which make you nasty too, maybe some resentment or something that happened on the street and they did the same to me, you know?…but anyway bit by bit, well I always had it in my head to do things right, but I've started to realize gradually and now I'm living as I'm living.

It is worth noting that Augusto and those who share this type of itinerary assign the "bad life" to some choice or decision of their own making. They think that they are "to blame," that they are "the worst" rather than perceiving that what happens to them might include circumstances beyond their control. In spite of blaming himself, Augusto has had a few brief periods in which he obtained work with a butcher and in a supermarket. His last job, which he lost over a month ago, was on a building site; the loss of it brought him back to the street.

> I came back because I was desperate, because I'd been out of work a week and I was broke and up to my neck, I owed money and so I came back and I said no, at one time I was going here and there getting up too all sorts... mind the cars I said to myself and so I started minding. And I didn't count the money, I just kept on and on...and then at the bus stop I counted the money and I wanted to cry because I didn't have anything. And I said no man no, I had nothing, but I still came here and at least I got a bit of money!

Although Augusto sees going back to the street as returning to a familiar place, the situation nevertheless causes him anxiety: "people think I'm going to rob them" or "a lot of them give me dirty looks." Similar to the previous cases, work assumes a purely instrumental meaning, but in contrast to the itineraries above, working on the street does not function as a means to organize daily routines. For him rhythm and intensity vary due to his needs—he does not work the same number of hours every day—so the regularity found in the above two trajectories is missing. He also feels he has no choice but to return to the street because of the scarce or non-existent family networks to help him.

> I sort myself out. I can't ask my mum for anything...she can't... She can't give me a hand, and my dad not at all and well, so ...I'm alone although...I always try to put a brave face on everything, everything. Sometimes everything gets you down, lots of things get you down and it's hard to pick yourself up and maybe you are...you have thoughts like 'yes, today I can do it,' 'I'm here today,' 'in the future'...and there's also the thought that 'no, no I can't'.... 'no, it's too late' and this and that and the other also bring you down.

As well as living on the street and being locked up, his impending paternity has now been added to the series of turning points shaping the course of Augusto's life. The assumption of a new role has given him a sense of urgency and the need to project a future that perhaps he could not see clearly before.

> I've got some urgent worries: I want to get something good, a real job. I've got a head for studying, I talk to people and I feel like starting my life, starting my house, my bit of land, some project for the future, stuff like that...I look at myself and say no to the other boys, they don't think like me, and well in the future, I don't just want secondary school finished, I want to do a course or something...like working with plants or something, something I'd like to study, I don't know, something. You really have to have qualifications to be someone in society, it's not enough just to know stuff yourself.

All the young people interviewed share conditions of extreme poverty—in terms of both income and structure—and scarce opportunities in the labor market. But other factors add to the additional and frequent instabilities: early parenthood, weak or nonexistent family ties, sporadic contact with school, weak emotional support, and recurring institutionalization. All these elements forge early trajectories in which weak social integration puts young people at extremely high risk, including risks to life itself (such as armed skirmishes with police, contemplation of suicide, etc.).

In summary, I outline a series of observations regarding the trajectories under study. The classification of the three types serves to show how, faced with similar structural conditions, small margins of difference appear that favor the creation of different trajectories, revealing clear constraints to social integration. While the biographies above show these possible paths, there is also a combination of common patterns in the makeup of the trajectories.

Firstly, when confronting the restrictions imposed by the local labor market, the subjects bring different strategies into play in which precarious, unstable, and short-term work is alternated with street work. In a highly uncertain context and given the great difficulty of finding formal work, the only known horizon that is familiar, certain, and stable is the street.

Faced with the demand for educational qualifications imposed by the real world on those looking for work, these young people are far from reaching them or even thinking about them as future possibilities. In some cases, the highest aspiration is to finish secondary school, while only a small number take this a step further and think about the possibility of higher education. However, those who can imagine this possibility are perhaps those with the least chance of making it a reality.

Looking back at the interview fragment with Augusto (18 years old), we can see that he mentioned wanting to study "about plants" at university, by which he meant a degree in biology. The desire to finish basic education is linked purely and exclusively to the possibility of obtaining formal work, since the idea of integration through a regular salary represents a very strong horizon for the present and future expectations of these young people. If anything will help them leave their present situation, it is to finish school and become regular wage earners.

When confronting the limitations imposed by background and social class, there is a significant element of self-blame for their social position and lives in general: bad decisions (Joaquin thinking about his early paternity), personal inabilities ("I'm lazy," "I'm useless at studying," expressed by Mauricio), or perceiving themselves as "bad" or "going the wrong way" (Augusto). These all point to the way the persistence of inequality is influenced by subjective dimensions.

Faced with the possibility of imagining and projecting their near future, these young people orient their trajectories toward a very limited horizon: they aspire to low-qualified, purely instrumental activities to achieve work stability, better working conditions, a regular wage, and access to social security and worker protections.

Final Reflections: From Childhood to Youth—Elements That Shape Vulnerable but Heterogeneous Life Courses

In this chapter, I began by outlining the challenges of the 2030 Agenda for Sustainable Development related to child labor. I particularly emphasized the need to contextualize the phenomenon and attempt to understand the network of relationships within which it takes place. I argued that general proposals to "eradicate child labor" without recognizing the heterogeneous and diverse experiences it encompasses can lead to erroneous social policies. In fact, none of the cases analyzed showed that the experience of work at an early age was the only factor shaping vulnerable trajectories; a combination of other factors was also involved. I therefore insist on the need for recognizing the complexity of problems affecting childhood as a whole, rather than an exclusive focus on one single factor.

This chapter has analyzed the construction of different biographical trajectories among a group of low-income youth who have worked on the street since early childhood, highlighting the heterogeneity of possible life courses. With respect to the shaping of these life courses, notwithstanding their shared structural constraints, I emphasized the role of different elements that motivate social action and contribute to the variations in the directions and outcomes of different courses. Studying the growth paths of these youths beginning in childhood allows us to comprehend the effects of social change, and the extent to which social measures might be successful, precisely given these constraints. My research shows that despite growing up in a more promising political, economic, and social context than that of the 1990s, these changes do not appear to have had much effect.

The life course perspective proposed by Elder (1994) to explain the ways in which childhood and youth trajectories are produced over time has been a very useful tool, in that both the trajectory and the transient nature of the approach itself allow us to observe the development of subjects' lives over time and the unequal appropriation of resources (material, affective, and symbolic), which explain the setting and accumulation of social disadvantage. The combination of the latter approach with the analytical model of Mora Salas and Oliveira (2014) enables consideration of the interplay between a wide range of elements, shedding light on what factors and situations are combined early on to produce vulnerable but heterogeneous trajectories. This identification allows us to observe different issues: on one hand, the levels of fragility and weakness in social bonds (with the weakest and most fragile clearly belonging to the third type of life course), and on the other hand, the finding that working on the street does not position the subjects within a homogenous and undifferentiated group, in contrast to common beliefs, but rather that this condition is processed, given meaning, and is combined with other factors in different ways.

As pointed out earlier, initiation into child labor did not of itself mark turning points in the biographies of those interviewed; however, these early experiences in the world of work influenced other circumstances that left imprints and marked out different life courses. This observation underlines the value of the heuristic approach used, emphasizing the weight of not one, but several different factors that over the course of time tend to reinforce the location of many children and youths in a disadvantaged position compared to other children of the same generation.

To be born and raised in a low-income home has long-term consequences. In fact, the young people interviewed have worked since they were young because of the daily needs of their families. However, to be male or female, to be the eldest brother or sister, to suffer neglect, sickness, or death of one of their parents, and receive little affection or support are other factors that greatly affect the biographies. When this develops in the context of scarce work opportunities for young people and adults, we find a combination of circumstances that make it difficult to leave the spiral of disadvantage that fixes them into subordinate positions within the social structure from an early age. Accordingly, the life trajectories are oriented toward a limited horizon: low-qualified activities chosen to enable access to steady, formal work, and not just any kind of work but rather those in which they feel comfortable—recalling the experience of

Joaquin in the call center, where he worked formally but could not stand the weight of social difference between himself and the other employees. If young people do not feel comfortable in a work environment, this subjective experience reflects an objective circumstance, and one that perpetuates inequality. In the end, the construction of subjective expectations and practices keeps them in the same place.

Notes

1. See "Brasilia Declaration on Child Labour" (ILO, 2013). Retrieved from www.ilo.org/ipecinfo/product/download.do?type=document&id=23480
2. The largest number of child workers belongs to the low-income sector.
3. The research was developed by a team of sociologists. For the fieldwork, a team of research assistants was added. For a detailed explanation concerning the methodological definitions of this study, see Rausky, Crego, Peiró, and Santos (2016).
4. The sequential mixed design is based on quantitative and qualitative strategies, specifically referring to a proposal of inquiry that addresses the object of study in different phases (two) where the methodological strategies are integrated. It is important to highlight that each phase is understood as a unit where the instances of conceptualization (decisions about what), methodologies (selection decisions, collection, and analysis), and inference are articulated.
5. Part of the results of the survey and its analysis can be found in Rausky, María Eugenia, Santos, Javier, Peiró, María Laura, and Crego, María Laura (2016).
6. For its construction, three variables were crossed: age group, sex, and type of work.
7. In the case of working with children, the approach was different from the one we carried out with the young people. As noted by specialists in childhood studies, although interviews with children can be held, they are usually shorter and are accompanied by other approaches such as observation that allows recognizing what cannot be verbalized, something that we emphasize for this age group.
8. See Bourdieu (2007), Giddens (1998), and Corcuff (2013).
9. Different classifications on work orientations can be found in the literature on the modes of valuing work. One of these refers to an instrumental or extrinsic vision of work and another refers to an expressive or intrinsic vision. The first looks at a vision of work that mainly values the material and economic rewards, especially the salary. The second looks at the value of intrinsic rewards that allow personal development and satisfaction and includes characteristics that permit social interaction between workers (Veira & Muñoz, 2004).

10. "Plan FinEs" is a flexible education program that allows people to finish their secondary school education who were unable to conclude within the institutional time frame. "Beca Progresar" provides a grant for further education studies. Both programs were designed under the government of Cristina Fernández de Kirchner (2007–2015).

Bibliography

Bayón, M. C. (2013). Hacia una sociología de la pobreza: la relevancia de las dimensiones culturales. *Estudios Sociológicos, XXXI*(91), 87–112.

Bertaux, D. (2005). *Los relatos de vida. Perspectiva etnosociológica*. Barcelona, Spain: Ediciones Bellaterra.

Blanco, M. (2011). El enfoque del curso de vida, orígenes y desarrollo. *Revista Latinoamericana de Población, 5*(8), 5–31.

Bottero, W. (2007). Social Inequality and Interaction. *Sociology Compass, 1*(2), 814–831.

Bourdieu, P. (2007). *El sentido práctico*. Buenos Aires, Argentina: Siglo XXI.

Carli, S. (2005). Infancia, cultura y educación en las décadas del 80 y 90 en Argentina. *Serie Documento de trabajo: Escuela de Educación*. Buenos Aires, Argentina: Universidad de San Andrés.

Carli, S. (2010). Notas para pensar la infancia en la argentina (1983–2001): figuras de la historia reciente. *Educacao em Revista, 26*(01), 351–382.

Casal, J., Garcia, M., Merino, R., & Quesada, M. (2006). Aportaciones teóricas y metodológicas a la sociología de la juventud desde la perspectiva de la transición. *Papers. Revista de Sociología, 79*, 21–48.

Colangelo, A. (2014). La crianza como proceso sociocultural. Posibles aportes de la antropología al abordaje médico de la niñez. Primeras Jornadas Diversidad en la Niñez. Hospital El Dique, Ensenada (Buenos Aires).

Corcuff, P. (2013). *Las nuevas sociologías*. Buenos Aires, Argentina: Siglo XXI.

Duek, C. (2014). *Juegos, juguetes y nuevas tecnologías*. Buenos Aires, Argentina: Capital intelectual.

Elder, G. (1994). Time, Human Agency, and Social Change: Perspectives on the Life Course. *Social Psychology Quarterly, 57*(1), 4–15.

Enriz, N. (2014). Juego, concepto y ordenamiento de una práctica escurridiza. *Espacios en Blanco – Serie indagaciones, 24*(1), 17–34.

Fitoussi, J., & Rosanvallon, P. (2003). *La nueva era de las desigualdades*. Buenos Aires, Argentina: Manantial.

Giddens, A. (1998). *La constitución de la sociedad*. Buenos Aires, Argentina: Amorrortu.

Hecht, A., & García, M. (2010). Categorías étnicas. Un estudio con niños y niñas de un barrio indígena. *Revista Latinoamericana de Ciencias Sociales, Niñez y Juventud, 8*(2), 981–994.

James, A., & Prout, A. (1990). *Constructing and Reconstructing Childhood: Contemporary Issues in the Sociological Study of Childhood*. London, UK: Routledge.

Kessler, G., & Espinoza, V. (2003). Movilidad social y trayectorias ocupacionales en Argentina: rupturas y algunas paradojas del caso de Buenos Aires. *Serie Políticas Sociales*, 66, Santiago de Chile, Chile: CEPAL.

Kessler, G., & Merklen, D. (2013). Una introducción cruzando el atlántico. In R. Castel, G. Kessler, D. Merklen, & N. Murard (Eds.), *Individuación, Precariedad, Inseguridad ¿Desinstitucionalización del presente?* (pp. 9–31). Buenos Aires, Argentina: Paidós.

Llobet, V. (2006). Las políticas sociales para una infancia vulnerable. Algunas reflexiones desde la psicología. *Revista de Ciencias Sociales, Niñez y Juventud, 4*(1), 4–20.

Llobet, V. (2012). Una lectura sobre el trabajo infantil como objeto de estudio. A propósito del aporte de Viviana Zelizer. *Desarrollo Económico, 52*(206), 311–328.

Llobet, V., & Litichever, C. (2010). Desigualdad e Inclusión Social. ¿Qué proponen los programas de atención a niños, niñas y adolescentes? In J. A. Trejo Sánchez, A. Itatí Palermo, & J. Arzate Salgado (Eds.), *Desigualdades Sociales y ciudadanía desde las culturas juveniles en América Latina* (pp. 217–234). Toluca, Mexico: Miguel Porrúa – UAEM.

Macri, M., Ford, M., Berliner, C., & Molteni, M. J. (2005). *El trabajo infantil no es juego. Estudios e investigaciones sobre trabajo infanto-adolescente en argentina (1900–2003)*. Buenos Aires, Argentina: Editorial Stella/ La Crujía.

Makowski, S. (2010). *Jóvenes que viven en la calle*. Mexico City, Mexico: Siglo XXI.

Mora Salas, M., & de Oliveira, O. (2014). Los jóvenes en el inicio de la vida adulta: trayectorias, transiciones y subjetividades. *Estudios Sociológicos, XXVII*(79), 267–289.

Muñiz Terra, L. (2012). Carreras y trayectorias laborales: una revisión crítica de las principales aproximaciones teórico-metodológicas para su abordaje. *Revista Latinoamericana de Metodología de las Ciencias Sociales, 2*(1), 36–65.

Noceti, B. (2006). Trabajo infantil y salud. Estrategias de fortalecimiento interinstitucional a favor de la comunidad. *Pluralidades. Quintas Jornadas Nacionales de Investigación Social de Infancia y Adolescencia. La Convención Internacional de los Derechos del Niño y las prácticas sociales*. Facultad de Ciencias Jurídicas y Sociales: UNLP.

Ortale, S. (2015). Acerca de la crianza. Reflexiones sobre el bienestar infantil. In J. Reichenbach, S. Fontana, & W. Gómez (Eds.), *Pediatría en Red. Portal de Educación Permanente en Pediatría* (pp. 116–120). La Plata, Argentina: Ministerio de Salud de la Provincia de Buenos Aires. Retrieved from http://www.ms.gba.gov.ar/ssps/Pediatria.pdf

Pautassi, L. (2007). La articulación entre políticas públicas y derechos, vínculos difusos. In X. Erazo, V. Abramovich, & J. Orbe (Eds.), *Políticas públicas para un estado social de derechos* (Vol. II, pp. 89–116). Santiago de Chile, Chile: Fundación Henry Dunant América Latina & Editorial LOM.

Pojomovsky, J. (2008). *Cruzar la calle. Niñez y adolescencia en las calles de la ciudad.* Buenos Aires, Argentina: Biblos.

Rausky, M. E. (2011). La calle y los niños: estrategias laborales en espacios públicos. *Avá. Revista de Antropología, 19*, 319–346.

Rausky, M. E. (2015). Los niños y niñas que trabajan: relaciones de género y generacionales. In A. Eguía, S. Ortale, & J. I. Piovani (Eds.), *Género, trabajo y políticas sociales. Apuntes teórico-metodológicos y estudios de caso en el Gran La Plata* (pp. 111–134). Buenos Aires. Argentina: CLACSO.

Rausky, M. E., Crego, M. L., Peiró, M. L., & Santos, J. (2016). Claves para pensar en la construcción de un objeto de investigación complejo: decisiones teórico-metodológicas en un abordaje multimétodo sobre niños/as, adolescentes y jóvenes que trabajan en las calles (La Plata, Buenos Aires, Argentina). *Empiria. Revista de Metodología de las Ciencias Sociales, 34*, 15–38.

Rausky, M. E., Santos, J., Peiró, M. L., & Crego, M. L. (2016). Trabajo callejero de niños/as, adolescentes y jóvenes: resultados del abordaje de una población de acceso complejo en la ciudad de La Plata, Buenos Aires, Argentina. *Papeles de Población, 22*(89), 9–41.

Rausky, M. E. (2009). Trabajo y familia: el aporte de los niños trabajadores a la reproducción del hogar. *Revista Trabajo y Sociedad, 12*, 1–17.

Remorini, C. (2015). El papel de los niños en la obtención, elaboración, circulación y consumo de alimentos en comunidades Mbya (Argentina). *Anthropology of Food, 9*, 1–15. Retrieved from: http://aof.revues.org/7770

Santillán, L. (2006). La construcción social del problema de la educación: un estudio antropológico desde la perspectiva y los modos de vida de los grupos familiares. *Intersecciones en Antropología, 7*, 375–386.

Santillán, L. (2007). La "educación" y la "escolarización" infantil en tramas de intervención local: una etnografía en los contornos de la escuela. *Revista Mexicana de Investigación Educativa, 1*(34), 895–919.

Saraví, G. (2007). Nuevas realidades y nuevos enfoques. In G. Saraví (Ed.), *De la pobreza a la exclusión. Continuidades y rupturas de la cuestión social en América Latina* (pp. 19–52). Mexico City, Mexico: CIESAS.

Saraví, G. (2015). *Juventudes fragmentadas. Socialización, clase y cultura en México.* Mexico City, Mexico: CIESAS.

Silva, R. (2014). *Los chicos en la calle: llegar, vivir y salir de la interperie urbana.* Buenos Aires, Argentina: Espacio Editorial.

Sirota, R. (2001). Emergencia de uma sociologia da infancia: evolucao du objeto e do olhar. *Cadernos de Pesquisa, 112*, 7–31.

Szulc, A. (2016). *La niñez mapuche: sentidos de pertenencia en tensión*. Buenos Aires, Argentina: Biblios.
Teddlie, A., & Tashakori, C. (2006). A General Typology of Research Designs Featuring Mixed Methods. *Research in the Schools, 13*(1), 12–28.
Thomson, R., Bell, R., Holland, J., Henderson, S., McGrellis, S., & Sharpe, S. (2002). Critical Moments: Choice, Change and Opportunity in Young People's Narratives of Transition. *Sociology, 36*(2), 335–354.
UN. (2015). *Transforming Our World: The 2030 Agenda for Sustainable Development*. Retrieved from https://sustainabledevelopment.un.org/post2015/transformingourworld
Veira, J. L., & Muñoz, C. (2004). Valores y actitudes del trabajo en Europa Occidental. *Revista Española de Sociología, 4*, 51–66.
Wagmiller Jr., R., & Adelman, R. (2009). *Childhood and Intergenerational Poverty. The Long-term Consequences of Growing Up Poor.* National Center for Children in Poverty, Mailman School of Public Health, Columbia University.

PART II

Youth, Poverty and Labor

CHAPTER 4

Working Lives of Youth in Poverty in Urban Argentina

Gonzalo Assusa and Mariana Chaves

Introduction

What characterizes those who work and live in poverty starting in adolescence or childhood? Is escape from poverty truly attainable? Which mechanisms, tools, and events make it possible to move away from a life trajectory of poverty, when employment alone is not enough to make this shift? What continuities or breakdowns can be identified in the trajectory in relation to the economic and political context, the events, and the available networks of assistance? Does labor beginning in childhood or adolescence accumulate disadvantage? Why and how? How do working conditions influence this dynamic? How is it influenced by gender? And finally, how does the symbolic dimension articulate itself as the creator of differences and inequalities among working and poor adolescents and young people?

G. Assusa (✉)
IDH-CONICET-UNC, Córdoba, Argentina

M. Chaves (✉)
CONICET, Facultad de Trabajo Social, Universidad Nacional de La Plata, La Plata, Buenos Aires, Argentina
e-mail: mchaves@fcnym.unlp.edu.ar

M. E. Rausky, M. Chaves (eds.), *Living and Working in Poverty in Latin America*, Governance, Development, and Social Inclusion in Latin America, https://doi.org/10.1007/978-3-030-00901-4_4

While some of these opening questions may seem impossible to answer, they challenge us to consider a range of angles, seeking to understand not only the lives of working children and adolescents in poverty and the phenomenon of working in poverty throughout the life course but also the design of policies to reduce inequality and bring greater dignity to the lives of individuals. The inconsistencies in confronting the issues of poverty and work—previously analyzed in the introduction of the book—are explored again in this chapter. Located in Argentina, our analysis centers on how people between 15 and 24 years old work and live in poverty. These young people have several years of working experience, since most of them began working during childhood or adolescence and are part of families—both nuclear and extended—with low incomes.

Methodologically, this text is based on complementary fieldwork by the two authors. Chaves' fieldwork was carried out in a suburban neighborhood of the city of La Plata (Province of Buenos Aires), and Assusa's fieldwork was done in different neighborhoods of the city of Córdoba Capital (Province of Córdoba).[1] Both conducted interviews and kept records of participant observation. Permanent Household Survey (PHS)[2] data were used for population analysis, including an initial characterization of the situation of working and poor youth in Argentina. The same data allowed us to make diachronic (over a period of time) and synchronic (regarding differences and inequalities among social classes) comparisons, to enable readers from other regions to understand the major trends in social conditions in Argentina. The richness of combining both data records and the complementary nature of quantitative and qualitative results provide a much wider framework for interpreting the phenomenon under analysis.

The interpretations that we make in this chapter are part of the tradition of researchers in the field of inequality study (Dubet, 2015; Goldthorpe, 2012; Reygadas, 2004; Therborn, 2015; Tilly, 2000), about life courses in general (Elder, 1994, 1998; Elder, Kirkpatrick, & Crosnoe, 2003), and for Latin America (Bayón, 2015; Mora Salas & de Oliveira, 2014; Saraví, 2009, 2015), in Argentina about social mobility (Bendit & Miranda, 2015; Busso & Pérez, 2016; Chávez Molina & Pla, 2013; Espinoza & Kessler, 2003; Salvia & Lindenboim, 2015), about youth's trajectory and work (Balardini & Miranda, 2000; Jacinto, 2002; Jacinto, Wolf, Bessega, & Longo, 2005; Miranda & Arancibia, 2017; Pérez & Busso, 2014, 2015; Piecke Goicochea, 2001); and about poverty, youth, and work (Assusa, 2017; Chaves, 2014a; Chaves, Fuentes, & Vecino, 2016; Efron,

Konterllnik, & Jacinto, 1996; Gallart, 2001; Macri & Van Kemenade, 1993; Saraví, 2006, 2015), to mention only the main areas for engaging in dialogue with the purpose of providing some answers on this issue.

This chapter is organized in four sections that allow us to show structural trends, peculiarities, and symbolic disputes in the accumulation of disadvantage and the construction of inequality networks. Following the Introduction, the second section uses statistical data to provide a portrayal of the living and working conditions of young men and women. The third section focuses on three trajectories analyzed from the life course perspective (Elder, 1994; Mora Salas & de Oliveira, 2014). Finally, the concluding discussion reexamines the opening questions in light of results obtained, public policies, and the 2030 Agenda for Sustainable Development.

Youth, Work, and Poverty in Argentina: Statistical Data as a Tool for Interpretation

The period in Argentina between 2003 and 2015 presents complexities and opposing trends[3]: in different areas and dimensions of social life—from the labor market and income distribution to health, education, and access to land—social inequalities have tended to reconfigure and reproduce themselves or reduce their gaps in dissimilar ways (Kessler, 2014). However, in analytical terms, this period can be interpreted as one of relative coherence and directionality. Views vary with regard to the labor market dynamic in the years previously mentioned (Benza, 2016; Palomino & Dalle, 2012; Quartulli & Salvia, 2012; Vera, 2013). However, there is certain agreement that this period is characterized by a discontinuity of the neoliberal model pursued during the 1990s and the remarkable contraction of workforce demand in that period.

After the crisis of 2001 and the devaluation of the national currency, a combination of measures led to a reorientation toward economic recovery, mainly deploying the fixed productive capacity that had remained inactive during the period of convertibility, leading to a considerable increase in the demand for unskilled labor during the first years of the postconvertibility period.[4]

The period beginning in 2003 saw unemployment and poverty reaching their highest levels in the country's history, with unemployment finally settling below 10% for almost all of 2015, with a progressive tendency to decrease, including during the years when job creation came to a standstill. Intergenerationally speaking, while the overall unemployment was on the decline, the differences between the unemployment indexes of young people (15–24 years old) and adults (25–64 years old) remained relatively stagnant over the entire period. The proportional relationship between unemployment in the two groups is about 2:1. This constitutes a worldwide trend, considered a public concern by international organizations (ILO, 2012, 2013).

Discussions around the dimensions of poverty are more complex: the Argentinian government's official poverty statistics have been a topic of considerable political dispute in recent years, their estimation being impugned, defended, and reconsidered by different sectors.[5] However, focusing on young people from poor families requires abandoning the statistical naivety that considers an age category ("youth") as a homogeneous collective. At the same time, it also requires moving away from a common epistemological position in public policy against poverty, which asserts that social exclusion, marginalization, and vulnerability can be eliminated simply by integration into the labor market while neglecting to consider the more complex forces behind the lack of material and symbolic resources in poor families. Because of this, we consider it necessary to show not only the unequal way unemployment affects young people at different positions within the social structure but also the variable nature of integration into a highly stratified labor market and its implications for access to social security systems.

Discussion about the complexity and multidimensionality of social inequalities is extensive in the social sciences, and an examination of the methodological disputes over the operation of an empirical construction of inequalities would make for an entire article in its own right. With a view to establishing certain parameters of international comparison and the aim of favoring critical dialogue with researchers from the greatest theoretical spectrum possible, we collected data considering the per capita income in families of young people between 15 and 24 years old as a stratified variable.

Stratification studies and social inequality enable categorizing individuals and families into specific social classes in a variety of ways. The classic perspectives on stratification, based on different theoretical frameworks (Crompton, 1997; Rivas Rivas, 2008), consider the socio-occupational category of heads of household as the closest proxy to the position of the agents in production relationships and, therefore, to their class position. Other research and reports published by international organizations have considered money income as the main inequality variable, due to the ease of using a numerical variable for these characteristics (Ferreira et al., 2013).

Considering that our research is not exclusively quantitative, we show some statistical trends on inequalities affecting young people by grouping them together according to their per capita income. Using the national PHS[6] for the second trimesters of 2004 and 2015, we grouped together the 30% of cases with the lowest income, the 10% of cases with the highest income, and the cases in between. In this way, we show how both advantages and disadvantages are unequally distributed and the way this uneven distribution represents a cumulative historical trend that has determined the strategies and experiences of young people and their families in the world of work (Saraví, 2009). Using these trends as a framework for interpretation, in the next section, we aim for a qualitative reconstruction of a number of specific life stories, exploring the articulation between the life courses, cumulative disadvantage, positions, trajectories, and class conditions of those young people who form part of the poorest 30%.

But first, we will analyze the resource distribution and the work-related "issues" among young members of families with different and unequal incomes. First, we address the major differences in unemployment rates, inactive population, and kinds of inactivity. This will enable us to see some initial trends in terms of labor participation and the care economy, to provide greater understanding of the issues surrounding this text. Then we will analyze data on medical coverage, social security enrollment, establishment size, job qualifications, and the use of technology to show the degree to which, even among those employed, the wide range of conditions, opportunities, remuneration, and protections available through work are highly unequal.

As shown in Table 4.1, even though unemployment decreased in every income group, youth from low-income families remain almost five times more likely to be unemployed than their high-income counterparts. To be

Table 4.1 Unemployed and inactive population among young people (aged 15–24) according to income group (2004–2015)

	Group of low incomes		*Group of medium and medium-high incomes*		*Group of high incomes*	
	2004	*2015*	*2004*	*2015*	*2004*	*2015*
Employed (from actives)	59%	75%	74%	85%	87%	94%
Unemployed (from actives)	41%	25%	26%	15%	13%	6%
Inactive (from AEP)	58%	73%	56%	66%	54%	55%

Source: Authors' own elaboration based on data from PHS 2004 and 2015

clear, unemployment is much lower in 2015 than in 2004. The context of integration in recent years is much less marked by the crisis and desperation among young people seeking workforce integration. However, as the life courses analyzed in the next section will show, unequal exposure to rejection and exclusion in the search for employment is a recurring theme throughout these years.

For the approach that we suggest, it is also necessary to consider the proportion of the so-called inactive members of this age group: while much less unequally distributed than unemployment, inactivity also affects mainly young people with low incomes, and particularly young women.

Focusing on this trend, Table 4.2 reveals that inactivity due to concentration on domestic labor ("housewife") among young people from low-income families is three times higher than the percentage of the same category among young people from high-income families. This trend leads—in relational terms—to a greater number of young people from poor families excluded from the labor market (whether unemployed or inactive); within this group, there is higher exposure to the type of activities that do not involve resource accumulation (such as obtaining educational credentials) that might "improve" the possibilities of labor integration in the future: many of them are young people outside of both paid employment and training practices.

In this way, we can evaluate how poverty exposes young people (but mainly young women) to much more complex choices and articulations than merely the choice between "studying or working." This can also be perceived through the unequal configuration of families. The average number of members under 10 in low-income families is almost ten times higher than the same average in high-income families. If we also consider the income differential, both the possibilities of attending domestic

Table 4.2 Type of inactivity for economically inactive young people (aged 15–24) according to income group (2004–2015)

	Group of low incomes		*Group of medium and medium-high incomes*		*Group of high incomes*	
	2004	*2015*	*2004*	*2015*	*2004*	*2015*
Student	69%	70%	83%	82%	92%	87%
Housewife	19%	16%	11%	10%	5%	6%

Source: Authors' own elaboration based on data from PHS 2004 and 2015

demands (such as by hiring a care assistant) and the dimension of these chores (the number of people in the house requiring care) make this activity much more arduous in low-income homes, due to the need for more working hours and/or human energy to attend the domestic management of a greater number of people.

As we have seen in a substantial part of our fieldwork, the care economy is a significant part of women's life since childhood: the unequal distribution of chores among siblings depending on their gender becomes broader as they grow older, encroaching into adolescence, and youth (Hernandez, Cingolani, & Chaves, 2015). Additionally, young women's work taking care of their siblings is frequently replaced—or overlapped—by taking care of their own children. Finally, the practical knowledge accumulated due to involvement in domestic chores within their own family develops, in many cases, into a resource for labor integration: many of young women's first employment experiences involve taking care of young children and older adults, in combination with cleaning tasks and related activities.

In this way, the trajectories of poor young people must constantly articulate between "studying," "working," and "providing care," depending on the cycles of accumulation and economic restriction within their families.

At the same time, even though period from 2003 to 2015 is characterized by an increase in formal employment among dependent workers, Table 4.3 reveals a similar process to the one observed in unemployment: informality decreased in every income group among young people, but it maintained an unequal structure that keeps more than the half of low-income young people in the informal sector (in comparison to a fifth of

Table 4.3 Social security indicators among young people (aged 15–24) according to income group (2004–2015)

	Group of low incomes		*Group of medium and medium-high incomes*		*Group of high incomes*	
	2004	*2015*	*2004*	*2015*	*2004*	*2015*
Without health coverage	73%	62%	41%	29%	14%	9%
Informal	95%	62%	66%	46%	41%	19%
Work in places of more than 40 people	19%	18%	17%	26%	28%	36%

Source: Authors' own elaboration based on data from PHS 2004 and 2015

high-income young people in the same situation). The smaller numbers of poor youth working for large employers (which, according to conventional wisdom, are considered to be the most subject to state oversight and, consequently, less inclined to be involved in the informal labor market) also offer evidence of the same dynamic.

While the sphere of employment activity does not of itself determine working conditions beyond hierarchies and job posts, the unequal distribution between spheres has significance for labor contexts with very disparate trends regarding the level of macroeconomic activity and the precariousness of job posts. While some areas like industry and commerce hold great influence over youth employment, their distribution by income group is rather homogeneous. Other areas, however, such as public administration, have a strong association with the high-income group, while domestic service and the construction sector are statistically associated with low-income young people. The last areas mentioned are characterized by a lack of job security as regards contract duration, formality of the job, and wages (Fernández Massi, 2014). According to 2016 data from the National Institute of Statistics and Census of Argentina (INDEC), the rate of informality in domestic services exceeds 74%, while in construction it exceeds 68%. As will be shown in later sections, the decisive step into these areas leaves an indelible imprint on the work experience of youth from poor families, with the appreciation and valuation systems specific to these spheres coming into play throughout their trajectories. What is more, their experiences in construction and domestic services are essential for practical job training and for understanding both the intergenerational relationship that regulates and articulates activities (work/care work) within their families.

The figures referring to health coverage in Table 4.3 point out a complementary process that feeds this trend. Despite the fact that the number of young people without health coverage decreased in every income group during the period from 2004 to 2015, it decreased to a lesser extent in the low-income group than in the medium- and high-income groups. This is due mainly to the ability of the family as a whole to access these kinds of resources: during this period, adults from medium- and high-income families were incorporated at much higher rates into formal employment, the main means of access to social security and worker protections, thereby benefiting their entire families. Meanwhile, not only young people but also adults from low-income families remained much more exposed to informal labor integration without social security during this period.

Table 4.4 Characterization of job posts among employed young people (aged 15–24) according to income group (2004–2015)

	Group of low incomes		*Group of medium and medium-high incomes*		*Group of high incomes*	
	2004	*2015*	*2004*	*2015*	*2004*	*2015*
Computer equipment and system operation	0%	2%	2%	10%	5%	26%
Qualified	35%	43%	47%	51%	52%	66%
Unskilled	61%	51%	42%	38%	18%	14%
Less skilled positions	96%	94%	89%	89%	70%	79%

Source: Authors' own elaboration based on data from PHS 2004 and 2015

Finally, if we consider only employed youth in each income group, we can see that (Table 4.4), even though there was a generalized process of improvement in job qualifications (i.e. growth in operational and professional positions), the number of low-income young people in unskilled jobs is three times higher than the number of high-income young people; also, the use of computer equipment and systems in their jobs is ten times lower than that among high-income young people. This implies participation in production areas with lower added value, with less-recognized job skills, and, consequently, lower remuneration and rewards of every kind in these positions.

To sum up, even when they are employed, low-income youth remain more exposed to precarious conditions, stigmatization, multiple kinds of pressure and demands (such as the pressures of care obligations), and exclusion from social security and worker protections, largely without access to resources through their families (such as health coverage).

Disadvantages related to their job positions are accumulated over the life courses of these young people, partly because their integration into precarious areas of the labor market is driven by a history of informal labor situations within their families. An individual's position in the social space according to his or her job post can be a factor in overcoming disadvantage, but it can also be completely the opposite: a continuity of disadvantages accumulating to the point where it becomes very difficult to curb the trend. The next section presents a number of life courses, highlighting both heterogeneity and regularity in these experiences.

Trajectories in Poverty Conditions and Work Experiences

The life stories of Yamila, Antonio, and Abel will help us show the reproduction strategies (Eguia & Ortale, 2004; Eguia, Ortale, Piovani, & Weingast, 2007; Gutiérrez, 2007, 2015) of the families where they grew up and their work experiences up to the present. Throughout their lives, these young people have belonged to the low-income sector of the population. Now they are between 18 and 24 years old and, in occupational terms, they would be described as an economically active population: at the time of writing, all three of them were informally employed in precarious jobs.[7]

Writing "low incomes" brings to mind the story of Yamila—a young woman who is now 23 with 2 children—who 8 years ago used the words, "so poor that you don't even have one peso," to describe life conditions when she was 15 and responsible for her 4 siblings. The expression "poor, as always" also comes to mind; it is used by Alicia Gutiérrez (2015) in her classic book of the same title. These two expressions carry two meanings that weave a single thread throughout this chapter: on one hand, the role of family relationships, and on the other hand, the history, the temporality of life in poverty.

Poverty as a relational condition is about the unequal distribution of innumerable resources, including devices, property, rights, opportunities, strategies, or even the very language used to describe distribution, dispute, or existence. The truth is that the relationship between access and hardship represents a sharp division in society—between malnourishment, exposure to cold, substandard living conditions, lack of toys, the inability to go to school, lack of access to quality medical care, the obligation to care for siblings or children, and not experiencing any of these situations. These descriptors, in addition to those listed in the first section of this chapter—as well as others to be outlined further on—allow us to place the individuals and their families within the social space in order to learn how they "managed" to survive in poverty over time and how they started working from an early age in order to achieve this. It is essential to know what jobs they did and their working conditions, as well as acknowledge subjects' capacity for agency, their networks, and the state or non-state support they were able to access or create.

Yamila

Yamila was born in the province of Misiones, in a town where the main activity is the cultivation of *yerba mate*; she describes it as "a place where people help each other" and adds "everybody is poor there, there aren't people with money like here." A few years later, her mother decided to separate from her father and they moved to the city of La Plata to live in the neighborhood where she was living when we talked to her. Even though this family migratory movement is one of the first crucial moments in her trajectory, there is another which she considers to be the most relevant, which represented a turning point in her life and forced her to grow up very suddenly. At the time, she was one of six siblings, the oldest of whom had stayed behind in Misiones. The youngest was two months old when the mother decided to leave the neighborhood on her own, leaving Yamila with all care responsibilities (the mother came back approximately two years later and left again several times): "from that day on I had to take on the role of the absent adult, and I was 8 years old." She threw herself into caring for her siblings, who were now her responsibility. She started working in the house of a neighbor, first running errands and then doing cleaning jobs; after a while she abandoned primary school. "I couldn't deal with everything, one day I stopped going; then, so did Osvaldo, and later, so did Marcelo," she said, referring to the brothers who followed her chronologically. Only the two youngest siblings stayed in school. They supported themselves by means of multiple strategies: Yamila's work (which continues into the present in a variety of jobs), her brother's occasional employment, help from neighbors, social programs, and integration into a social organization with community centers for babies, children, and young people. These state and community support systems and these children and adolescents' own capacity for agency made possible their survival without being institutionalized.

Yamila's trajectory from an early age set her on a continuous course of cumulative disadvantage. She never stopped working, except during certain weeks or months when she was unemployed. However, all her jobs have been in the informal sector without access to social security; consequently, despite having 15 years' work experience, she has been unable to participate in the retirement system, health coverage, workplace accident insurance, or have access to any other benefit available to some employees (e.g. unionization, loans, co-insurance, among others). Her jobs have included running errands, cleaning houses, attending clients in a pizza kitchen, sweeping the streets and plots of the city, assisting nurses, and finally, her current job, taking care of a sick elderly lady. However, her path has allowed her to accumulate certain kinds of capital. First, as social capital, she benefits from relationships with neighbors and with the social organization where she is a participant. Her economic capital consists of the lot where she has lived as a squatter with her mother and her siblings, as well as the fruits of the different income transfer programs which she has strategically articulated to obtain a little more money with each successive month. Thirdly, as cultural capital, she has studied to become a nursing assistant in a public hospital. Despite having all this experience at just 23 years old, Yamila is still living in poverty. Now she has two young children, she rents a house for the three of them in the same neighborhood, and she is able to support her family with the money she earns as a care worker (informal skilled paid work), together with the payments she receives from social programs (*AUH*,[8] *Plan Más Vida*,[9] and a municipal contribution by the childhood and adolescence department) and the aid from the social organization in which she still participates.

Antonio

Antonio graduated from a public high school near his home and is one of the few in the neighborhood to achieve this milestone despite experiencing homelessness during several periods of his life. He was born and raised in the same place. He did not have much to eat and was often exposed to the cold. He lives with his mother and is the oldest of three siblings. While at school he was supported by his mother, by a social organization he has attended since he was a child, by an income transfer program (*AUH*), and, of course, by his own determination. All of his siblings are still in school, although one of them has attended intermittently since he started high school.

Living conditions have been hard for the family: they live as squatters on a plot which they share with an uncle and his family; it has flooded on occasion and the building, fragile at first, can now be considered vulnerable, and it has always been small. Antonio's mother has always had intermittent and precarious jobs. She experienced gender-based violence at the hands of one of her partners, also causing Antonio to experience family violence. Continuing his education was connected to his strong desire to obtain a "formal" job and to turn that schooling capital into economic capital. However, that goal has not yet been achieved—by enrolling in the police force or armed forces as Antonio had planned—since he was rejected by both of them.

Antonio started working outside his home when he was 16 years old. He used to be partially responsible for taking care of his siblings and the house, as well as searching the neighborhood for clothes and food from churches, soup kitchens, and organizations. He started working in a refrigerator repair shop, but received hardly any money and eventually grew fed up: "it was unfair, I didn't even get one peso." A variety of different jobs followed, all of them precarious, inconsistent, and sporadic: as a gardener, builder's apprentice, and painter. At the community organization, he acquired informal training in graphics; despite some difficulties, he completed his training and started working at the printing house run by the same NGO. Like Yamila and 95% of low-income young people, he has no social security because he has never had formal employment (see Table 4.3). Antonio made a classic bet on schooling, an investment that has not yet brought returns, and neither his family trajectory nor the labor market have provided the structural conditions necessary for obtaining such a return. Now 20, he still lives with his mother and siblings. Antonio and his mother combine their incomes and some occasional contributions from the father of his siblings, together with money transfers from social programs (*AUH, Plan Más Vida*) and the aid of a social organization (clothes, food, mediation with government agencies, educational and recreational activities for children and young people).

Abel

The third life story is Abel's. He was born and raised in the neighborhood where he lives with his mother, his father, and four younger siblings in a house made of wood and cement with repairs made of cardboard and nylon. He completed up to the penultimate year of high school, but dropped out after failing a number of classes. He plans to finish school someday "because the certificate is good to have," he tells us, revealing his hope of overcoming the accumulation of disadvantages keeping him down. His mother is his role model, having finished her own high school through the *FinEs2*[10] program. Reproduction strategies in the family's home combine the income earned by his father, who works in construction, with his mother's work in the house and the raising of the children, as well as social program benefits (*AUH, Más Vida*), donations of clothes and food by neighbors, and income from Abel's own work.

At the age of 12—the same time he started high school—he began working in a neighborhood bakery: "I cleaned sheet trays the whole morning after baking." He was paid very little, but "you couldn't get many other jobs at that age." It lasted "around two years." Many other times he helped his father working as his builder's assistant; in that job he sometimes earned his own money, but at other times it was his father who received all the money, which was used for the household. There were times when he did not work, but the need to do so always existed: "I had to work to help my family, or, at least, get money to meet my expenses." He became interested in the esthetic production on the body, such as piercings and tattoos, and he approached the field by learning the profession with the help of an older tattooist. He started investing in equipment and inks with what money he could save from odd jobs, until he equipped himself with working tools and clients. Now he is 18 and works as a freelance tattooist, as well as working a number of other informal jobs.

As mentioned before, Yamila, Antonio, and Abel are part of the "low-income" group of the population characterized in statistical terms in the previous section, where we could visualize differences by income regarding inequality in employment opportunities, categories of inactivity, access to social security, and job characteristics (see Tables 4.1, 4.2, 4.3, and 4.4).

In order to make some general interpretations about the three stories—and somehow include many others that were not told here but share similarities with the ones presented—we will consider Mora Salas and de Oliveira's (2014) analytical axes, overtaking and deepening Elder's approach (1994): (1) family environment; (2) occurrence and timing of life events; (3) critical moments; (4) family, social, and institutional supports; and (5) choices, decisions, expectations, and future plans. This will enable us to identify the ways in which disadvantages are either accumulated or overcome, challenging the notion that work "per se" or "any" job is enough to achieve the eradication of poverty.

As regards the family environment, we are talking about domestic units who have been living in poverty for at least three or four generations (the earliest historical records only go this far, although this does not imply that people in general had better living conditions in the more distant past). Labor situations that contribute to this cycle include the scarcity of formal employment, low salaries—always—precarious working conditions, and the booming informal economy, which provides no access to social security. Labor informality is a constant in poor families. Yamila's grandparents live within a locally based agricultural economy in the Northwest of the country; her mother migrated to La Plata as an adult and transitioned her working trajectory from rural work to urban work in services. Some of Abel's and Antonio's grandparents were born in La Plata, while others also had their origins in the country's Northwest. The two men and their parents were born in the neighborhood where they continue to live to this day.

In previous research (Chaves et al., 2016), we showed how a family's "progress" and improvements in living conditions are structured around four elements: (1) Access to land and/or housing, measured by property, possession, and type of materials; (2) Access to infrastructure and services: electricity, water, gas, drains, pavement, transport, health, and education; (3) Integration into non-rural employment, greater occupational choices, better working conditions, and symbolically better-regarded jobs; (4) Access to public programs: social support, health, and education. The family and class trajectory conditions of the young men and women who participated in this research socialized them into a working environment from a young age which demands effort, physical strain, and working precariousness, as well as imposing gender-based social divisions in employment based on traditional gender roles. This reproduces the scheme of working outside the house for men and inside the house—or inside and outside—for women.

Argentina has seen an increase in the intergenerational accumulation of school-based qualifications.[11] The families of these young people are no exception to this trend. While this accumulation of educational capital represents one way to overcome disadvantages, the case of Antonio, and that of many others, serves to illustrate that it is another thing entirely to translate this progress into economic gain similar to that achieved by youth at other income levels, with the search often ending in frustration. Yamila's situation is the bleakest, since she has not finished primary school. Many young people are in the same situation: their desire and intent to finish their schooling are genuine; however, they cannot find an institutional offering that fosters them or that might be compatible with their paternity or maternity situations and/or jobs.

The occurrence and timing of life events is the second axis of analysis. In the cases studied, we considered births, deaths, beginning of workforce participation, and union of partners as life events. The three cases described show an early entry into the workforce: their working careers outside their houses start when they are between 8 and 16, and if we include work done inside the home, it begins even earlier in two cases with the care of siblings, feeding the family, and house cleaning. The time spent taking care of others is a factor that produces significant inequality in comparison to children and young people from other social positions. There is an accumulation of disadvantage of several aspects: by obstructing schooling, influencing early processes of responsibility and autonomy, and narrowing of the possible spectrum of work opportunities (with job searches subordinated to the times that care work leaves available).

Yamila's life reveals the incidence of maternity as a life event. She imagined that the birth of her first child would mean emancipation from her mother, ending her responsibilities to care for her siblings and support her family: "I thought that if I had a child I would be able to leave and wouldn't have to support them anymore." But that autonomy came at the cost of further accumulation of disadvantage: she did not stop taking care of others, merely shifting from one subject of care to another, and she could not gain time "to go back to school" or "go out and have fun." Consequently, this life event appears to have had a double effect: on one hand, it had the positive result of overcoming the disadvantage of being subordinated to her mother and the achievement of economic and housing autonomy; on the other hand, it nonetheless contributes to the accumulation of disadvantages, since she is still left caring for others and supporting them economically.

Crucial moments constitute the third axis of analysis. Certain life events are also crucial moments, but that is not the case in any of the life stories told here. Yamila's own perception of the crucial moment that represents a turning point in her life was "becoming responsible for my sister." Her life and the lives of her siblings became disorganized and organized again due to her mother's departure. According to these young people's descriptions, fathers and/or mothers who do not take care of their children, either temporarily or permanently, produce crucial moments in their life trajectories. It is worth noting a gender-based difference in the perception of adults' roles, as the absence of the father is normalized, and therefore perceived more as a life event than a crucial moment (but, of course, not in every case). Such an idea is based on a patriarchal conception of whose responsibility it is to care for children, one which dominates the Western cultural matrix.

In relation to the fourth axis, support, we have previously established that family incomes are not only based on incomes, payments for work, money transfers, or benefits from social policies[12] but also on "contributions" by relatives and friends, as well as cultural, political, social, sport-based, and religious organizations. The focus of our research on young people in La Plata with ties to a community organization has made it possible to study the influence of the organization, and some of its adult mentors, on the lives of these young people and on the reproduction strategies used within both their families of origin and their own families. Health and educational institutions are insufficient at the margins where society's poorest live their lives; they are characterized by crumbling infrastructure and often by negligent attention (Chaves, 2014b). Nonetheless, those who manage to attend and remain in school gain meaningful experiences and combine trajectories of "doing well" intermittently with "doing badly," possibly because of longer interruptions of schooling, as in Abel's case. Adult mentors who provide meaningful support also work in the areas of health, school, and sport, but universally the most influential support is that provided by the nuclear family and particularly the mother figure.

In our analysis of the three life courses, we have described situations and processes of accumulation and dispossession of capital. We have shown different positions within the social space and the variety of social roles performed by these young people in their daily lives. Drawing on these analyses, we could interpret some of the situations described as creating or eliminating advantages and disadvantages. Bearing in mind that these families are situated among the poorest 30% of Argentinian families, the construction of trajectories in the analyzed sector shows heterogeneity, but also many recurring themes. The permanence in the role of workers is one constant; another, to be discussed below, is the representation of a hard life, based on a strong perception of effort, which contrasts with the idea held by many in Argentinian society about poor young men and women. What is described both by outsiders but also inside poor neighborhoods as laziness, apathy, or "*ni-ni*" (Spanish for a young person who "neither works nor studies") is translated in practice into a wide range of ways to combine work, study, and care work.

Conclusion

It may seem obvious, but given the current context, obvious does not mean unnecessary: labor market integration does not necessarily imply social integration into decent living conditions that reverse and overcome poverty. Different forms of exploitation and the inequality networks in which young people participate determine whether conditions of poverty worsen, stay the same, or are opened to real possibilities for change. The situations of the families and young people studied in La Plata and in Córdoba Capital are not exceptions among working class youth in large urban centers in Argentina, but rather the rule.

Exposure to labor exploitation and a lack of decent wages are common themes in working class trajectories. Their activities are carried out in jobs and industries which are badly paid and, in many cases, poorly regarded by society. These jobs are informal and offer no health coverage, meaning that access to quality health services for this working population is limited, setting the foundations for precarious lives. As sustained by Therborn (2015) and Bravo Almonacid (2015), you live less when you are poor. Also, in a way, integration in the labor market starting in childhood or adolescence produces premature exhaustion of human energy. Moreover, when jobs do not provide payments into retirement programs, employees are left without the economic support of social security when they grow old. The endless cycle of precarious employment and the impossibility of moving out of the informal economy keep these young people, and usually their parents, for the most part, trapped within the most vulnerable positions in the social space.

The young people who participated in the research are imbricated in networks of inequality (Reygadas, 2004) that both reproduce their condition of poverty and their positions of subordination in various areas, as they allow to identify the youth agencies, "the efforts" (Saraví, 2009, Jacinto et al., 2005, Roberti, 2016; Chaves, 2016) and the strategies they carry out to live.[13]

Ways to get out of poverty do exist, but they do not depend exclusively or even mostly on the subjects. As we have endeavored to show throughout this chapter, the wide range of conditions, opportunities, rewards, and protection available through work are deeply unequal in nature and must be disclosed. This concept has been the driving force behind this research, for both the urban-based population analysis and the case studies of Yamila, Antonio, and Abel. Our focus has been on wage earners and occasional workers living in poverty, who come from families in the same situation, on trajectories pointing them toward a continuity or even a worsening of their condition. As such, while workforce participation is necessary, it is not sufficient on its own to produce decent living conditions. It has long been acknowledged that the "sale of labor" does not provide enough resources for its own reproduction. However, a substantial improvement in the conditions of the state's organization of care work could result in improvements in the lives of children, teenagers, and young men and women who take care of others. The same is true of the creation of protection systems for young and adolescent workers, which would also go a long way toward ending some of the effects of cumulative disadvantage.

Data on the strategies used by young men and women to combine care work, studies, and work allow us to conclude that, if certain disadvantages can be overcome, perhaps through obtaining access to basic rights and decent working conditions, a positive effect will be passed over into other areas. It is necessary to imagine, design, and implement measures that carry a real possibility of creating compatibility between the different social roles held by these young people: father, mother, student, worker, and care worker, among others. It is also important to bring recognition and validation to the role of poor young men and women in care work, as it represents a fundamental contribution to their families' reproduction strategies.

We would like to mention one more thing before making reference to the 2030 Agenda for Sustainable Development: the moral value of work and how work, "the attitude towards work," or "working culture" (Assusa, 2016; Chaves, 2016; Chaves et al., 2016) are used by several social agents to build a sense of moral belonging in communities. The young people studied here also do this—on one hand, by internalizing meritocratic dichotomies that distinguish between "hard working people and layabouts"; on the other, disputing the meaning for a positive recognition of their situation in the face of the classic stigma that young poor people do not work.

To sum up, in this chapter we have sought to contribute to the characterization of life courses of young people whose work trajectories began in childhood or adolescence and who live in poverty. We also intended to contribute to the visibility of work trajectories which, having started at childhood and in poverty, imply an accumulation disadvantage which cannot be reversed simply through blame or individual responsibility, fragmentary public policies, "the free market," destiny, or chance. In accordance with the United Nations' 2030 Agenda for Sustainable Development, we intend to spread knowledge that could influence the implementation of measures to fulfill those goals: zero hunger, no poverty, decent work and economic growth, and gender equality—to mention just 4 of the 17 goals. However, these cannot be achieved without a deep transformation in exploitative relationships and inequality networks in which the lives of the young people in this research take place—as well as all the other men and women who, like them, work hard and continue leading lives of poverty.

Notes

1. Chaves' data about trajectory were collected in the context of a socio-community activity with young people, which included accompanying them through their lives and activities in a social organization. It was financed by National Scientific and Technical Research Council (*CONICET*) and National University of La Plata (*UNLP*) research grants and *UNLP* National Community Extension and Volunteering Activities and University Policies Office. Assusa's work is part of several research projects financed by the *CONICET* and National University of Córdoba.
2. The Permanent Household Survey (PHS) is the main statistical source in Argentina to monitor data related to socioeconomic and working indicators. It gathers information on urban centers, most of which have more than 100,000 inhabitants. This source is representative—taking necessary precautions—of a country like Argentina, which has more than 90% of its population in urban spaces. This must be taken into account if international comparisons are to be made, mainly in the Latin American region, where countries like Brazil, Mexico, and Bolivia have 14%, 21%, and 30% of rural population, respectively (according to World Bank data from 2015).
3. The period 2003–2015 is defined as a time of neodevelopmentalist policies by several authors (O'Connor, 2009; Féliz, 2015, among others). The national government had the same political line: Peronism. The first presidency was Néstor Kirchner's (2003–2007), and then Cristina Fernández de Kirchner was president for two periods (2007–2015). In 2015, this administration was defeated in the polls by Mauricio Macri—whose party is called *Cambiemos* (alliance between Republican Proposal (*PRO*) and Radical Civic Union)—and a period of neoliberal policies began.
4. The period characterized by the "Convertibility Plan" in Argentina has to do with the monetary policy of the 1990s, which was developed during the presidency of Carlos Menem and the interrupted presidency of Fernando de la Rúa. The crisis of the neoliberal model in the country led to a complementary crisis of the political representation system in 2001, which only stabilized in 2003 due to the beginning of Néstor Kirchner's presidency, even though some of the specific policies coming out of the crisis had already started in 2002. Most of these measures implied returning to policies of economic deregulation and enormous flexibility in the labor market beginning in the 1990s. Because of the drastic modification that this change produced on economic policies and the dynamic of workforce demand, reconstruction of working policies, and distributive struggle, alternative categories are used to characterize a period difficult to describe: postconvertibility, postneoliberalism, neodevelopmentalism, and so forth. For further information about the characterization of the "project" that began in 2003, see Feliz (2012).

5. In 2007 the national government took control over *INDEC* [Spanish for National Institute of Statistics and Census of Argentina] and modified the calculation of CPI. This rate, apart from being useful to analyze basic consumer goods and, consequently, the lines of poverty and extreme poverty, adjusted the payment of interest on the foreign debt. The manipulation of this rate was a significant topic of discussion for the public and the media and cast doubt on the transparency of the entire National Statistical System during the last years of presidency of the Victory Front bloc. A group of private studies analyzing the measurement of these figures became visible in recent years, among which the Argentine Social Debt Survey by the Catholic University of Argentina stands out. At the same time, it has been suggested that there was a certain manipulation in the unemployment figures, namely, a kind of search that checked cases of "dubious" activity or unemployment. The most critical estimate holds that the differences produced by these revisions may oscillate between 0.5% and 1%.
6. The Permanent Household Survey (PHS) is the main statistical source in Argentina for monitoring data related to socioeconomic and working indicators. It gathers information on urban centers, most of which have more than 100,000 inhabitants. This source is representative—taking necessary precautions—of a country like Argentina, which has more than 90% of its population in urban spaces. This must be taken into account if international comparisons are to be made, mainly in the Latin American region, where countries like Brazil, Mexico, and Bolivia have 14%, 21%, and 30% of rural population, respectively (according to World Bank data from 2015).
7. For definitions and discussions about precarious and informal labor and jobs in Argentina, we suggest Beccaria, Carpio, and Orsati (2000), Battistini (2009), and Bertranou, Jiménez, and Jiménez (2013).
8. [Spanish for Universal Child Allowance]. It is a conditional income transfer program for underage (18 years old or less) people attending school, having medical checkups done, and whose parents have no formal or freelance work. For further information, see Social Security Observatory (2011).
9. A Conditional Cash Transfer Program financed by the State (State and Buenos Aires Province) which has maternity integration requirements (at least two children) and the lack of a formal work or freelance work. For more information, see http://planmasvida.com
10. "*Fines2* Program (Spanish for High School Completion Plan) is a national policy, managed by provinces, whose objective is to guarantee the completion of high school education by young people and adults who could not do so for a number of reasons" (for further information, see Crego & González, 2015: 3).

11. Information can be found in the Information System on Educational Trends in Latin America (*SITEAL*, IIPE-UNESCO, http://www.siteal.iipe-oei.org) and in the National Department of Information and Assessment of Educational Quality (*DINIECE*), Ministry of Education: http://portales.educacion.gov.ar/diniece/
12. In the analyzed period, we identified a positive impact caused by the Universal Child Allowance income transfer policy, Provisional Inclusion Plan (Bravo Almonacid, 2015), and the policies related to work cooperatives in urban maintenance administrated by the State and municipal authorities (Crego & González, 2015).
13. See chapters in this book about Argentina written by María Eugenia Rausky, focusing on children and teenagers, and by Débora Gorbán and Ana Tizziani, dealing with paid women domestic workers.

Bibliography

Assusa, G. (2016). *La 'cultura del trabajo': sentidos, clasificaciones y distinciones en torno al trabajo entre jóvenes de clases populares en Córdoba* (PhD Thesis). National University of Cordoba, Cordoba, Argentina. Unpublished.

Assusa, G. (2017). *Jóvenes trabajadores: Disputas sobre sentidos, apropiaciones simbólicas y distinciones sociales en el mundo laboral.* Buenos Aires, Argentina: Grupo Editor Universitario.

Balardini, S., & Miranda, A. (2000). *Juventud, transiciones y permanencias. Pobres, pobreza y exclusión social.* Buenos Aires, Argentina: CEIL/CONICET.

Battistini, O. (2009). La precariedad como referencial identitario. Un estudio sobre la realidad del trabajo en la Argentina actual. *Psicoperspectivas, VIII*(2), 120–142.

Bayón, M. C. (2015). *La Integración excluyente.* Mexico City, Mexico: Bonilla Artigas/IISUNAM.

Beccaria, L., Carpio, J., & Orsatti, A. (2000). Argentina: informalidad laboral en el nuevo modelo económico. In J. Carpio, E. Klein, & I. Novacovsky (Eds.), *Informalidad y exclusión social* (pp. 139–160). Buenos Aires, Argentina: FCE/SIEMPRO/ILO.

Bendit, R., Hahn, M., & Miranda, A. (2008). *Los jóvenes y el futuro. Procesos de inclusión social y patrones de vulnerabilidad en un mundo globalizado.* Buenos Aires, Argentina: Prometeo.

Bendit, R., & Miranda, A. (2015). Transitions to Adulthood in Contexts of Economic Crisis and Postrecession. The Case of Argentina. *Journal of Youth Studies, 18*(2), 183–196.

Benza, G. (2016). La estructura de clases argentina durante la década 2003–2013. In G. Kessler (Ed.), *La sociedad argentina hoy* (pp. 111–139). Buenos Aires, Argentina: Siglo XXI/Fundación OSDE.

Bertranou, F., Jiménez, M., & Jiménez, M. (2013). *Informalidad, calidad del empleo y segmentación laboral en Argentina* (Working Documents, 2). Buenos Aires, Argentina: ILO Country Office for Argentina.

Bravo Almonacid, F. (2015). *Envejecer en la pobreza: Prácticas y representaciones de personas mayores tendientes a su reproducción cotidiana en ámbitos domésticos y extradomésticos* (PhD Thesis). National University of La Plata, Buenos Aires, Argentina. Available from: http://www.memoria.fahce.unlp.edu.ar/tesis/te.1354/te.1354.pdf

Busso, M., & Pérez, P. (2016). *Caminos al trabajo: el mundo laboral de los jóvenes durante la última etapa del gobierno kirchnerista*. Buenos Aires, Argentina: Miño y Dávila.

Chaves, M. (2014a). Cotidianeidad juvenil en la pobreza: una lectura desde las desigualdades omnipresentes. In s/d, *XI Argentine Congress of Social Anthropology*, National University of Rosario. Rosario, Argentina.

Chaves, M. (2014b). Haciendo trámites con los pibes y las familias: barreras de acceso y micropolíticas públicas. *Escenarios, 14*(21), 15–23.

Chaves, M. (2016) "El esfuerzo": usos en la construcción de fronteras, lógicas de merecimiento y redes de desigualdad con jóvenes de sectores populares en un barrio de La Plata. In M. Rozas Pagaza, III (Ed.), *Latin American Social Work Forum*. La Plata, Argentina: School of Social Work, National University of La Plata. Available: http://www.trabajosocial.unlp.edu.ar/uploads/docs/chaves_gt_24.pdf

Chaves, M., Fuentes, S. G., & Vecino, L. (2016). *Experiencias juveniles de la desigualdad. Fronteras y merecimientos en sectores populares, medios altos y altos*. Buenos Aires, Argentina: Grupo Editor Universitario. (2017) Edición Digital. Buenos Aires, Argentina: CLACSO-GEU. Available: http://biblioteca.clacso.edu.ar/clacso/gt/20171218041618/Experiencias_juveniles_de_la_desigualdad.pdf

Chávez Molina, E., & Pla, J. (2013). *Desigualdad y movilidad social en el mundo contemporáneo aportes empíricos y conceptuales: Argentina, China, España, Francia*. Buenos Aires, Argentina: Imago Mundi.

Crego, M. L., & González, F. (2015). Nuevas oportunidades como experiencia. Jóvenes y desigualdad en el caso del Plan FinEs2 en el Gran La Plata, *Cuestiones de Sociología, 13*. Retrieved from: http://www.cuestionessociologia.fahce.unlp.edu.ar/article/view/CSn13a03

Crompton, R. (1997). *Clase y estratificación. Una introducción a los debates actuales*. Madrid, Spain: Tecnos.

Dubet, F. (2015). *Por qué preferimos la desigualdad*. Buenos Aires, Argentina: Siglo XXI.

Efron, R., Konterllnik, I., & Jacinto, C. (1996). *Adolescencia, pobreza, educación y trabajo: el desafía es hoy*. Buenos Aires, Argentina: Editorial Losada.

Eguia, A., Ortale, M. S., Piovani, J., & Weingast, D. (2007). La pobreza en Argentina: nuevas realidades, nuevos conceptos. In A. Camou, M. C. Torti, &

A. Viguera (Eds.), *La Argentina democrática: los años y los libros* (pp. 241–280). La Plata, Argentina: UNLP-Prometeo.

Eguia, A., & Ortale, S. (2004). Reproducción social y pobreza urbana. *Cuestiones de Sociología, 2*: s/n°. Retrieved from: https://www.cuestionessociologia.fahce.unlp.edu.ar/article/view/CSn02a01/5792

Elder, G. (1994). Time, Human Agency, and Social Change: Perspectives on the Life Course. *Social Psychology Quarterly, 57*(1), 4–15. doi: https://doi.org/10.2307/2786971. Stable URL: http://www.jstor.org/stable/2786971

Elder, G. (1998). The Life Course as Developmental Theory. *Child Development, 69*(1), 1–12. https://doi.org/10.2307/1132065.

Elder, G., Kirkpatrick Johnson, M., & Crosnoe, R. (2003). The Emergence and Development of Life Course Theory. In J. T. Mortimer & M. J. Shanahan (Eds.), *Handbook of the Life Course* (pp. 3–19). New York, NY: Kluwer.

Espinoza, V., & Kessler, G. (2003). *Movilidad social y trayectorias ocupacionales en Argentina: rupturas y algunas paradojas del caso de Buenos Aires.* Santiago de Chile, Chile: CEPAL/ECLAC. Retrieved from: http://www.cepal.org/publicaciones/DesarrolloSocial/5/LCL1895PE/lcl1895eP.pdf

Féliz, M. (2012). Proyecto sin clase: crítica al neoestructuralismo como fundamento del neodesarrollismo. In AAVV. *Más allá del individuo. Clases sociales, transformaciones económicas y políticas estatales en la Argentina contemporánea* (pp. 7–44). Buenos Aires, Argentina: Editorial El colectivo.

Féliz, M. (2015). *Argentina neodesarrollista: debates sobre el modelo.* La Plata, Argentina: EDULP. Available at: http://www.memoria.fahce.unlp.edu.ar/libros/pm.383/pm.383.pdf

Fernández Massi, M. (2014). Una mirada sectorial sobre las inserciones laborales precarias de los jóvenes en Argentina. In P. Pérez & M. Musso (Coord.), *Tiempos contingentes: inserción laboral de los jóvenes en la Argentina posneoliberal* (pp. 33–52). Buenos Aires, Argentina: Miño y Dávila.

Ferreira, F., Messina, J., Rigolini, J., López Calva, L. F., Lugo, M. A., & Vakis, R. (2013). *Panorámica general: La movilidad económica y el crecimiento de la clase media en América Latina.* Washington, DC: World Bank Latin American and Caribbean studies.

Gallart, M. A. (2001). *El desafío de la formación para el trabajo de los jóvenes en situación de pobreza en el Gran Buenos Aires.* Buenos Aires, Argentina: CENEP.

Goldthorpe, J. (2012). De vuelta a la clase y el estatus: por qué debe reivindicarse una perspectiva sociológica de la desigualdad social. *Reis, 137*, 43–58. https://doi.org/10.5477/cis/reis.137.43.

González, F. (2014). Dinámicas desiguales de inserción laboral: Posiciones en el mundo del trabajo, estrategias de búsqueda y mecanismos de acceso a empleos en jóvenes estudiantes del Plan FinEs2 en la ciudad de La Plata. In A. Viguera (Ed.), *VIII Conference of Sociology of the National University of La Plata.* Ensenada, Argentina. Available at: http://www.memoria.fahce.unlp.edu.ar/trab_eventos/ev.4445/ev.4445.pdf

Gorbán, D. (2014). *Las tramas del cartón. Trabajo y familia en los sectores populares del Gran Buenos Aires.* Buenos Aires, Argentina: GORLA.

Gutiérrez, A. (2007). Herramientas teórico-metodológicas de un análisis relacional para los estudios de la pobreza. *Ciencia, docencia y tecnología* (35), 15–33.

Gutiérrez, A. (2015). *Pobre' ... como siempre: Estrategias de reproducción social en la pobreza.* Villa María, Argentina: Eduvim.

Hernandez, C., Cingolani, J., & Chaves, M. (2015). Espacios con edades: el barrio y la pobreza desde los niños/as y jóvenes. In M. Chaves & R. Segura (Eds.), *Hacerse un lugar. Prácticas, circuitos y trayectorias juveniles en ámbitos urbanos* (pp. 123–146). Buenos Aires, Argentina: Biblos.

International Labour Office. (2012). *The Youth Employment Crisis: Time for Action.* Retrieved from: http://www.ilo.org/wcmsp5/groups/public/%2D%2D-ed_norm/%2D%2D-relconf/documents/meetingdocument/wcms_175421.pdf

International Labour Organization. (2013). *Global Employment Trends for Youth 2013 A Generation at Risk.* Retrieved from: http://www.ilo.org/wcmsp5/groups/public/@dgreports/@dcomm/documents/publication/wcms_212423.pdf

Jacinto, C. (2002). Los jóvenes, la educación y el trabajo en América Latina. Nuevos temas, debates y dilemas. In M. Ibarrola (Ed.), *Desarrollo local y formación: hacia una mirada integral de la formación de los jóvenes para el trabajo* (pp. 67–102). Montevideo, Uruguay: CINTERFOR/ILO.

Jacinto, C., Wolf, M., Bessega, C., & Longo, M. E. (2005). Jóvenes, precariedades y sentidos del trabajo. In *s/d 7° National Congress of Labor Studies.* Argentine Association of Specialists in Labor Studies, Buenos Aires, Argentina. Available at: http://www.aset.org.ar/congresos/7/02007.pdf

Kessler, G. (2014). *Controversias sobre la desigualdad. Argentina, 2003–2013.* Buenos Aires, Argentina: Fondo de Cultura Económica.

Labrunée, M. E., & Gallo, M. E. (2005). Informalidad, precariedad y trabajo en negro. Distinción conceptual y aproximación empírica. *Realidad Económica, 210*, 60–76.

Macri, M., & Van Kemenade, S. (1993). *Estrategias laborales en jóvenes de barrios carenciados.* Buenos Aires, Argentina: Centro Editor de América Latina.

Ministerio de Trabajo, Empleo y Seguridad Social de la Nación. (2017). *Informe Jóvenes y trabajo.* Buenos Aires, Argentina. Retrieved from http://www.trabajo.gob.ar/downloads/estadisticas/Jovenes_y_trabajo_2017.pdf

Miranda, A., & Arancibia, M. (2017). El futuro está incompleto: la construcción de trayectorias laborales sobre principios de siglo 21. *Trabajo y Sociedad, 28*, 195–217.

Mora Salas, M., & de Oliveira, O. (2014). ¿Ruptura o reproducción de las desventajas sociales heredadas? Relatos de vida de jóvenes que han vivido situaciones de pobreza. In M. Mora Salas & O. de Oliveira (Coords.), *Desafíos y paradojas. Los jóvenes frente a las desigualdades sociales* (pp. 245–312). Mexico City, Mexico: El Colegio de México – Centro de Estudios Sociológicos.

Noel, G. (2014). Presentación Las dimensiones morales de la vida colectiva. Exploraciones desde los estudios sociales de las moralidades. *Papeles de Trabajo, 8*(13), 14–32.

O'Connor, E. A. (2009). *El neodesarrollismo en la Argentina: un enfoque de desarrollo e integración regional* (PhD Thesis). Argentine Catholic University, Buenos Aires, Argentina. Retrieved from: http://bibliotecadigital.uca.edu.ar/repositorio/tesis/neodesarrollismo-argentina-enfoque-desarrollo.pdf

Observatorio de la Seguridad Social. (2011). *Asignación universal por hijo para protección social: una política de inclusión para los más vulnerables.* Buenos Aires, Argentina: ANSES. Retrieved from: http://observatorio.anses.gob.ar/archivos/documentos/AUH%20para%20Protecci%C3%B3n%20Social.pdf

Palomino, H., & Dalle, P. (2012). El impacto de los cambios ocupacionales en la estructura social de la Argentina: 2003–2011. *Revista del Trabajo – Nueva Época, 8*(10), 205–224.

Pérez, P. (2011). Jóvenes, estratificación social y oportunidades laborales. *Lavborarios, 24*, 134–153.

Pérez, P., & Busso, M. (Eds.). (2014). *Tiempos contingentes: inserción laboral de los jóvenes en la Argentina posneoliberal.* Buenos Aires, Argentina: Miño y Dávila ediciones.

Pérez, P., & Busso, M. (2015). Los jóvenes argentinos y sus trayectorias laborales inestables: Mitos y realidades. *Trabajo y sociedad* (24), 147–160.

Piecke Goicochea, E. (2001). *Los jóvenes y el trabajo: la educación frente a la exclusión social.* Mexico City, Mexico: Universidad Iberoamericana.

Pla, J., & Chávez Molina, E. (2010a). *Mobility or Social Reproduction in a Poor Quarter of Buenos Aires.* In Spring Meeting of the Research Committee on Social Stratification and Mobility (RC28) of the International Sociological Association. Haifa, Israel.

Pla, J., & Chávez Molina, E. (2010b). *Determinantes de la movilidad social de un barrio periférico del Gran Buenos Aires.* In II International Encounter Political Theory and Practice in Latin America. National University of Mar del Plata, Mar del Plata, Argentina. CD-ROM.

Quartulli, D., & Salvia, A. (2012). La movilidad y la estratificación socio-ocupacional en la Argentina. Un análisis de las desigualdades de origen. *Entramados y perspectivas, 2*(2), 15–42.

Racynski, D., & Serrano, C. (1985). *Vivir la pobreza. Testimonio de mujeres.* Santiago de Chile, Chile: PISPAL-CIEPLAN.

Reygadas, L. (2004). Las redes de la desigualdad: un enfoque multidimensional. *Política y Cultura, 22*, 7–25.

Rivas Rivas, R. (2008). Dos enfoques clásicos para el estudio de la estratificación social y de las clases sociales. *Espacio Abierto, 17*(3), 367–389.

Roberti, E. (2016). Los sentidos (des)centrados del trabajo: hacia una reconstrucción de los itinerarios típicos delineados por jóvenes. *Ultima década, 24*(44), 227–255.

Salvia, A., & Lindenboim, J. (2015). *Hora de Balance: proceso de acumulación, mercado de trabajo y bienestar. Argentina 2002–2014*. Buenos Aires, Argentina: EUDEBA.

Saraví, G. (2006). Biografías de exclusión: desventajas y juventud en Argentina. *Perfiles Latinoamericanos, 28*, 83–116.

Saraví, G. (2009). *Transiciones vulnerables: juventud, desigualdad y exclusión en México*. Mexico City, Mexico: CIESAS.

Saraví, G. (2015). *Juventudes fragmentadas: socialización, clase y cultura en la construcción de la desigualdad*. Mexico City, Mexico: FLACSO-CIESAS.

Therborn, G. (2015). *Los campos de exterminio de la desigualdad*. Buenos Aires, Argentina: Fondo de Cultura Económica.

Tilly, C. (2000). *La desigualdad persistente*. Buenos Aires, Argentina: Manantial.

Vera, J. (2013). Informalidad y segmentación laboral desde la perspectiva estructuralista: una aplicación para la argentina (1992–2010). *Lavboratorio, 25*, 11–34.

CHAPTER 5

Work and Schooling in the Life Course of Poor Young People in Rio de Janeiro

Ana Karina Brenner and Paulo Carrano

Introduction

One challenge inherent in investigating the diverse life courses of young people is viewing age not only as biological phases but also as representations and fields of symbolic disputes traversed by specific aspects of life in a variety of social places. It includes understanding processes of social individualization, but also the vectors that unify socializing standards in a world that has become simultaneously globalized and exclusionary, in which tradition is confronted by enlarged fields of possible choices, but where the absence of vital support limits the ability to achieve full exercise of these choices by all.

We will address the processes of poor young people going into adult life, taking the school-work relationship as the main vector. The empirical basis of our discussion comes from quantitative and qualitative data

A. K. Brenner (✉)
State University of Rio de Janeiro, Rio de Janeiro, Brazil
e-mail: ana.brenner@uerj.br

P. Carrano (✉)
Federal Fluminense University, Niteroi, Rio de Janeiro, Brazil
e-mail: paulo.carrano@pq.cnpq.br

M. E. Rausky, M. Chaves (eds.), *Living and Working in Poverty in Latin America*, Governance, Development, and Social Inclusion in Latin America, https://doi.org/10.1007/978-3-030-00901-4_5

obtained through the study *Jovens Fora de Série*[1] (young outliers) about young high-school students in the city of Rio de Janeiro between 2013 and 2015.

This chapter begins by exploring theoretical thinking on youth, on processes of individuation in the context of current societal changes and on different life courses. Next, we present and analyze research data in the light of this conceptual framework. The collection, tabulation and analysis of the survey made it possible to get a summary table of itineraries for schooling, social standpoints, family and labor experiences and so on, all serving to bring objectivity to the life courses. Narratives by two youths are presented and interpreted in an attempt to highlight subjective dimensions of the biographical trajectories.

Young People in the Face of the Biographical Challenge

While most youths need to overcome objectively precarious conditions that are interposed in their lives, those from the poorest sectors of our societies are faced with the additional challenge of producing their own subjectivity under conditions of great material and symbolic scarcity. Social risks arise on the scale of systemic crises; however, they inevitably have a direct impact on specific collectivities and individual bodies. Young people are held responsible for choices made under conditions of palpable restrictions produced by a structural framework of inequalities, cyclical economic crises and socio-spatial and cultural limitations which they inherit from their families, limiting or even preventing them from sharing in the purported benefits of consumer societies.

The singularities observed in the life courses are within the sphere of social regularities that, while they are not necessarily predictable before they occur, need to be inventoried within the specific contexts where they take place. Despite the wide range of no-longer linear arrangements for the transition toward adult life, many personal strategies are used in the search for autonomy in the context of highly individualized societies with high margins of autonomy in the making of oneself, combined with dramatic contexts of insecurity and uncertainty regarding the future. According to the *biographical model* (Beck, 2010), young people in a high-risk society must be active creators of biographies socially inscribed in objective conditions and producers of personal constraints in the fulfillment of their choices.

It is difficult to measure the relative weights of biographical choices in the face of the real and often scarce "structures of opportunities" (Filgueira, 2001) promoted by the State, the market or society. Likewise, there is not a single, recognizable pattern beyond the institutionalization of life courses and regularities in the processes of social individuation. This is an ongoing effort that must involve different fields of investigation.

Schwartz, Côté, and Arnett (2005) conducted a study with young people in their transition to adult life, seeking to understand the relationship between how identities are formed and what they called "agency" in the individuation process. Even though issues related to identity are continuously addressed, the role of personal agency and individuation in the process of forming an identity during adolescence are not yet well understood. The highest levels of agency may have positive associations with exploration and flexibility of commitments, rather than conformity, although these characteristics may erroneously lead young people to be labeled as "lazy." Despite the existence of new arrangements which enhance the possibility of getting to adult life (related to the career, world perspective, etc.), there is a decline in collective support for the forming of identities (Arnett, 2000, 2001). Some young adults seem prepared to make their own way toward the roles and responsibilities of adult life, in a stable and coherent manner and committed to their identities. Others will need external help in the form of intervention or support in order to make the transition to taking on new roles and responsibilities.

Singling Out the Life Courses

Following the decline of institutional networks, the support systems available to young people making the transition to adulthood also became weaker. According to Camarano, Mello, Pasinato and Kanso (2004), an analysis of national demographic data from 1982 through 2002 shows a tendency for non-linear transitions toward adult life in Brazil: for example, having children prior to marriage, or marriage prior to entry into the workforce. Another key example is the disjunction in the path traditionally leading from schooling to higher education to the workforce. In this respect, there is agreement among the authors of studies on youth (Bois-Reymond, 2008; Calvo, 2005; Leccardi, 2005; Pais, 2001; Reguillo, 2013; Sposito, 2005) that the life course became unstable and the personal itineraries less predictable. The greatest challenge of any future research may be to determine the implications of the changes taking place in the course of this "late modernity."

The individual is upheld by a set of both material and symbolic support systems (Martuccelli, 2007a, 2007b). Paradoxically, for a person to become "decentralized," individualized and to distinguish him- or herself from the social world, it is necessary to become integrated into social networks in a practical way. Studying the individuation of young people as they experience youth and the transition to adult life demands looking at the concrete way they set themselves on a life course. However, one cannot disregard the relationships between their biographies and global social constraints and changes that affect the lives of all, even though not everyone experiences these changes directly or reacts to them in the same way. In this vein, Caradec and Martuccelli (2004) do not ignore that individuals are located within social places determined according to their social class of origin and the socializing processes they went through. Yet, the authors highlight the impossibility of merely deriving individual itineraries according to these standpoints, social places or *habitus* of class and socialization.

Deriving itineraries and biographies from social determiners would be a theoretical-methodological position incompatible with the analysis of contemporary societies. Therefore, what is now known as a sociology of individuation denotes something that no longer believes in analyses that established an alleged direct relationship between the dynamics of social destinations and individuality. We maintain that young people from underprivileged classes, even when they take common social standpoints—or even shared generational destinations as Mannheim (2005) has pointed out—experience singular *life courses* (Elder, 1994).

Uncertain Transits Toward Adult Life

Young people extend youth because they cannot find appropriate ways to achieve a social and economic transition to adult life. Therefore, they remain in their parents' home by choice, extend their schooling or experience economic dependence on their families due to declining job opportunities within the scenario of worldwide structural unemployment.

Without ignoring other possible perspectives on youth, authors emphasize the processes of transition toward adult life and focus their analyses on different cultural and historical processes that define the new generations of adults (Attias-Donfut, 1996; Dubet, 1996; Galland, 1996; Pais, 2003). The combination of a variety of perspectives on youth issues constitutes an attempt to answer the question of when someone is no longer young and reaches adult life. The answer, which cannot be considered final, depends both on the indicators related to the changes experienced by the biological body and on the objective social data and the representations that each society assigns to the concept of youth and young people. In other words, it is about the objective age, measured in years, in combination with the social representations that are made about specific age-related milestones.

The passages between the times of childhood, adolescence, youth and adult life can be understood as "societal agreements." Somehow, societies establish intersubjective agreements and cultural norms that define the way "youth" is conceptualized or represented (the juvenile condition). In some societies the rituals of passing to adult life are well-defined and involve specific social rituals. In our urban societies, especially, the frontiers are less and less visible, with markers for generational passage becoming increasingly blurred.

Certain milestones once used to mark the end of youth and the moment a young person was joining the adult world have become ambiguous in this respect: school graduation, getting a job, moving out of the parents' home, getting one's own place to live and raise a family, getting married and having children. These are "stations" of an idealized juvenile itinerary, but no longer serve as defining characteristics of the "transition from youth to adult life." The loss of linearity in this process can be seen as one of the marks of coming of age in the current era. Instead of linear transitions, coming of age now takes a number of forms, described by Pais (2003) as "*yo-yo*," reversible or labyrinthine.

It is important to keep in mind the diverse ways in which today's young people live their youth and also to inventory the constantly shifting "points of entry" into adult life. Young people live tangible experiences that are more or less close to the "juvenile condition" represented by the ideal or dominant concept.

Educational inequalities, resulting in low rates of high school and higher education completion in Brazil, enhance the heterogeneousness of what can be called "transition structures."[2] Young people, especially those from poor families, face an uncertain itinerary as they search for opportunities in the workforce; the available jobs are often precarious and lack protections and provide little or no possibility of starting or advancing in a professional career. Informal work represents a greater proportion of opportunities available to lower income workers with limited power as consumers. Higher levels of educational attainment generally coincide with greater chances of getting a formal job—a reality of crucial importance to young people, considering that youth unemployment in Brazil is, on average, three times higher than for the rest of the population.

In this perspective, it is possible to say that the social constraints which define a given structure of transition (the process of changes into different situations in life) interfere with the *creation of the social itineraries* of young people, in the formation of their "ways of life" (Guerra, 1993) and in their possibilities for making sense of the future. The expression "life course" highlights the positions taken by an individual throughout his or her life and which characterize his or her *biography*.

Bois-Reymond (2008, p. 57), in a comparative study on parenting, agency and social change among European young people, highlights the convergence of sociological analyses that acknowledge the transformation in the standard life cycle of young people to what he called "individualized biographies." Today's young generation is confronted with social change and suffers from a lack of models to show them how to deal with such changes.

Extended educational careers lead to increasingly longer periods of youth and delay the attainment of the previously well-defined status of adulthood with the markers of economic independence and family roles acquired as mothers and fathers. Thus, the juvenile life course is no longer stable, but rather mirrors the turbulence of societies. This is the meaning of the "yo-yo" metaphor to describe these life courses. Young people experience situations that make them feel they are not the ones in charge of managing their own lives, most notably in terms of access to the labor market and the free choice of an occupation and working hours. Many young people cannot lead an independent life, as they lack sufficient income to afford their own housing.

In Europe, Bois-Reymond (2008) emphasizes the mechanisms of social selection in the segmented educational systems and labor markets have an even more profound impact on youths from ethnic minorities. These young people become dependent on their families and relatives, forced to take jobs that are underpaid, unsafe and irregular in the hope of a better future. The social capital expressed in support networks is crucial: young people with access to such resources are the ones who find the best opportunities and feel more responsible for their lives.

Youth, Schooling and Work

Since the global crisis of the 1970s that led to the deregulation of the workforce, described by Ulrich Beck (2010) as "the un-standardization of wage work," the markets responded as could be expected, following the logic of maximizing profit for private benefit in the relationship between capital and labor. However, the combined support of the state and multiple social institutions proved insufficient to uphold poor young people's transitions toward adult life. In societies where work has become more flexible but also precarious and unprotected, where the notion of progress and career disappear and social guarantees are no longer taken for granted as battles already won by classes and organizations of workers, entry to the labor force becomes more and more uncertain and individualized. The shift to workforce outsourcing, the declining importance of trade unions and the market predominance of recruitments companies that intermediate workforce set the tone for the fragmentation of the labor field.

One cannot deny the place of work in building a social life and individuality. However, it is clear that work no longer plays the same role in promoting societal integration that it once did, especially in urban societies. Work identity is combined with other societal dimensions related to gender, race, generation or territory and culture. A number of studies on the relationship between young people and labor have underlined that these other points of reference have gained significance in defining a working identity, at the expense of the workplace and professional qualifications. Within this framework, it is possible to point out the elements that contribute to the weakening of worker identity such as the weight of informality, neglect of workers' rights, the instability of itineraries that are no longer predictable as they were when the term "career" was coined, the plurality and heterogeneity of activities, whether due to high job rotation or concomitance in daily, weekly or monthly working shifts. All of this is added to the strong attraction of the time-spaces of consumption and the cultural significance of individual and collective leisure-time behaviors in the construction of juvenile subjectivities.

Youths from underprivileged classes undertake a hard and unprotected struggle that combines work and school. However, it must be said that in the current climate of uncertainty and the declining predictability of trajectories, even young people who stay in school learn to distrust the power of diplomas and the validity of formal school knowledge in their search for work. Their goal is to obtain protected jobs that are characterized by formal hiring processes, including registry in the social security system, and are a "steady and permanent job" that will provide them with a salary and enough free time to live their lives.

In the face of the imperative to meet objective needs and build their own field of autonomy, the "making of oneself" takes place amid powerful economic and symbolic exclusions which tend to be aggravated in the absence of support systems in the form of effective structures and public policies to aid in reconciling the worlds of family, school and work.

Even in the face of serious restrictions to accessing social security and the scarcity of real job opportunities, young people seek alternatives and invent their lives in diverse, creative ways.

Young People in the Recent Brazilian Economic Cycle

Between 2006 and 2017, the Brazilian economy experienced a series of major fluctuations. Between the second term of the Lula administration and the impeachment of President Dilma Rousseff, Brazil enjoyed some of the greatest prosperity in its history, but the country also faced an unprecedented political crisis (Carvalho, 2018). While the poorest sectors saw some increase in their incomes, coupled with decreased rates of unemployment, high levels of social inequality fed the growth in violence (UNDP, 2013–2014).

From the perspective of Brazil's youth, changes in the educational system had a significant impact. On one hand, access to public higher education was expanded and affirmative action programs—such as racial and social quotas—introduced, providing greater access to a larger number of young people from underprivileged sectors. Increases in family income allowed many youths, mainly teenagers, to leave the labor market and focus exclusively on their studies (Menezes, 2015). Advances in consumer products enabled more people to gain access to ICTs (especially mobile phones), with a direct impact on expectations, the spread of information and forms of collective action.

For Fleury (2013), the reduction in poverty, resulting from both economic growth and policies aimed at improving salaries and social assistance, contributed to the climate of optimism and the consolidation of Brazil's democratic institutions. Yet, the impact of reduced inequality was weakened by the continued failure to provide the poorest people with access to quality public services in areas such as education, health, transportation, sanitation and housing.

By the end of 2012, the brief cycle of prosperity in Brazil had run its course. This could be perceived in the low rates of economic growth and the subsequent rise in unemployment which was, as always, felt most profoundly by Brazil's young people. Also, the decline in family income has also forced many in this group into the labor market (Menezes, 2015).[3]

Specifically regarding the level of occupation by young people[4]—measured by the ratio between those who were working in the week of reference and the total amount of youths—we see that between 2005 and

2014 there was some stability among 25–29 years old and among 18–24 years old, but there was a steep fall in the level of occupation among adolescents between 15 and 17 years old (from 31.0 percent to 23.1 percent), and this is consistent with the percentage increase in those only attending school. Between 2014 and 2015, youth employment rates fell in all age ranges, going from 57.5 percent down to 52.5 percent of all young people, a more noticeable drop than that seen in the employment rate of the population as a whole.

Unemployment among black youth may be 40 percent higher than for their white counterparts in the metropolitan areas of Brazil. Young black women are the segment most affected by the lack of jobs. In terms of income distribution between white and non-white youths,[5] whites make up the majority in the income ranges higher than two minimum salaries, while non-whites are the majority among those with earnings lower than two minimum salaries, as well as those with no income at all.

In the period from 2005 through 2015, there was no significant change in young people's school attendance (36.2 and 36.5 percent, respectively). Disaggregation by age groups shows that the percentage of adolescents between 15 and 17 years old attending school increased from 81.6 percent to 85.0 percent. In the context of this age group, who would ideally be expected to be attending high school, we emphasize that there was a change in the profile of young people attending school between 2005 and 2015. In this period, the percentage of those who studied and worked simultaneously dropped and there was an increase in those going to school only; this potentially means that they had more time available to focus on their studies.

Outstanding Young Outliers: Research on Schooling and Life Courses

In 2013 we conducted a *survey* in 14 high schools in the public state education system, located in 4 areas of the capital of Rio de Janeiro.[6] A total of 593 questionnaires were given to young people, in a non-probabilistic sample, selected on the basis of personal criteria regarding the elements that are most representative of the population (Costa Neto, 1977, p. 45). Thus, our data comes from a specific case study and, while it does not allow for generalizations, it nonetheless provides significant information to identify the dynamics of the profile of young students called Young outliers applicable to other contexts as well as with the qualitative phase of the research (narrative interviews and photographic reflexive devices).

Out of the 593 young respondents, 7 were between 15 and 17 years old, 503 were between 18 and 24 years old and 83 were between 25 and 29 years old; in addition, 61.6 percent studied in the category called *Youth and Adult Education*[7] and 36.9 percent were in *Program Autonomy*,[8] considered by the state school system as individuals with a mismatch between their age and the grade they were attending.

The survey consisted of a structured self-applicable questionnaire, with closed questions and a few open questions that interviewees could freely answer, making a total of 85 questions. The ethical criteria, established for scientific research, were respected and the data confidentiality was ensured.

Following the tabulations and the analyses of the survey, some recurrent profiles of students were listed and then, of the participants who had responded positively to the invitation at the end of the questionnaire to participate in the next step of the research, we selected 19 youths for the second, qualitative stage of the study. Interviews took place on site at participants' schools, and all of them were filmed to make the full-length research film *Fora de Série* ["Held back but…." (www.filmeforadeserie.com)].

Also, a third step of the research was to analyze the material obtained from the filmed narrative interviews; this involved following two of the young interviewees as they carried out their everyday life routines: work, family life, leisure and free time.[9] Each of the two youths was given a camera to take photographs that they considered representative of their lives, on the understanding that the young participant would return for a new meeting with the researchers to talk about the images they had produced.

Below we present the overall data of the profile of the young interviewees in the survey and, next, followed by specific traits from the biographical trajectories of the two young people we followed in the process of this research and its accompanying film.

The gender balance was almost equal among the young people who took the questionnaire, with 51 percent male and 49 percent female. The age ranges are distributed between 15 and 17 years old (1.2 percent), 18 and 24 years old (84.8 percent) and 25 and 29 years old (14 percent). The majority (41 percent) self-identify as brown and 20 percent as black, 26 percent consider themselves white, 3 percent identify as Indians and 5 percent as Asian. As a proportion of the overall national population, black people make up 53 percent and whites 45.4 percent.

In this study, 16.8 percent of young people had a family income of up to one minimum salary (270 US dollars), and 29 percent had a family income ranging from 270 to 540 US dollars per month. Average family size was four people.

Regarding the differences in average income between white and black youth, 25 percent of black youth subsisted on one minimum salary compared to 19.4 percent of whites. Sixty-eight percent of black youth lived on up to two minimum salaries, while 56 percent of whites lived at the same income level. Data show that despite the tendency of young people overall to have low incomes, black youth are at a particular economic disadvantage compared to whites. This scenario of economic vulnerability, which is replicated within families and disproportionately affects black youth, tends to exercise adverse effects on the ability to complete school without interruptions.

The research obtained critical data regarding the differences in sex, age, work and income. Among those who had never had a job, 13 percent were male and 20 percent were female. Women in the study started working later, for lower wages, at the same jobs taken by men. Over half the young women who worked (61.5 percent) received up to one minimum salary, while 39 percent of young men got the same compensation. It must be noted that the occupations are spread evenly between the sexes—a little more than half the sample of both sexes are work as providers of services or as salespeople in stores and markets. A total of 6.4 percent of males earned between two and five minimum salaries, while 3.4 percent of females received earnings within the same range.

We observed a correlation between incompletion of elementary/middle school and having worked and studied simultaneously. Of the youth who had never needed to combine work and study, 83 percent were able to complete middle school. In spite of the fact that working and studying at the same time is an obstacle in the academic itinerary, in this group the phenomenon appears less likely to be linked to failure than to giving up. As regards failure, other factors may be involved. This result reflects studies by Cacciamali and Braga (2002) revealing that the reasons for the age-grade discrepancy, as well as for drop-out rates, are not the same causes leading young people into the labor market but rather others originating in the pedagogical system itself: for example, levels of age-grade mismatch tend to be high, whether youths have a job or not.

If, on one hand, work is not the strongest influence leading to a disparity between age and school grade, poverty, on the other hand, may have a powerful impact on academic performance. Andrews and Vries (2012) studied 5500 Brazilian cities and towns, where poverty was the variable explaining the discrepancy and drop-out rate in 60 percent of cases. The thesis that poverty can only be overcome by means of school education (Easterlin, 1981;

Hanushek, 1995) is relativized by evidence that it is not possible to improve educational attainment without overcoming poverty (Andrews & Vries, 2012). It is within this context that one can say that economic inequalities constrain young people's possible horizons for action in their relationship with school and the world of labor (Sposito, 2005).

Out of interviewees who said they both worked and studied at some point in their school careers, 30 percent abandoned school while in middle school. Data also show the ages at which they started working: 4.9 percent reported starting work before 10 years of age, while 21 percent began between 10 and 15 years old, and 41 percent between 16 and 18 years old. Such data demand reflection that significant obstacles must still be overcome to eradicate child labor and protect adolescent workers in Brazil, in order to ensure that these situations do not hinder the schooling of poor children and teenagers.

In high school, the impact on the drop-out rate of having worked and studied was emblematic. Of those who had already worked and studied, 58.1 percent never left school, while the number rose to 74.6 percent for those who had never worked. The percentage of those combining work and study was relatively proportional among Young outliers in relation to those who do not work.

However, there are differences in terms of the drop-out rate. Those who work and study face greater difficulty for remaining in school. Asked about the motivation for giving up, the significant number of 34.7 percent indicated work as the principal reason.

Only 11.4 percent of respondents said they were "studying only." Of the others, 17.8 percent said they were looking for a job; 43.1 percent said they already had a steady job; 10.4 percent declared they do odd jobs and 1.7 percent said they did household chores. Out of those who worked, 47 percent had a wage, while 11.1 percent said they got nothing in return for work. Considering the daily working hours, the largest group (22.5 percent) worked between 6 and 8 hours a day, followed by 15.8 percent who worked more than 8 hours a day (above the maximum time of 44 hours per week, as provided by the Federal Constitution), 9.4 percent worked 4–6 hours, 4.4 percent worked 2–4 hours and 2.2 percent worked up to 2 hours.

Between 2005 and 2015, working conditions of people in Brazil between 15 and 29 years old adopted characteristics of the ILO's definition of decent work, at least in two of its dimensions. Regarding monthly income from all work, the percentages of young people working without pay dropped from 11.6 to 6.1 percent, those who were paid up to ½ minimum salary fell from 11.7 to 8.2 percent and those who received between ½ and 1 minimum salary went from 24.8 to 22.7 percent, while the percentage of youths earning 1–2 minimum salaries went up from 32.6 to 43.8 percent. In addition, 13.7 percent of young people no longer worked more than 44 hours per week—that is, above the normal working hours set forth by paragraph XIII of Art. 7 of the 1988 Federal Constitution of Brazil—and instead, a total of 50.9 percent of employed youth were working 40–44 hours per week in 2015 (PNAD, 2015a, 2015b).

A total of 27.2 percent of youth had jobs with no formal hiring practices and 10.5 percent did odd jobs. These figures clearly show the problems of informal labor, underemployment and precarious occupations to which young people with little professional training are subject. It is possible to perceive that 17.9 percent of those who claimed to be looking for a job are strongly inclined to join this category of unprotected workers.

For youths involved in the special system *Youth and Adult Education*, returning to school seems to represent a singular moment of reclaiming the meaning of school, which is fed by dreams and future projections. The experiences they had in other places and moments allow these young people to understand the importance of school, of its codes and languages, to achieving a better place in society.

When many of these youths have experienced the obstacles caused by the lack of school credentials, either in the labor market or their social life, they reconsider the interruption of their studies and returning to school becomes an option. Thus, school is rediscovered as an indispensable way to achieve a better position in their social contexts.

Zago (2000) says that school acquires meaning for the subjects when school experience appears on the horizon of their life expectations. Thus, there is a specific moment when studying gains real instrumental purpose, and turns into a key element in resuming life plans, frequently after several years of interruption in their school itinerary.

Curiously, when work and study are correlated with future expectations, this simultaneous realization favorably influences what young people project. One sees that those who have already reconciled their school commitments with the world of work had higher expectations of furthering their education, either by getting a university diploma in the medium term or even taking a professional training course. The expectations among this group of achieving a job in the public service and its corresponding stability are also higher. In the portion of those who never reconciled work and study, we observe a higher percentage of those who solely wish to find a job and those who hope to earn money with their own business. This is also the group that gathers the largest portion of those with no plans whatsoever for the future at the time of the research.

The Trajectories of Antonio and Fernanda[10]

Here we present two experiences narrated by youths in biographical interviews conducted in 2014. These interviews were complemented by observing them in their everyday activities as well as the photographic records utilized in the research that occurred in 2015. The script of the interviews was personalized, prepared based on the responses given in the questionnaire.[11] In the interviews, we attempted to gain an in-depth perspective of a reflexive sociology (Melucci, 2005) adopted as a theoretical and methodological assumption. In this regard, by personalizing the script by using what had been learned about life itineraries (work, schooling, leisure, family structure, sociability) based on responses to the questionnaire, the dialogue between the interviewer and the interviewee was better able to reach core issues of the life course of the youths without typical definitions or issues of general interest that were at the margin of their individual experiences. The proposal to use a camera (to photograph what might represent what had been lived) also allowed for deeper reflection; talking about their photographs made the youths confront their own stories, enabling them to describe crucial events of their lives as they had experienced them, but in the context of a listening dialogue with the researchers.

The principle of the dialogue interview is based on what La Mendola (2009) defined as a process of giving life to the interview, that is, to handle it not only as data collection or the recording of speeches but mainly to consider it as a quality relationship between the researcher and the individual being researched. This perspective undertakes a particular form of listening and apprehension of social representations and relationships that does not ignore the societal frameworks of the interviewees. The dialogue interview is not prescribed to all, nor is it used homogeneously. It is done differently from one person to another because it seeks the consciousness of oneself and the reflection about one's own existence. There is, therefore, what one might call a centering game—research preoccupations—and openness—space for the narrative dimension in the *adventure* of listening to the other.

Our attempt is to articulate the trajectories with social contexts that have been, to a certain extent, described in previous sections. The analyses below follow a methodological orientation based on a tradition that is concerned with keeping together and linking the subjective and objective dimensions of the contents narrated (Alexander, Giesen, Munch, & Smelser, 1987; Dubar, 1998; Pais, 2005).

We utilize two key elements of analysis in our attempt to understand the experiences narrated: *tests and existential supports* (Martuccelli, 2007a). *Tests* are deemed to be the social challenges faced by individuals in the processes of individuation or the making of themselves; they are socially produced and unequally distributed. And *supports* may be defined as the relationship between subjective resources the individuals manage to articulate in order to uphold themselves and the existing social surroundings in the form of networks and material and symbolic supports; a support, therefore, is not defined just as a material support, it may also be expressed in an emotional relationship, a representation—a literary character, for example—that contributes to supporting the individual in the tasks of upholding him- or herself in the world.

Antonio

Antonio, who is black, was 24 years old and lived with his mother at the time of the interview (2014). He was taking the fourth and last module of *Youth and Adult Education* in a school in district of Santa Cruz, in the outermost west area of the city of Rio de Janeiro. He worked as a freelance bricklayer. In his childhood, he lived in the neighborhood of Santa Teresa in the center of the city, so for him, the move to Santa Cruz meant isolation and limitation of his cultural possibilities, due to the difficulties of mobility and access to the city and its opportunities. He never knew his father and grew up with his mother who worked most of her life as a domestic servant. He was the fourth child in a family with seven children. He began working with his older siblings when he was 7, and when he was 9 he ran away for the first time and lived on the street. He says he ran away because he could not stand the pressures to reconcile work and school, or the precarious situation within his family. On the street he discovered the meaning of freedom to him. For some time, Antonio worked bagging products in a market and selling candy on the street, then later as a doorkeeper and as a salesperson in stores, but it was in the construction industry that he achieved a sense of accomplishment. For him, "it is much more rewarding to have the feeling that you are building something." After a few attempts interrupted by failure and dropping out, he completed middle school at the age of 19 and then took a technical course on masonry (where he also learned to design buildings). He said his first experience in construction had been when he was 11 or 12, when he helped a neighbor and one of his brothers and, after that, another relative. He also mentioned that he started working in a construction because, at that age, shyness and shame made it difficult for him to work on the street. He is delighted with the possibility of designing his own home (that he is building with the help of friends) and that other people build things based on their plans. “Tearing down is easy, building is the real thing.” He describes experiences of racism, especially at school, and how long it took for him to understand the systems within Brazilian society that attempted to undermine his worth as a person. He mentioned that by comprehending the meaning of racism, he was in a better position to defend himself or take attitudes of indifference in the face of the grievances caused by racism’s symbolic violence and its mechanisms of subordination. While still in preschool, he found ways to express his sensitivity in craftwork and in the arts which, according to him, turned out to be an antidote to the world of child labor and the feeling of abandonment he experienced being the fourth of seven children: “it is very difficult for a mother to focus and provide care to everyone if she has seven children.” In his youth, drawing was his most consistent artistic expression. All of his sketches convey his initials—ANG—which, in his opinion, are a form of highlighting his identity.

Fernanda

Fernanda, who is white, was 21 years old at the time of the interview (2014) and lived with her current partner and 5-year-old son in a rented house in a favela in the center of the city of Rio de Janeiro. She worked a formal job (with social security benefits) during the day and went to school in the evening for the second-to-last period of *Youth and Adult Education*. Her partner stayed with the child so that she could go to night school. At the age of 14, she made to leave her home by her father when he found out that she was dating; she went to live with an aunt in Jacarepaguá, a district far away from the center of the city, in a wooden house with precarious structural conditions. In order to help with expenses at her aunt’s place, she started working at night in a hot-dog food truck and gave up school because she got too tired of the long night shifts. She recalls the day she decided to drop out of school: “the rent was overdue and I was very tired of working overtime. I decided to increase my working hours and give up school. School would be helpful but only in the future, at that moment I needed to work.” She suffered countless physical assaults by her father, going forward and backward to her parents' home after being forced out at the age of 14 years. Fernanda says her mother never spoke on her behalf and, according to her, the only way to escape indefinitely from this domestic violence was by becoming pregnant as her father would finally expel her permanently from home. However, she was also beaten by the partner with whom she lived and by whom she got pregnant when she was 15 years old. Her son was born when she was 16, after which time she lived alone, working to support the child; her mother helped her in secret, without the knowledge of her father. The lack of family support and public policies for the care of her baby made it very difficult to go back to school. She worked as a cleaner and as a waitress until she was offered a job in naval communication company, a turning point in her life. This job encouraged her to go back to school, to speak correctly, to learn and get to know things she had never thought existed. As a result of having this job, she made new plans: to finish high school (she was still in middle school when she took this job) and go to university, with a stipend from her employers to support her studies. She took the admissions test for Brazilian public universities but did not pass, explaining that her schooling did not provide her with the conditions necessary to do so and that she herself was not in a position to prepare herself if left to her own devices. While participating in the research study, Fernanda always showed she had alternative plans for herself. She bought, through public funding, an apartment in a building still under construction outside the favela she intended to train as a flight attendant and was seeking professional development in the company she worked for by taking advantage of the opportunities she was offered. Using the camera given to her by the research team, Fernanda photographed a dining area, representing her work as a domestic servant, and also several doors of the houses where she had lived and places where she had worked. She spoke of the emotions invoked by being for the first time at the door of her current job, which meant a great deal in overcoming so many of the tests she had already gone through in her life.

The Common Test of Working and Studying

Having to work while still a child or at the beginning of adolescence is a persistent challenge for poor young people in Brazil. According to the 2017 ongoing PNAD (National Survey of Households), 1.8 million children and teenagers in Brazil between 5 and 17 years old were working, out of a population of 40.1 million people in this age range. Brazilian legislation establishes the minimum working age at 14 years old for the position of apprentice or in formal non-dangerous jobs, but these are not characteristic of the working conditions of most youth, which are more accurately described as child labor.

Antonio faced such challenges when he was still seven years old in the company of his older siblings. Fernanda faced this challenge alone on night shifts at the age of 14. For Antonio, the purpose of working was to help with the household expenses; for Fernanda, the objective was to support herself autonomously even when living at her aunt's home and then while living alone with her child.

For Antonio, despite its precariousness—with its lack of stability, permanence, social security benefits and labor rights—his work as a bricklayer grants him a "creative" identity, as he values so highly the possibility of building something; this has its highest expression in the fact that he can, with his own hands, build his own home. However, the working relationships and conditions are not favorable to him. Being underpaid for work he values so highly is disappointing, whereas the need to confront employers who delay payment or do not pay the previously agreed amount is outrageous.

Fernanda got a job that has provided her with stability, social mobility and cultural, social and economic capital. She says she was amazed by the job opportunity since only well-trained people worked in that company, whereas she was still going to middle school and made several mistakes in her native Portuguese language. But she faced the challenge of learning in service, through service and on behalf of service.

Both dropped out of formal education when they were in middle school and their stories express a condition highlighted by the quantitative data collected in the research: 35 percent of all respondents had left school while in middle school, at a time when they had to combine working and studying. National data on schooling among the Brazilian population indicate that 51 percent of people older than 25 did not complete middle school. It is known that leaving school is a more decisive factor than academic failure in the truncation of basic education. As shown by the youth in this study, going back to school represents an effort to overcome the structural constraints that led them to drop out in the first place and also shows the importance of *Youth and Adult Education* as a public policy in providing schooling to those whose age no longer match the regular school grade.

Research by Costa (2011) on the meaning of returning to school for young by the education for young people from *Youth and Adult Education* emphasizes that going back to school equates with a bet on reconfiguring life plans and dreams postponed by adverse circumstances. Resuming schooling gains a new meaning for those who are experiencing it for the second, third or more times. Thus, one may say that the return to school is related to the meanings given by youth to their schooling, related to future projections and reformulations of their life plans.

The answers collected through the survey reinforce how difficult a task combining study and work continues to be, notably for poor young people for whom work means survival, and not merely education and training for life as is the case for middle-class and elite youth in Brazil. However, the meanings of these relationships in the experiences of the young people need to be problematized. A significant portion of the individuals investigated do not necessarily see this reconciliation negatively. Among the respondents, 17.3 percent said that reconciling work and study allowed for their personal growth, while 2.3 percent said they could go back to school because they were working.

Conclusion

The life course approach employed in the research study enabled the establishment of interfaces between objective, clearly defined social standpoints in the biographical itineraries and the narrative materials of individuals revealing the subjective dimensions of their experiences. The demographic settings of schooling, work and income together with the primary survey data in our research demarcate both the social positions taken by Brazilian youth and the common tests they face in the space-time dimension of being young. The experiences recalled by Antonio and Fernanda single out the aforementioned objective positions; they are biographies that clarify contexts. Such recollections are not intended to represent entire groups of the population. They are, above all, landmarks to understand the place of *agency* in relation to social constraints.

The dilemmas inherent in balancing both study and work are a characteristic aspect of being poor and young in Brazil, although it is possible that the experiences gained through labor relations have solidified participants' belief in the importance of academic achievement in the search for economic and social improvement. For these youths, work and school are not mutually exclusive but rather, as already noted by Sposito (2008), they are projects that overlap. One may say that both play a crucial role in shaping young people's expectations for the future. Being complementary to each other, school and work intertwine to produce future expectations and make life plans come true.

There is an apparent paradox in the links between improvements to socioeconomic conditions and the persistence of labor among young people, especially adolescents. In a more favorable socioeconomic context, work could represent more than a means of subsistence. The need that pushes adolescents toward the labor markets would also be made up of other considerations, such as the search for independence and autonomy, or the value families assign to work as an element in the education of their children, and also as a means to build discipline and to control juvenile free time in underprivileged milieus.

Not all young people live their youth as a time of transition and preparation for the responsibilities of adulthood. In other words, for underprivileged youth the responsibilities of "adult life," especially the "pressure" to get a job, as well as the experiences of pregnancy, maternity and paternity, arrive without the benefit of a period of transition, during their time of youth.

Society sees itself marked by unprecedented societal processes as a consequence of global changes. A historical age of *temporal acceleration* is apparently creating a *new youth* (Leccardi, 2005). Such youth takes place in contexts of new life choices brought forth by scientific-technological development and new cultural patterns in the relationships between generations. There are risks and uncertainties unleashed by a process of globalization characterized by unequal opportunities and by fragile institutional bonds. The contemporary speed has decisive consequences, not only for the life of institutions but also for the making of biographies, both of them forced to blend continuously.

Notes

1. This research has been funded by FAPERJ—Foundation for Research Support of the State of Rio de Janeiro.
2. By contrast, in Chile, for example, the structure of transition is partly homogenized among several sectors of youth, resulting mainly from the changes taking place in education that universalized access to high school. The high rates of secondary education completion, together with the fact that 12-year schooling has recently become mandatory, somehow led most young people to go through a similar structure of transition up to the age in which secondary education is usually completed (León & Soto, 2007: 51).
3. The economic crisis worsened at the beginning of Dilma's administration in 2015 and was aggravated by what has been called a judicial-parliamentary coup that ended with the impeachment of a president without proof

of a crime of liability. Vice-President Michel Temer took over and opened the doors to resuming the neoliberal agenda in Brazil. This was characterized by privatization of public companies, 10-year cuts in public expenditure and the passing of the law of labor reform that withdrew rights, promoted dismissal and encouraged precarious and underpaid hiring. The year of 2016 was marked by an increase in youth unemployment.

4. The Youth Statute (Act No. 12,852, of 05 Aug 13) considers young the person who is between 15 and 29 years old. According to the National Research by Domicile Sampling—PNAD—2015, the Brazilian population is 204.9 million people, and 23.6 percent of the total population is considered young.
5. The demographic category "non-white" also includes, in addition to black people (known as black and brown people), indigenous and Asian people.
6. Dividing the city by areas took place as a way to maintain the proportional criterion of the sample among the units of neighborhood analyses.
7. The category Youth and Adult Education is a specific type of education—a modality—that ensures the right to education to people who did not have access to school or could not remain in the so-called right age group. To be included in this modality of education, you must be over 18 years of age. The acronym of this modality is EJA, in Portuguese "Educação de Jovens e Adultos."
8. Program to accelerate schooling for young people of high school age (15–18 years old) who not match the expected grade for their current age.
9. At this stage of the research, all participants had already completed high school in the EJA modality.
10. Names have been changed to ensure the information remains confidential.
11. It should be reiterated that the questionnaire was anonymous, except in the cases of those who agreed to participate in the second (qualitative) stage of the research when biographical interviews were filmed. This allowed personalization of the scripts.

Bibliography

Alexander, J., Giesen, B., Munch, R., & Smelser, N. J. (dir.). (1987). *The Micro-Macro Link*. Berkeley, CA: University of California Press.

Andrews, C. W., & Vries, M. S. de. (2012). Pobreza e municipalização da educação: análise dos resultados do IDEB (2005–2009). *Cadernos de Pesquisa*, São Paulo, *42*(147), 826–847.

Arnett, J. J. (2000). Emerging Adulthood: A Theory of Development from the Late Teens Through the Twenties. *American Psychologist, 55*, 469–480.

Arnett, J. J. (2001). Conceptions of the Transition to Adulthood: Perspectives from Adolescence to Midlife. *Journal of Adult Development, 8*, 133–143.

Attias-Donfut, C. (1996). Jeunesse et conjugaison des temps. *Sociologie et sociétés, 28*, 1.

Beck, U. (2010). *Sociedade de risco: rumo a uma outra modernidade*. São Paulo, Brazil: Ed. 34.

Bois-Reymond, M du. (org.). (2008). *Young Parenthood, Agency and Social Change*—UP2YOUTH "Thematic Final Report" Young Parenthood. Leiden, The Netherlands: University of Leiden. 163 p. Retrieved from http://www.up2youth.org/downloads/task,doc_download/gid,71/index.html

Cacciamali, M. C., & Braga, T. (2002). *Educação e trabalho da população jovem: diagnóstico e políticas* (pp. 11–15). São Paulo, Brazil: Ministério do Trabalho e Emprego.

Calvo, G. (2005). El envejecimiento de la juventud. *Revista Injuve – Autonomia de la juventud em Europa, 71*, 11–19.

Camarano, A. A., Mello, J. L., Pasinato, M. T., & Kanso, S. (2004). *Caminhos para a vida adulta: as múltiplas trajetórias dos jovens brasileiros*. Rio de Janeiro, Brazil: IPEA. Discussion Text 1038. Retrieved from http://repositorio.ipea.gov.br/handle/11058/1876

Caradec, V., & Martuccelli, D. (2004). *Matériaux pour une sociologie de l'individu: perspectives et débats*. Lille, France: Presses Universitaires du Septentrion..

Carvalho, L. (2018). *Valsa brasileira: Do boom ao caos econômico*. São Paulo, Brazil: Editora Todavia.

Costa, Mariane Brito da. (2011). Começar de novo: um estudo sobre percursos biográficos de jovens na EJA/Mariane Brito da Costa – 2011. 129 f. Thesis advisor: Paulo César Rodrigues Carrano.

Costa Neto, P. L. de O. (1977). *Estatística*. São Paulo, Brazil: Edgard Blücher.

Dubar, C. (1998). Trajetórias sociais e formas identitárias: alguns esclarecimentos conceituais e metodológicos. *Educação e Sociedade, 19*(62), 13–30.

Dubet, F. (1996). Des jeneusses et des sociologies. Le cas français. *Sociologie et societé. Les jeunes, 28*(1), 13–22.

Easterlin, R. A. (1981). Why Isn't the Whole World Developed? *The Journal of Economic History, 41*(1), 1–19.

Elder, G. H. Jr. (1994). Time, Human Agency, and Social Change: Perspectives on the Life Course. *Social Psychology Quarterly, 57*(1), 4–15. Retrieved from http://www.academia.edu/2520553/Time_human_agency_and_social_change_Perspectives_on_the_life_course

Filgueira, C. H. (2001). Estructura de oportunidades y vulnerabilidad social: Aproximaciones conceptuales recientes. In CEPAL (Ed.), *Seminário vulnerabilidad*. Santiago de Chile, Chile: CEPAL.

Fleury, S. (2013). Do Welfare State ao Warfare State. *Conjuntura Política Brasileira*. Dossie temático, *2*, 97–102.

Galland, O. (1996). *Les jeunes* (5e ed.). Paris, France: La Découverte.

Guerra, I. (1993). Modos de vida: novos percursos e novos conceitos. *Sociologia—Problemas e Práticas, 13*, 59–74.

Hanushek, E. A. (1995). Interpreting Recent Research on Schooling in Developing Countries. *The World Bank Research Observer, 10*(2), 227–246.

La Mendola, S. (2009). *Centrato e aperto. Dare vita a interviste dialogiche*. Torino, Italy: Utet Università.

Leccardi, C. (2005). Facing Uncertainty: Temporality and Biographies in the New Century. *Nordic Journal of Youth Research, 13*(2), 123–146.

León, O. D., & Soto, F. (2007). *Los desheredados. Trayectorias de vida y nuevas condiciones juveniles*. Valparaíso, Chile: Ediciones CIDPA.

Mannheim, K. (2005). El problema de las generaciones. *REIS—Revista española de investigaciones sociológicas, 62*, 193–242.

Martuccelli, D. (2007a). *Cambio de rumbo: la sociedad a escala del individuo*. Santiago de Chile, Chile: Lom.

Martuccelli, D. (2007b). *Gramáticas del indivíduo*. Buenos Aires, Argentina: Losada.

Melucci, A. (2005). Busca de qualidade, ação social e cultura—Por uma sociologia reflexiva. In *Por uma sociologia reflexiva: pesquisa qualitativa e cultura*. Petrópolis, RJ: Vozes.

Menezes, N. (2015). *Renda dos pais e trabalho dos jovens*. Retrieved from http://www.valor.com.br/imprimir/noticia/3917642/opiniao/3917642/renda-dos-pais-e-trabalho-dos-jovens

Pais, J. M. (2001). *Ganchos, tachos e biscates: Jovens, trabalho e futuro*. Porto, Portugal: Ambar.

Pais, J. M. (2003). *Vida cotidiana: enigmas e revelações*. São Paulo, Brazil: Cortez.

Pais, J. M. (2005). *Traços e riscos de vida. Uma abordagem qualitativa a modos de vida juvenis*. Porto, Portugal: Ambar.

Pesquisa Nacional por Amostra de Domicílios: *síntese de indicadores 2014*/IBGE, Coordenação de Trabalho e Rendimento. Rio de Janeiro, Brazil: IBGE, 2015a.102 p. Retrieved from https://biblioteca.ibge.gov.br/visualizacao/livros/liv94935.pdf

Pesquisa Nacional por Amostra de Domicílios: *síntese de indicadores 2013*/IBGE, Coordenação de Trabalho e Rendimento. 2 ed. Rio de Janeiro, Brazil: IBGE, 2015b. 296 p. Retrieved from https://biblioteca.ibge.gov.br/visualizacao/livros/liv94414.pdf

Pesquisa Nacional por Amostra de Domicílios: *síntese de indicadores 2016*/IBGE, Coordenação de Trabalho e Rendimento. Rio de Janeiro, Brazil: IBGE, 2017. Retrieved from https://www.ibge.gov.br/estatisticas-novoportal/sociais/habitacao/17270-pnad-continua.html?edicao=18264&t=sobre

Reguillo, R. (2013). *Culturas Juveniles: Formas políticas del desencanto*. Buenos Aires, Argentina: SigloVeintiuno Editores.

Schwartz, S. J., Côté, J. E., & Arnett, J. J. (2005). Identity and Agency in Emerging Adulthood: Two Development Routes in the Individualization Process. *Youth & Society, 37*(2), 201–229.

Sposito, M. (2005). Algumas reflexões e muitas indagações sobre as relações entre juventude e escola no Brazil. In H. Abramo & P. P. Branco (Eds.), *Retratos da juventude brasileira: análises de uma pesquisa nacional* (pp. 87–128). São Paulo, Brazil: Fundação Perseu Abramo.

Sposito, M. (2008). Juventude e Educação: interações entre a educação escolar e a educação não-formal. *Educação & Realidade, 2*(33), 83–98. Retrieved from http://seer.ufrgs.br/index.php/educacaoerealidade/article/view/7065/4381

Zago, N. (2000). Processos de escolarização nos meios populares: as contradições da obrigatoriedade escolar. In M. Nogueira, G. Romanelli, & N. Zago (Eds.), *Família e escola: trajetórias de escolarização em camadas médias e populares* (pp. 19–43). Petrópolis, Brazil: Vozes.

PART III

Adulthood, Poverty and Domestic Paid Work

CHAPTER 6

"You Can't Have It All": Patterns of Gender and Class Segregation in Paid Domestic Work in the City of Buenos Aires

Débora Gorbán and Ania Tizziani

Introduction

In Argentina, as in many countries in Latin America, domestic service is one of the main sources of employment for working-class women, who often face very limited job options. Like other forms of highly feminized and undervalued work that are considered to be "unskilled" occupations, domestic service generally entails low incomes, inadequate or absent social protections, and highly unfavorable working conditions. It has been studied as a critical space for the analysis of structures which promote inequalities of gender, class, ethnicity, nationality, or citizenship (Gutiérrez Rodríguez, 2010; Parreñas, 2001; Romero, 2002; among other studies).

D. Gorbán (✉)
ICI-UNGS/CONICET, Buenos Aires, Argentina
e-mail: dgorban@campus.ungs.edu.ar

A. Tizziani (✉)
CONICET, National University of General Sarmiento (UNGS), Buenos Aires, Argentina
e-mail: atizzian@ungs.edu.ar

M. E. Rausky, M. Chaves (eds.), *Living and Working in Poverty in Latin America*, Governance, Development, and Social Inclusion in Latin America, https://doi.org/10.1007/978-3-030-00901-4_6

The work histories and experiences of the women who work in this area reveal the restrictions and strong conditioning factors that disadvantaged women come up against as they try to enter the world of work.

In this chapter, we analyze the labor histories of women who have mainly worked in domestic service, in the hope of expanding the study of gender- and class-based segregation patterns in the world of work. We will pay particular attention to two factors that are at the core of the configuration of these inequalities. First, we look at the intersection between these women's roles in the labor market and their family dynamics, and its effect on their work histories—in other words, how their unpaid, reproductive work within their homes articulates with paid work outside the home. Second, we examine the characteristics of the jobs that make up the universe of occupations to which women with lower educational capital have access. Through this analysis, we are hoping to answer the following questions: In workers' accounts, which factors shape their employment histories? What factors influence their decision-making with regard to the world of work? How do they combine their domestic responsibilities and their paid work? What strategies do they use to acquire skills or training and move between different jobs and employment areas? How do they view and evaluate the different jobs they have held?

This study is based on a research project that we have been carrying out since 2009, which focuses on experiences and working conditions among domestic workers in the City of Buenos Aires. As part of this project, we carried out qualitative fieldwork in different stages, which included in-depth interviews with domestic workers and employers. We contacted the workers through different organizations that are connected with this sector (labor unions, associations, training centers), and we also interviewed authorities from these organizations and observed the activities that are run on their premises. Additionally, we carried out observations and informal interviews in different city squares and parks, where we met domestic employees whose profiles varied but who mainly (although not exclusively) performed childcare tasks. In this chapter, we focus on the stories of adult women in order to observe their journeys through life, reflecting on how the latter are affected and shaped by different events related to family and work.

The chapter is organized into four sections. The first section presents the main issues that emerge from the social sciences literature on gender and class inequality in the labor market. In the following section, we analyze the life path and employment history of a worker who has been employed in domestic service for her entire working life. This will allow us to identify the conditioning factors that have shaped such paths and will shed light on the degree of flexibility available to workers and the multiple geographic and occupational mobility strategies that they develop. The third section examines these mobility strategies in greater detail. To this end, our analysis includes the experiences of workers who have also held other types of jobs, to explore how these alternative routes emerge and how they are perceived and valued. Based on these observations, the conclusion puts forward some guidelines for rethinking public policies that will contribute to improving these women's role in the labor market from the vantage points of decent work and gender equality, both of which are highlighted in the 2030 Agenda for Sustainable Development adopted by the United Nations in September 2015.

Labor Paths, Conditioning, and Segregation

Different studies have drawn attention to the continued existence of marked segregation by gender and class in the Argentinian labor market in recent decades (Cortés, 2012). On one hand, despite improvements in the country's employment indicators toward the end of the first decade of the 2000s, significant gender inequalities persist (Bertranou and Casanova, 2013; Cortés, 2012; Novick, Rojo, & Castillo, 2008). As in other countries in Latin America, female workers are more affected by unemployment, underemployment, and precarious and informal employment than their male counterparts (CEPAL, 2014). Similarly, different studies argue that the country's occupational structure is divided into male and female territories, that high wage gaps persist even among workers in higher-ranking positions with similar education or skill levels, and that women are less likely to be employed as supervisors, managers, or executives (Novick et al., 2008).

A broad range of studies emphasize that one of the core elements in the configuration of these gender inequality patterns is the huge overlap between reproductive and productive labor in women's life paths and the articulation of employment decisions and family dynamics (Barrancos and Goren, 2002; Wainerman, 2002; among others). The weight of the social responsibilities that women bear as part of their reproductive labor limits both their opportunities for performing paid labor outside the home and the type of jobs to which they have access. At the same time, ongoing gender stereotypes that differentiate roles, skills, and knowledge differently for men and women (and assign different values to these) also contribute to restricting the universe of occupations accessible to women (Novick et al., 2008).

As a consequence, urban women in Argentina are employed mainly in trade and services, in activities that are viewed as "typically feminine," that is, those that are defined as an extension of the reproductive tasks that are socially attributed to women. This extension of traditional female gender roles into the world of wage work contributes to normalizing the precariousness of the labor conditions that define these occupations (Georges, 2011: 111). For middle-class women, teaching, social services, and health-care are the sectors with the highest representation, whereas for working-class women with lower levels of formal education, domestic and care services are the most common form of work (Contartese & Maceira, 2005; Dávalos, 2013).

These differences in women's labor integration depending on their socioeconomic sector point to the need to analyze these gender segregation patterns in conjunction with the ways that other inequalities are configured, particularly those related to class origins. Low-income women have the most limited options when entering the world of work and do so in more unfavorable conditions. This is mainly due to the limited resources available to them in managing the reproductive responsibilities to which they are socially assigned. The impact of these responsibilities on women's labor paths undoubtedly depends on arrangements and negotiations within homes, but also on unequal access to services outside the home, whether they are operated by the state, the community, or the market. In other words, working-class women have little or no access to services such as paid domestic work, daycare or nurseries for children, institutions that care for the sick and the elderly, access to domestic technology, and so on (Jelin, 2010). Additionally, the fact that the supply of such services is largely defined by market mechanisms contributes to reproducing these patterns of segregation by gender and socioeconomic sector in the labor market.

The specific problems that working-class women face within the labor market have been analyzed in different studies, notably those that focus on the relationships between gender, work, and poverty (Barrancos & Goren, 2002; Gallart et al., 1992; Valenzuela, 2003). These draw attention to the lower involvement of women from less privileged sectors in paid activities outside the home in comparison to women from the middle and upper classes. Indeed, the labor histories of working-class women are characterized by an intermittent presence in the labor market. Alternations between periods of employment and unemployment and frequent transitions to inactivity shape these discontinuous, unstable employment paths, which are closely linked to stages in the family life cycle. Low-income women are much more likely to leave the labor market when they get married and particularly when they have children than women with higher incomes (Cerrutti, 2002). Furthermore, they find it especially hard to make paid activities compatible with domestic and care responsibilities within their own homes. To do so, they turn to part-time or flexible labor activities or work by the hour, which is often precarious, informal employment. They also deploy a series of family-based strategies to respond to their own care needs, which may involve other members of their household or family (mainly women) and other community networks. When these impromptu caregivers are girls or young women in the same family, such strategies may seriously restrict their schooling and opportunities for engaging in further education or training.

The positions of working-class women in the labor market cannot be separated from the characteristics of the jobs to which they have access. These are generally activities that rank low in the occupational structure and offer low salaries, disadvantageous labor conditions, and limited career development opportunities. These characteristics affect the value and meaning that women ascribe to such work, which they often do not perceive as being a real job but rather a way of "helping out" with family finances (Cerrutti, 2002). Skills and qualifications also play a major role in defining the set of occupations available to working-class women: low levels of formal education and employment paths dominated by occupations that are considered unskilled (and which do not provide workers with new skills) contribute to the confinement of working-class women to lower-quality occupations (Barrancos & Goren, 2002).

The fact that immigrant status is more common among domestic workers than other wage workers also plays a part in these workers being subject to more disadvantageous circumstances in the labor market. In Argentina, migrants from other South American countries (the main origin of immigration flows) are employed in the lowest-ranking positions within the occupational structure: those with low skill requirements, low salaries, and where informal conditions are prevalent (see "Migraciones laborales en la Argentina," ILO, 2015). Numerous studies on domestic work in the United States and European countries show that restrictive immigration policies and barriers to obtaining legal resident status in destination countries effectively confine these workers to informal positions with no legal protection from extreme exploitation (Parreñas, 2001; Hondagneu Sotelo, 2007). However, in Argentina, inclusive immigration policies mean that very few immigrants from other countries in South America lack a legal immigration status. For this reason, various studies attribute migrant workers' difficulties in accessing jobs to other dynamics related to the structure of inequalities. Pizarro argues that the allocation of immigrants from certain countries to the most adverse jobs is justified through cultural hierarchies and ethnic or national discrimination based on racial prejudice (Pizarro, 2012: 24; see also Mallimaci, 2011).

In the case of domestic service, these stigmatizing racial associations have deep historical roots due to their direct association with slavery and the influence of colonization processes on the historical structure of such occupations.[1] These racial marking processes were extended through immigration flows that have always played an important part in this domestic work. Initially, these flows were internal, but then extended to neighboring countries. In Argentina, this racialization has contributed to deepening class inequalities (Gorbán & Tizziani, 2014) and the ways that these articulate with the disadvantages that working-class women face in entering the labor market and remaining there.

In the following section, by analyzing the life and employment path of a domestic worker, we will attempt to identify how these different issues are intertwined. To do so, we will use the concept of trajectories, based on what Elder (2003, cited in Blanco, 2011) calls the "life course perspective," which focuses on the paths through different interdependent areas of people's lives. In this focus, the relationship between family and work is at the core of the analysis of life trajectories. These two spheres are understood as "dynamic, interrelated processes" (Elder, 2003, cited in Blanco, 2011). This perspective places particular emphasis on the time factor and prioritizes the individual and their movements in the context of their sociohistorical circumstances and family configurations. Accordingly, these personal trajectories unfold in the context of the specific place and time that shape them and also develop in relation to specific events (timing) that happen at particular points in individuals' lives (Blanco, 2011). In the next section, we reconstruct Ana's trajectory and explore these aspects of her experiences.

Ana's Story: Family, Work, and Migration

Ana is originally from Paraguay. Now 38, she has lived in Argentina since she was 15. Her story is similar to those of many female immigrants whose search for work takes them to big cities in foreign countries. While their reasons for emigrating vary, the lack of available work and low wages in their countries of origin are commonly cited as motivations. Historically, Paraguay has been a significant source of immigration flows to Argentina, involving typical cycles of ebbs and surges (Cerruti, 2002; Pacecca & Courtis, 2008).

Ana is not the only member of her family to leave her home town: four of the six siblings in her family left the rural area where her parents still live to move to Buenos Aires. The first to leave was her sister Ornella, who went to live with an aunt in Greater Buenos Aires when she was 16. After brief spells in Buenos Aires, two more of her sisters, Federica and Juana, emigrated to Spain, where they still live. Ana's sister Lila moved to a town near her parents' home after getting married and still lives there with her husband, who works for a butcher. The two youngest children, Mariana and Benicio, lived with their parents until they were 18. Mariana then began to work in Esperanza as a live-in maid for a family that she knew. Benicio has not moved and does odd jobs around town, ranging from selling lottery tickets to agricultural labor. Ana says that they are the only two in the family who "were lucky enough" to finish high school, as she and her older sisters only managed to finish primary school, except Ornella, who did not even get that far.

Obstacles to continuing their education are a constant, common problem for working-class women. As we observed in this case, this is not merely because they enter the labor market early, but also because of the tasks that they have to perform within their families from a young age. These include not only looking after younger siblings, which is almost always the responsibility of older girls, but also cleaning and other domestic chores, as well as productive activities. In Ana's family, these tasks ranged from fetching drinking water from a nearby stream to looking after chickens and collecting eggs, weeding a plot of land, or harvesting vegetables from the garden that provided a large share of the family's food. All of these activities required significant physical effort and were part of Ana's routine since the age of six.

Although Ana says that she started her first job at the age of 11, working for a family near Asunción for whom she did cleaning and childcare work in return for board and schooling, her working life really began much earlier, as we described in the previous paragraph. As was also the case with the other women that we interviewed during our fieldwork, Ana's account contained countless mentions of tasks that are normalized and invisibilized. The work in question, be it care work or productive work, is not acknowledged as actually being work. Indeed, the debate around care work has only really become part of the public agenda in recent years, and its recognition as work is still hotly disputed. Furthermore, as Zelizer argues (2012), the care work that is performed by boys and girls is even more problematic as they are supposed to be recipients of care rather than caregivers. Even when children must perform different care tasks, the moral legitimacy of which varies, adults and children set limits around what they believe to be appropriate or inappropriate relationships in care work (Zelizer, 2012). In line with Zelizer, we observed that children's care work may take a wide variety of forms depending on the networks of social relationships within which it takes place. Whether or not such work is acceptable or inadmissible depends on the relationship context—in other words, it depends on *who* the work is for and *where* it takes place. Work that happens within an intimate, family space is more acceptable as it is perceived as "help." This is the case in Ana's story.

The possibility for her to attend school is framed as being unavoidably connected to work. Work was the necessary condition for her to be able to continue her education. The work in question was unpaid, and her employers were families in cities near the rural area where she lived. The tasks that she carried out for them were similar to those that she and her sisters had been performing in their own home and their grandmother's home since they were little. This narrative is not unusual: it reappears continually in the labor histories of women who are employed in paid domestic service and also in the stories of many women from low-income homes.

> I had a really bad time at that house [in Asunción, where she started working at the age of 11]. I went there because I wanted to go to school, I wanted to do something with my life. I didn't want to become a maid because all my classmates were able to keep going to school. Their parents had other sources of income and could let their children go to school. But mine couldn't, because my family is very poor, and my father couldn't afford it. But I wanted to go to school. So I went to work there and I had a terrible time. I cried all the time because they made me… I was only 11 and I had to clean the bathrooms. It was awful.

As Ana's account reveals, the possibility of a better future, as represented by education, is interrupted by her experience of work. Indeed, her experience at the time was not just about the possibility of going to school but about making this compatible with the demands of her daily work in the household of two adults and three children where Ana had to cook, clean, iron, and look after children who were nearly as old as she was. "Dealing with it" was the condition for being able to finish her education, but Ana was unable to. Ana perceives the interruption of her formal education as a factor that strongly conditioned the jobs she could potentially do. In her account, she says that, unlike her cousin, who "dealt with" mistreatment from her employers and became a schoolteacher, the only option for her was domestic service.

Q: *Can you imagine what your life would have been like if you hadn't left Paraguay?*

A: I can't imagine it (laughs). I don't even want to think about it, if I had stayed in Paraguay I would have run away eventually. In fact, I did run away. I came to work here [in Argentina] for a year, then I went back and stayed in Paraguay for six months. I got myself a boyfriend who was a real drunk. I imagined what my life would be like there, having loads of children and ruining my life. Because life in the countryside is like that, you have loads of children and ruin your life. That's what I think mine would have been like if I'd stayed in Paraguay.

Ana's story is marked by different migration experiences—first, the move from her village to different towns and cities in Paraguay, then from Paraguay to Argentina. She sees this move as a turning point, especially in relation to the options open to her in Paraguay, even though she continued to work in the same sector after emigrating. As Mallimaci observed in her study of Bolivian women migrants, in this case, migration does not represent a way into the labor market: the women in question have always worked, so "migration does not signify a change in the presence or absence of work in their lives although it does significantly transform the type of work that they do" (Mallimaci, 2009: 8). In Ana's case, the forms of work that she would carry out changed over the course of her labor history, but they were always within the domestic service sector. She began by "helping out" at home and working for other families in exchange for food, lodging, and schooling and then found employment as a paid domestic worker in the City of Buenos Aires. She reached Buenos Aires through a network of women in her family already working in domestic service there and living in the west of Greater Buenos Aires. After a brief spell working at a bakery owned by an uncle, which she recalls as difficult experience due to the "tough" work it involved, the unusual hours, and how badly her extended family treated her, she was hired by a high-income family in the City of

Buenos Aires as a live-in cleaner. One of her aunt's friends recommended her for the job and became one of the first people to help her understand how things worked in Argentina. Four years later, Ana found out that she was pregnant and was forced to resign not long before her baby was born; not being formally employed, she lacked basic rights such as maternity leave.[2] Her time out of the labor market was short, however, because her difficult relationship with her son's father meant that she was forced to go back to work to earn a living. She went back to work weekends for the same family at their house in a gated community outside of Buenos Aires. When her son turned one, she started working as a live-in maid for a sister-in-law of her former employer in a high-income neighborhood. Over the next few years, she was hired in three other houses, where she did cleaning work and looked after children from Monday to Friday. Ana was able to remain in the labor market after becoming a mother because she hired a neighbor to look after her son during his early years. However, in 2002, she was involved in a traffic accident after leaving work. After this, she stopped working as a live-in maid and switched to combining one steady job where she worked eight hours a day as a domestic worker with other jobs where she worked by the hour for different employers.

Her continued experience in this sector meant that Ana became proficient not only in the different cleaning, cooking, and childcare tasks required of her by her employers but also in the negotiation of working conditions, the role of labor unions, the legal framework that applied to her work, and other information that defines relationships and practices in the world of domestic service.[3] Collectively, this represented a pool of knowledge on which she could draw in negotiations with her employers and which would enable her to improve her own working conditions from one job to the next (Tizziani & Gorbán, 2015). This learning is central to the labor paths of Ana and other domestic workers analyzed as part of this study, as it correlates with access to some sort of job stability. Likewise, even though such knowledge is not synonymous with vertical social mobility, it leads to workers accessing what are seen as "better" jobs, which improves their horizontal mobility within the sector (Tizziani, 2011). This, in turn, represents concrete improvements to their working conditions: shorter hours, established breaks, paid travel expenses, a formal contract, access to benefits, and so forth. Although all of these factors remain largely dependent on employers' "good will," workers use the information available to them not only to negotiate better conditions but also to reject jobs that are not in their interests.

As can be seen, our analysis of Ana's personal and labor history overlaps significantly with the life course approach on which other chapters in this book are based. Entering into a dialogue with this perspective allows us to draw attention to certain factors that we believe are central to how Ana's life trajectory is organized. First, as mentioned above, the different spheres of her life are profoundly interrelated: her family of origin, work, education, and experiences of migration. Ana's account of her labor history and the directions, changes, and choices that have shaped it are inseparable from what has taken place in those different spheres and the way in which they are interwoven: the social and economic vulnerability of her family of origin, the continual presence of work (which was unpaid within her own home), and her early entry to the labor market, which cut short her education. Her transition to paid work outside the home, at an earlier age than is generally expected in other social classes and contexts, had long-term consequences: it is one of the main limitations that Ana points to regarding future job opportunities. This is the first disadvantage that she experienced, which then triggered and became articulated with other gender- and class-related limitations in what Elder (1998) termed "cumulative disadvantage."

However, these structural conditions do not "explain" her entire trajectory. In particular, the experience of migrating to the City of Buenos Aires is a turning point in Ana's account, an event that she chooses to reconstruct step-by-step as a watershed moment that opened up the horizon of possibilities available to her in different spheres. This break with the life that she says she would have led "in the countryside" enabled her to organize her relationships with partners and family life differently. It also opened up opportunities and gave her access to learning and experience that would play a fundamental role in improving her working conditions within domestic service.

We should stress that although there is indeed an "accumulation of disadvantages" (Elder, 1998) that condition the way that Ana's trajectory has unfolded, these cannot be analyzed in a linear fashion. In other words, even in the social and historical contexts that have shaped Ana's story, there are certain points when a profound disadvantage subsequently comes to represent a possible turning point. In the face of such possibilities, Ana makes choices and decisions that allow her to improve her employment and living conditions over time. Her ability to choose despite strong conditioning factors is the point we wish to stress here. As we will show in the following section, even within the limited employment alternatives available, there are margins of choice that are constructed in the transition between different work and life experiences.

Labor Horizons: Beyond Domestic Service …

Ana's story has significant points in common with the social and labor histories of many of the female workers that we interviewed during our fieldwork. However, although domestic service is an immediate possibility for finding paid employment, it is not always the only option on the labor horizons of the women with whom we talked. In fact, it is rarely the only job that they have done: Margarita sold clothing door-to-door in Lima before arriving in Buenos Aires and becoming a live-in domestic worker; Laura worked at a service station before moving from Asunción to a farm in Pilar, north of the City of Buenos Aires, where she started to work as a live-in maid; Mariana worked at a poultry shop 15 kilometers outside of Asunción before emigrating to Argentina and taking on paid domestic work; Andrea moved to Buenos Aires from La Paz with her entire family at the age of 13 and began work as a presser in a textile factory when she was 17 before switching to domestic service.

Both migrant and non-migrant female workers have usually performed cleaning tasks and care work (for both children and the elderly) in both domestic and nondomestic spaces throughout their labor histories. Indeed, at the time of our interviews, some of the women to whom we talked were combining part-time cleaning work in private homes, buildings, offices, or small shops. Dora describes a labor history of several decades in domestic service that she interrupted for four years to set up a daycare service. Margarita's brief experience in domestic service was punctuated by six months working as a nursing assistant at an aged care facility. Elina worked for many years as a cleaner in clinics and an aged care facility before switching to domestic work at the age of 58.

How do they see these other types of work in relation to their current jobs in domestic service? Dora was "happy looking after those children" when she set up her daycare service. In contrast, Mariana's description of her former work experience is loaded with ambiguity that emerges in her description of the work she did at the poultry shop where she worked: "we killed the chickens and processed them. We were murderers!" When we carried out the interviews, Andrea had been working for six months as a full-time live-out maid, performing domestic tasks, cooking, washing, and ironing as well as taking care of a six-month-old girl. She describes her current job as "easy-going," in terms of the physical effort involved, in comparison to her previous job pressing children's clothing at a textile factory in the neighborhood of Palermo in Buenos Aires. Margarita describes her switch to domestic service and her experience at an aged care facility in the City of Buenos Aires as follows:

> I look after old people. I've worked for four different people and I've never been fired. One of my employers died but the family recommended me for another job. I took the job and worked there for a year. Then I worked in an old people's home for six months, but I got very tired, it was really hard work because I had to look after 35 patients by myself and we had to do everything, change them... So, no. They paid minimum wage and the work was so hard that it really killed your waist, even now I'm still feeling the effects from it because sometimes my waist hurts and all that.

Throughout their employment histories, the labor experiences of these women occur within a set of occupations with shared characteristics. First, they are all activities that are seen as "unskilled" and largely go unrecognized in society. Some are examples of small-scale, informal, independent business initiatives that have little prospects of growing or developing, such as Margarita selling clothes or Dora's daycare in her own home. Others are examples of informal, cash-in-hand jobs, such as Andrea's position at the textile factory, or short-term, unstable contracts such as Elina's jobs at clinics and aged care facilities. As can be seen from Margarita's account, all are low-quality occupations that are marked by instability, unfavorable labor conditions, long working hours, and an intense pace.

Even though domestic service is one of the lowest-ranking jobs in the occupational structure, it often features in the accounts of the women we interviewed as a choice that makes sense given the limited universe of job options to which they have access. As can be seen from Ana's story in the previous section, the learning that workers acquire throughout their experience in the sector allows them to access jobs that have advantages over other possible employment options. By consolidating labor relationships, developing their social networks (which often includes contact with labor unions), and learning to manage relationships with employers, these workers can play an active part in defining the core aspects of their daily labor practices.

The labor mobility strategies mentioned by these workers—that is, the projects that will offer them a way out of both domestic service and the other occupations they have held—are oriented toward occupations that are more widely recognized and appreciated in society. These mobility strategies are long-term projects and invariably entail major changes in their education or professional training. In their discourse, it is the acquisition of new educational qualifications that will allow them to improve their position in the labor market. In some cases, these projects imply obtaining a high school leaver's certificate. In others, they are about accessing training and professional qualifications, often in relation to beauty care or other personal services (hairdressing, waxing, manicures, etc.)—training options that are open to women with low levels of formal education. Even though such strategies appear repeatedly in the accounts of the workers we interviewed, not all of them are able to put them into practice. On one hand, much of this professional training has to be paid for and the prices are often high in relation to the low wages of domestic workers. On the other, they require an investment of additional time on top of the already long work days that are the norm in the sector, as well as the domestic and care work that these workers carry out within their own homes.

Liliana worked in domestic service for nearly two decades before setting up a small hairdressing salon in the neighborhood of Barracas in Buenos Aires. Her experience illustrates these mobility strategies, their meanings, and the strong factors that condition workers' possibilities for implementing them. Liliana was 40 when we interviewed her and was living in an apartment in the neighborhood of Nueva Pompeya with her three-year-old son. After several experiences working in domestic service in Asunción, Paraguay, where Liliana was originally from, she started work at a textile factory where she stayed for five years. That was when she decided to train as a hairdresser, "because I wanted to have a profession." The timing of this decision was not insignificant. Her job at the textile factory was "eight hours a day," Liliana says. She had always been a live-in domestic worker up to that point, so her working hours at the factory meant that she had considerable extra time, which allowed her to attend the hairdressing course for three hours a day. Liliana insists that it was a "long" course, one that lasted two years, "not like those ones that you finish in six months and then don't learn how to do anything." She then complemented it with other shorter training courses several years later, when she was living in Buenos Aires and working in domestic service again.

For several years, before she started her business, she alternated between jobs at other hairdressing salons and in domestic service: although the former was what she wanted to do, the latter, where she had the bulk of her experience, brought in better pay and more stability.

> Before, when I was working at that hairdresser's, I had to be there from nine in the morning till nine-thirty at night and I didn't earn much. When you work like that, as an employee at a hairdresser's, they pay you a percentage, say 40% of whatever jobs you do. I got paid 40% there. If there were days when nobody came in and you didn't do anything, then you didn't get paid.

> So, you don't get a fixed salary at a hairdresser's so it makes more sense to... In fact, I started working for them [at the hairdresser's] and after four months I was offered a live-in job that would pay me more, so it made more sense because I would earn a fixed salary and not just so much percent. So anyway, I stopped working there [at the hairdresser's], I told them I'd got another job and I left.

Eventually, she stopped working in domestic service after managing to set up her own business in the City of Buenos Aires, where she works alone doing hairdressing, waxing, and manicure. Liliana sees this as a step up in her work history: "I like this job more because I'm the boss," she says. This change has less to do with her income level, which is only slightly higher than domestic work, and is more centered on the fact that owning her own business means that she can do the job she trained for and receive greater social recognition for it. Accordingly, what Liliana values about her new situation is her independence and the fact that she can choose her own hours and have more time off, which is fundamental for her since she is separated from her partner and lives alone with her son. This independence comes at the cost of income instability, the most problematic aspect of her work as a hairdresser. This emerges clearly when she compares it with her prior experience in domestic service:

> The disadvantage when you're in hairdressing is that you don't have a fixed monthly wage.
>
> *Q: Especially in comparison with live-in work, because there are other women who work by the hour and their pay also varies...*
>
> No, but sometimes you work at someone's house and they pay you by the month, not by the hour, you go every day and they pay by the month so they have to give you paid holiday time, a bonus salary, and a monthly wage. So that's something that I miss, because before if I didn't work... Let's say I get sick, that's something that worries me a lot because if I get sick or something like that then I won't be earning any money. That worries me because I have to pay the bills, the rent, I have to feed my son, I have to eat too, all that. When you have a stable job, you know that even if you're sick, if you're not working, if you're on bed rest, you get paid all the same. When you work for yourself, if you don't work, you don't get paid.

Liliana's account reveals a core feature of certain upward labor trajectories among women who work in domestic service. The transition to self-employment, to a job that enjoys a higher social status with the need for specific training, is valued in terms of their family life and day-to-day activities, even if it does not necessarily imply a significant improvement in working conditions. Even though Liliana's income as a hairdresser might be higher than what she would have earned in domestic service, it is still one of the lowest in the labor market, which makes it even harder for her to manage the instability that is typical of freelance work or self-employment. Moreover, the independent nature of her work implies the absence of certain protections and social benefits, such as bonuses, holiday pay, sick pay, and maternity leave, which heighten instability. As such, working-class women's prospects for labor mobility are limited to a circuit of jobs in which they always have to give something up.

Final Considerations

In this chapter, we have sought to provide an in-depth analysis of gender and class segregation in the labor market by studying the labor paths of different working-class women who are mainly employed in domestic service. We have focused on observing the limitations and structural conditioning factors that shape these workers' trajectories but have also examined their opportunities for maneuvering within this space and achieving margins of autonomy.

Our inclusion of the dimension of time, through the life course approach, has allowed us to emphasize the deep interconnections between the different life spheres in which these women's trajectories unfold. This overlap is a core component of the way in which gender and class inequalities are configured. The labor paths of more disadvantaged women cannot be analyzed without considering their family dynamics, how these have affected their education, and their experiences of migration. As we saw in Ana's story, these different spheres articulate with one another and reinforce a series of initial disadvantages.

Indeed, the burden of unpaid work within their homes and paid activities outside the home interrupts these women's educational journeys from an early age, thus shaping the universe of jobs available to them. This universe is limited to unstable, precarious, informal jobs with low pay, which tend to be perceived as "typically female." A core factor that reinforces these conditioning factors is the lack of public or community care institutions for children, the elderly, or those with disabilities. As has been observed in the literature, those from sectors of society with greater purchasing power can make up for the absence of such services by paying for them privately. The absence of these institutions constitutes a form of inequality that persists throughout the lives of working-class women. In Ana's case, this conditioning factor can be observed during both her childhood and her adulthood. In all the employment histories studied here, domestic work and reproductive work, the fundamental impossibility of accessing care services, and the precarious, unstable conditions that characterize the jobs accessible to these women reinforce both the gender and class inequalities that were already present in their families of origin.

However, none of these circumstances prevent these women from developing tactics and strategies for mobility and identifying room for maneuvering with the potential to modify the direction of their own work and life paths. As they did for Ana and many others, these strategies may include geographic mobility: migration experiences (often alone and at a young age) are part of a quest for new opportunities. These searches are not limited to employment but also span multiple dimensions of their daily lives: romantic relationships, family structure, the possibility of engaging in some kind of training, and so forth. These movements cannot be analyzed in a linear fashion, in terms of an evolution toward "better" situations: there are advances and setbacks, vacillations that cannot always be interpreted as "positive" or "negative" in themselves. What we wish to highlight is the importance of these women's ability to make decisions and take action, despite the limitations they face.

These movements also include mobility tactics between different jobs. This mobility entails long-term strategies and significant investments of both time and money that often take the form of new educational qualifications. In Liliana's view and that of many of the women we interviewed, "having a profession" and "getting out of" domestic service signified a major change in their trajectories: it implied, on the one hand, greater independence and autonomy in the way they went about their daily work and, on the other, performing a job with a higher social status. However, these exit strategies did not cancel out the main problems that they faced in these other occupations that are also "typical" of working-class women: instability and a lack of rights and benefits. If one feature is common to all of these trajectories, it is that they mainly involve precarious labor activities.

As such, these women's attempts to pursue training and education are limited by two factors. On one hand, not all of them are able to put these strategies into practice due to the financial costs involved and the difficulty in fitting them around productive and reproductive labor responsibilities that they cannot delegate. As we mentioned above, the lack of accessible care services for people working in this sector makes it hard for them to finish formal schooling and to pursue other forms of training that open up new employment opportunities. Even the best-educated workers or those who have successfully managed to complete training and qualifications face a world of work where the conditions for feminized occupations are highly disadvantageous.

The results of our research suggest that conditions of gender and class inequality are being perpetuated for these women, affecting both the employment and training possibilities open to them. Accordingly, it is our opinion that policies to improve women's situation in the labor market, and especially policies to bring them out of poverty, will only be effective if they offer an integral response to the disadvantages that affect the different spheres we have pointed to: the responsibilities associated with reproductive labor and their effects on women's training and education options and working conditions. An improvement in employment conditions for jobs that are further down the occupational hierarchy would undoubtedly require changes in legislation, new regulations, and better oversight. However, a policy that aims to improve working conditions should include measures that guarantee the provision of care services and access to the same. Only an integrated approach to these issues will enable the creation of real possibilities of decent work for more vulnerable women.

Notes

1. Until slavery was abolished in the Río de la Plata in 1813, African slaves or descendants of the African diaspora mainly worked as wet nurses, laundresses, or in domestic service (Langa Pizarro, 2011). Toward the end of the nineteenth century, after successive military campaigns to colonize those parts of what is now Argentina that were then still held by indigenous populations, indigenous women and children were "viewed as spoils of war and handed out to [white] households for domestic service" (Lobato, 2007). Their placement with families in big cities was conceived as part of a policy for "civilizing" indigenous peoples.
2. At the time when we did this fieldwork, and the periods that Ana has discussed so far, the legislation did not contemplate such rights for domestic workers.
3. Until very recently, this work was excluded from the general frame existing for labor laws, and it was regulated through a special structure which created restricted rights and benefits to cover house help workers vis-à-vis salaried workers. In 2013 a new law was passed (Act 26844, special work contract

items for house help workers in private houses) which aims to harmonize working conditions in this sector with those established by the general legal framework. Among the most important transformations is access to maternity leave. This leave was not supported under the previous law, whereas the new law addresses full salary indemnity, as well as laying off due to presumed pregnancy, while also covering work risks (on the impact of said transformations, see Pereyra, 2017). As to union organizations, as per MTE and SS Registers, in the years 2015, 17 groups were identified for home help workers nationwide, although we did not have access to exact data regarding membership. The two organizations located in Buenos Aires City were established over half a century ago. However, several studies point out that their political weight was historically low (Birgin, 2009; Gogna, 1993; Cárdenas, 1986).

Bibliography

Barrancos, D., & Goren, N. (2002). Género y empleo en el Gran Buenos Aires. Exploraciones acerca de las calificaciones en mujeres de los sectores de pobreza. In F. Forni (Ed.), *De la exclusión a la organización. Hacia de la integración de los pobres en los nuevos barrios del conurbano bonaerense* (pp. 207–230). Buenos Aires, Argentina: Ciccus.

Bertranou, F., & Casanova, L. (2013). *Informalidad laboral en Argentina: segmentos críticos y políticas para la formalización*. Buenos Aires, Argentina: ILO.

Birgin, H. (2009). Sin acceso a la justicia: el caso de las trabajadoras domésticas en Argentina. In M. E. Valenzuela & C. Mora (Eds.), *Trabajo doméstico: un largo camino hacia el trabajo decente* (pp. 261–284). Santiago de Chile, Chile: ILO.

Blanco, M. (2011). El enfoque del curso de vida: orígenes y desarrollo. *Revista Latinoamericana de Población, 5*(8), 5–31.

Cardenas, I. (1986). *Ramona y el Robot. El servicio doméstico en barrios prestigiosos de Buenos Aires (1895–1985)*. Buenos Aires, Argentina: Ediciones Búsqueda.

CEPAL. (2014). *Panorama social de América Latina*. Santiago de Chile, Chile: United Nations.

Cerrutti, M. (2002). Trabajo, organización familiar y relaciones de género en Buenos Aires. In C. Wainerman (Ed.), *Familia, trabajo y género. Un mundo de nuevas relaciones* (pp. 105–152). Buenos Aires, Argentina: UNICEF/Fondo de Cultura Económica.

Contartese, D., & Maceira, V. (2005). *Diagnóstico sobre la situación laboral de las mujeres*. Buenos Aires, Argentina: Subsecretaría de Programación Técnica y Estudios Laborales, MTEySS.

Cortés, R. (2012). Políticas laborales y transferencias de ingresos: ¿estrategias complementarias? *Voces del Fénix, 5*, 44–51.

Dávalos, P. (2013). La Asignación Universal por Hijo desde la perspectiva de los hogares perceptores. *Estudios del Trabajo, 45*, 5–32.

Elder, G. H. (1998). The Life Course as Developmental Theory. *Child Development, 69*(1), 1–12. Blackwell Publishing. Retrieved from: http://www.jstor.org/stable/1132065.

Gallart, M. A., Moreno, M., Cerrutti, M., & Suárez, A. L. (1992). *Las trabajadoras de villas. Familia, educación y trabajo* (Cuaderno del CENEP 46). Buenos Aires, Argentina: CENEP.

Georges, I. (2011). Entre discriminação e reconhecimento: as trabalhadoras domesticas de São Paulo. In R. Cabanes, I. Georges, C. Rizek, & V. da Silva Telles (Eds.), *Saídas de emergência. Perder/ganhar a vida em São Paulo* (pp. 95–113). São Paulo, Brazil: Editorial Boitempo.

Gogna, M. (1993). "Empleadas domésticas en Buenos Aires". E. Chaney & M. García Castro Mu*chacha, cachifa, criada, empleada, empregadinha, sirvienta y más nada* 81–98. Caracas, Venezuela: Nueva Sociedad.

Gorbán, D., & Tizziani, A. (2014). Inferiorisation and Deference: The Construction of Social Hierarchies in the Context of Paid Domestic Labour. *Women's Studies International Forum, 46*, 54–62. Retrieved from: https://doi.org/10.1016/j.wsif.2014.01.001.

Gutiérrez Rodríguez, E. (2010). *Migration, Domestic Work and Affect.* London, UK: Routledge.

Hondagneu- Sotelo, P. (2007). *Domestica: Immigrant Workers Cleaning and Caring in the Shadows of Affluence.* Berkeley, CA: University of California Press.

ILO. (2015). *Migraciones laborales en Argentina. Protección social, informalidad y heterogeneidades sectoriales.* Buenos Aires, Argentina: ILO.

Jelin, E. (2010). *Pan y afectos. La transformación de las familias.* Buenos Aires, Argentina: Fondo de Cultura Económica.

Langa Pizarro, M. (2011). Las negras rioplatenses: entre la invisibilidad y el mito. *Altre Modernità, 6*(11), 163–176.

Lobato, M. Z. (2007). *Historia de las Trabajadoras en Argentina (1869–1960).* Buenos Aires, Argentina: Edhasa.

Mallimaci Barral, A. (2009). Estudios Migratorios y Perspectiva de Género. Apuntes para una Discusión sobre la relación entre los Géneros y las migraciones. *Revista Estudios Digital, 22*, 1–14.

Mallimaci Barral, A. (2011). Las lógicas de la discriminación. *Nuevo Mundo, Mundos Nuevos.* Retrieved from: https://doi.org/10.4000/nuevomundo.60921.

Novick, M., Rojo, S., & Castillo, V. (Eds.). (2008). *El trabajo femenino en la post convertibilidad. Argentina 2003–2007* (Documentos de Proyecto). Santiago de Chile, Chile: CEPAL.

Pacecca, M. I., & Courtis, C. (2008). *Inmigración contemporánea en Argentina: dinámicas y políticas* (Serie Población y desarrollo, 84). Santiago de Chile, Chile: CEPAL.

Parreñas Salazar, R. (2001). *Servants of Globalization: Women, Migration, Domestic Work.* Stanford, CA: Stanford University Press.

Pereyra, F. (2017). *Trabajadoras domésticas y protección social en la Argentina: avances y desafíos pendientes*. Buenos Aires, Argentina: ILO.

Pizarro, C. (2012). (Des)marcaciones de la bolivianidad en los hornos de ladrillos de dos localidades argentinas. *Temas de Antropologia y Migracion, 3*, 23–39.

Romero, M. (2002). *Maid in the USA*. New York, NY/London, UK: Routledge.

Tizziani, A. (2011). El servicio doméstico en la ciudad de Buenos Aires. De la movilidad ocupacional a las condiciones de trabajo. *Revista Trabajo y Sociedad, 17*(XV), 309–328.

Tizziani, A., & Gorban, D. (2015). Circulación de información y representaciones del trabajo en el servicio doméstico. *Cuadernos del IDES, 30*, 108–125.

Valenzuela, M. E. (2003). *Mujeres, pobreza y mercado de trabajo. Argentina y Paraguay*. Santiago de Chile, Chile: ILO.

Wainerman, C. (2002). *Familia, trabajo y género. Un mundo de nuevas relaciones*. Buenos Aires, Argentina: UNICEF/Fondo de Cultura Económica.

Zelizer, V. (2012). "El "niño invaluable" revisitado", estudio introductorio de Llobet, Valeria: Una Lectura Sobre El Trabajo Infantil Como Objeto De Estudio. A Propósito Del Aporte De Viviana Zelizer. *Desarrollo Económico, 52*(206), 311–328.

CHAPTER 7

The Restructuring of Labor in Cuba (2008–2016) and Paid Domestic Workers: Broken or Reconstructed Labor Trajectories?

Magela Romero Almodovar

The Context

At the beginning of the twenty-first century, a process of economic recovery began in Cuba, with the State gradually resuming its role as the main provider of jobs. A central feature of this process was the promotion of employment in social services and other fields requiring specialized study, including emerging training programs in social work, nursing and teaching, as well as others focused on the sugar industry. These measures improved the employment prospects of women and other socially disadvantaged groups such as youth, the working class, Afro-Cubans, mestizos and others. The approval and implementation of these measures marked a departure from the country's history of reducing social spending during times of crisis or recovery.

M. Romero Almodovar (✉)
Sociology Department, University of Havana, Havana, Cuba
e-mail: magela@ffh.uh.cu

M. E. Rausky, M. Chaves (eds.), *Living and Working in Poverty in Latin America*, Governance, Development, and Social Inclusion in Latin America, https://doi.org/10.1007/978-3-030-00901-4_7

However, as pointed out by Echevarría (2013, p. 137), although this strategy helped to mitigate the immediate effects of the crisis, including the lack of job creation in productive sectors, other issues—many of them dating back to the 1980s and 1990s—were left unsolved.[1] Underemployment featured foremost among these long-term problems, being closely related to the lack of articulation between training, required job skills and results. Unlike in the past, employment quality no longer depended on the job, qualification or social importance of an activity, but on other transcendental aspects such as the economic space in which the employment link took place.

As an issue involving a range of different spaces, it is clear that while numerous organizations have attempted to address this work by disadvantaged sectors, the results have been to disrupt, oversimplify and dehumanize their realities. This occurred mainly during the readjustment during the 1990s, as part of an effect that can be described as both harmful and inevitable, while the physical, economic and social working conditions underwent a simultaneous, asymmetrical segmentation (Martin, 2015). These working conditions show, even on the margins of multi-spatiality, the most visible dysfunction of the Cuban labor reality: the failure of the basic function of work as a means of earning a living, due to the insolvency of the national currency in which salaries are paid, as well as the inadequacy or obsolescence of facilities and equipment (Martín, 2000). These circumstances have had a direct impact on the world of work and workers, most affecting those without access to the freely convertible national currency ("the CUC").[2] In the new climate, opportunities to access well-paid jobs depend as never before on management by the individual, involving high risks for those with little capital or access to information networks—disproportionately black people, young people, the disabled and women. Real-life consequences include increased marginalization, vulnerability and poverty, all of which are linked to the proliferation of informal and illegal activities to satisfy individual and family needs, as well as the precariousness which such activities bring to the lives and well-being of those involved (Echevarría, Díaz, & Romero, 2015; Espina, 2012; Zabala, 2010).

The labor reality described above is a product of a deformed, dependent and underdeveloped economic structure, intersecting with a set of issues that are gaining urgency in the current scenario: the country's insertion as an outlier into the globalized, neoliberal economy; the combination of the international economic crisis with the internal crisis and obstacles stemming from the United States' economic blockade that hinder the country's progress within the world economic system, low productive efficiency and so on.

In response to this scenario, the country's leadership has proposed a process for updating the socioeconomic model, taking as its starting point: (1) Cuban society's indisputable strengths and (2) a set of guidelines that will guide this change. For example, the characteristics of Cuba's labor force are notable strengths, particularly considering the numerical magnitude, age structure and level of education of its population and the high rate of higher education completion among 40-year-olds[3] (Torres, 2013; Martin, 2015). With regard to the new guidelines, the most significant include a plan to emphasize export substitution, as well as the reorganization of the system of ownership over the means of production, granting a broader, complementary space to different forms of non-State property (mixed, foreign capital, cooperative, small private property) to promote job and income creation. The State's role is also set to change, with a reduction in its role as owner, producer and central planner; the role of municipal government is expected to increase; social policy mechanisms focused on vulnerabilities are to be expanded, based on the construction of a universal tax system that would include all economic actors and social groups that generate and receive income (Espina, 2012).[4]

These guidelines and other principles behind the reforms are included in the Economic and Social Policy Guidelines (*Lineamientos de la política social y económica* or "LPES"), the objectives of which are to strengthen the functioning of the non-State sector of the economy, to boost the agricultural sector, to expand the self-employment sector and the promotion of cooperatives in non-agricultural sectors and to establish indicators for the improvement of big business, the State and the development of urban cooperatives (PCC, 2011; Pérez, 2013; Triana, 2012). Following the approval and implementation of the above guidelines, a number of changes have taken place involving significant reorientation of the country's employment and social security policy; one of the most relevant has been the abandonment of the decades-old principle of full employment.[5] The impact on the employment sphere is highly visible, signifying a "turning point" for many (Blanco, 2011), bringing about a sea change in the lived realities of both individuals and entire social groups.

Paid domestic workers comprise one group that has been visibly impacted by these changes. It is worth noting that paid domestic work constitutes a *sui generis* labor option, since in many ways it is incompatible with established social policy. This is due to the peculiar nature of the labor relationships that are established between the actors involved, which relates not only to the singularity of the space in which they arise but also to the model of domestic production.[6] This chapter aims to address the scarcity of research on this social phenomenon while highlighting its importance as an object of discussion. This work takes into account socioeconomic and gender inequality gaps that are reconfigured in this process, taking as a reference the concept of labor trajectories, based on the theoretical-methodological approach of the life course (Blanco, 2011; Elder, 1998).

The results presented in this chapter are part of a broader doctoral research project developed by the author between 2009 and 2016 (Romero, 2016), which aimed to explain the relationship between the transformations in employment policy and changes in labor relations in paid domestic work in Cuba (1960–2015), emphasizing its current behavior in the Miramar Popular Council. This inquiry delved not only into the characteristics of the workers in the informal economic space[7] but also into the stories and labor dynamics of workers belonging to other spaces, such as the self-employed, workers belonging to the PALCO employer agency and those belonging to the CIMEX agency. A remarkable amount of information and analysis was obtained from the incursion into these four spaces; however, due to the global overrepresentation of paid domestic workers in the informal sector, this chapter focuses on the way in which these transformations have affected their daily lives, as well as the discontinuity and instability of their labor trajectories. The starting premise was as follows: changes in employment policy have a significant impact on the labor trajectories (both individual and collective) of disadvantaged groups, affecting not only the level of work but also overall quality of life.

Data collection techniques used were interviews with subjects, semi-structured questionnaires, interviews with key informants, interviews with experts and the analysis of regulatory documents on Cuban employment and social security policy. The discussion drawing on this material is not intended to be absolute or all-encompassing, as it is impossible to reproduce completely the dynamics and diverse perceptions of fragmented lives framed within the framework of a system of unequal powers. However, it is hoped that personal experiences will provide some clues, so as to better understand the world of paid domestic work in Cuba and the processes that have influenced its (re)configuration up to the present.

The Workers Studied: Who Are They?

The socio-demographic profile of the selected sample exhibited heterogeneity within a range of shared characteristics. Most of the interviewees were from Havana (10 out of 14), while the rest came from other provinces of the country. This result shows a major change compared with the typical characteristics of domestic workers prior to 1959. At that time, a significant percentage of those who did this work in Havana came from other provinces, many of them without any kind of lodgings in the capital, so finding work also meant obtaining housing and other necessities for living. Now, it is far less common for this work to be carried out on a full-time basis; in the sample studied here, none of the interviewees were engaged full time.

All of the interviewees were found to reside in the Playa Municipality; this area provides them with proximity between home and work, allowing them to avoid the problems that exist with public transportation (a recurring theme when discussing the advantages of this job); it is also common for them to be hired by neighbors or other members of the local community who are personally acquainted with their moral conditions, skills and disposition to domestic work. The sample group was racially diverse with a slight predominance of white participants (7) compared to Afro-Cubans (5) and mestizas (2). This is likely a reflection of the specific characteristics of the Miramar context (People's Council of the Playa Municipality), considering the research showing that elsewhere in Cuba this occupation is predominantly carried out by poor black women (Zabala, 2010).

The fact that most of these women (10 out of 14) are not currently in a permanent relationship suggests that income from their jobs is needed to provide not only for themselves but also for their children and extended families; the average number of children per woman in the group is 1.3. The women are aged between 33 and 72 years old, with only one less than 40 years old, implying that this is not the job of choice for young people; in contrast, domestic work in other Latin American countries is predominated by younger women with low educational attainment.

In this group, educational attainment ranged from middle school to higher education, a fact that speaks to the impact of educational policies on Cuba's female population. This characteristic also serves to distinguish these employees from their predecessors in the national context and their counterparts in other parts of the world. It was found that more than half of the sample had completed high school level or graduated from university in a range of disciplines such as primary education, nursing, culinary arts and other less traditional areas such as agricultural sciences, chemistry, technical drawing and others. Specialized knowledge is one aspect that usually affects the economic and social status of this job as well as the remuneration received, especially when it is related to the tasks involved. However, the situation is not entirely advantageous in terms of continuing education, since the self-management of this process is generally limited by both their work and personal agendas. Participants describe understandable feelings of frustration with regard to their levels of education or specialization because they aspired to more prominent fields of employment. These feelings are clearly expressed in the following statements: "I got 5 points (maximum possible grade) at University but my mind has atrophied, I have become stupid and sometimes they tell me that I could not be so smart when I do not know anything about computers or cell phones now" (Case 4), or "I feel like a preschool student, I feel like an ignorant person, but the truth is that I'm so tired that I just want to bathe and sleep. I cannot read or watch TV, I am becoming an ignorant" (Case 5). It should be noted that accounts such as those referenced are more common in women who have reached a higher level of education, a reality described by one expert as a major social problem affecting women's work: "The problem here is the under-utilization of a whole generation of human capital created during the decades of the Revolution; it is being wasted in jobs well below the real potential of these workers." Notwithstanding these difficulties, these workers' high levels of educational attainment can be considered one of the key factors in understanding the logic of their trajectories and the relationships established between domestic workers and employers, as well as their questioning attitudes toward the segregatory practices imposed by employers.

The income they receive for their work ranges between 16.00 CUC and 200.00 CUC per month.[8] Differences are observed between those whose employers are foreigners and those who provide services to other Cubans, with the former being better paid. However, most (11 out of 14) of these workers describe themselves as satisfied with their wages, citing, among other reasons, the fact that they are earning better than other workers doing the same job, that their wages give them the ability to provide for themselves and their families, that they are commensurate with the requirements of the job and so on. Nonetheless, other workers claim dissatisfaction with their pay, describing it as too low and disproportionate to the effort required, and even arguing that compared to the earnings of domestic workers in other countries, this amount could be considered exploitative. Clearly, workers' perceptions of their wages were more closely related to their employers' living conditions than to their own. Their assessments were directly linked to their own inferences as to their employers' incomes, with those working for foreigners assuming that the latter should be prepared to pay as they would have done in their own countries.

On the Trajectories and Journeys from Broken and/or Reconstructed Work Histories

This study, framed within what is sociologically known as the "life course approach," allows us to observe "how a family, economic or other event that an individual faces changes the likelihood that other events will take place in their existence" (Courgeau & Leliévre, 2001, p. 15 cited by Blanco, 2011, p. 7) and also how these events, when they have a macro-structural nature, provoke individual responses in the micro-social sphere that can be very similar to those of others within the social or occupational group to which s/he belongs.

Recent research has shown that changes in the Cuban labor market have led to major changes in the lives of women as a collective. These changes are visible in aspects such as labor mobility, types of contracts and working hours, the intensity of the same, working conditions and the way relationships are established between actors who make up the surrounding system of labor relations, among other aspects. The labor reforms mentioned above have led, likewise, to the growth of informal work, especially in those spaces where the centrally planned economy is not capable of fully satisfying the most pressing needs of the population, such as those associated with domestic work. The work activities involved in these services are highly feminized and demand skills for which most women have been educated throughout their lives. This learning takes place through socialization, through which they are trained to perform household chores since childhood. This process occurs first with specially designed children's games, then with the assignment of domestic responsibilities. Over time, the development of these skills can become an easy gateway into the labor market, this being an option that allows many women to earn sufficient income to meet their own needs and those of their families.

An analysis of 14 informal domestic workers working for the Miramar Popular Council of the municipality of Playa enabled corroboration of this thesis. For the majority, entering the informal space as domestic workers has constituted a safety valve during periods of worsening economic crisis. At times, the ongoing crisis has become a part of Cubans' everyday lives, especially when it overlaps with labor restructuring processes, most recently at the beginning of the 1990s and from 2008 to the present. These periods have constituted a significant turning point in the lives of many, and especially those of these working women, due, above all, to the ruptures imposed on their work trajectories. This change brought major transformations, not only to their lives as workers in the public sphere but also in other spheres of their present and future lives. They became more inclined to opt for precarious jobs in the informal market, not only because of the impossibility of accessing the security and social protection system through such employment but also because they usually constitute socially and economically devalued spaces, which provide a means for survival even as they enhance social inequality (whether by class, ethnicity or gender). Paid domestic work is just one of the alternatives mentioned above, and while it may not necessarily, at least in Cuba, be synonymous with low pay, it still leads to situations of vulnerability and instability which shine through in the descriptions of feelings, imaginings and genuine possibilities of achieving upward social mobility.

How the women who make up the sample of this study applied for this alternative and what their journeys had been until then constitute key questions for this exercise, as well as how the relationship between individual time, family time and historical-social time is expressed in each of their journeys.

Despite their differences, participants in the study describe similar life and work experiences, with points of connection related to individual and family episodes that occurred within the framework of concrete personal and historical-social moments. This reality could be identified from the reconstruction of their work histories through the collection of longitudinal personal information of a retrospective nature. The exercise made it possible to visualize the existence of three fundamental stages in their journeys, which can be summarized as follows: workforce entry and relative job stability, a "temporary" exit from the labor market and labor reintegration as a domestic worker in the informal sector. Below follows the analysis of the characteristics of each of these stages.

Workforce Entry and Relative Job Stability

For most of the women in this study, entry into the labor market took place during the 1970s and 1980s, a period characterized by the consolidation of the achievements gained after the triumph of the Cuban Revolution. These achievements included the eradication of illiteracy, the emergence of a socially and politically organized population, considerable improvements in labor and salary conditions and strong union representation to protect a system of guarantees that were unthinkable in the past. Large sectors of the population who had been living in poverty prior to the Revolution began to experience increased social mobility, almost always as a direct result of the transformations in their labor reality. Entire socio-occupational groups who had worked in conditions of near-slavery prior to the Revolution either disappeared or were considerably reduced.

These decades also saw significant progress in women's rights, resulting from the social policy at the time aimed at their empowerment, as well as the establishment of full employment with clear protections and social security guarantees. The central role of the State in the regulation of the labor market and the implementation, within the framework of the United Nations Decade for Women, of numerous programs to promote their participation in the public sphere were among the factors favoring the achievement of these goals. The main expression of women's participation was through employment in formal and State economic spaces,[9] an achievement made possible thanks to the work of organizations such as the Federation of Cuban Women, whose intentions to promote greater female autonomy were translated into the establishment of strategies for training, employment and promotion of women, as well as for promoting balance between work and family responsibilities.[10]

Under the circumstances of the time, women were able to find employment that not only fit their professional profile but allowed them a certain stability regarding their work experiences. This was evident in the cases studied: of the 11 women who were old enough to have entered the job market at that time, 9 managed to do so, and despite accounts by 2 women of some fluctuations between positions held, they continued to be employed by State entities. This condition not only guaranteed their inclusion in the country's political project but also the enjoyment of rights such as annual paid holidays, maternity leave, the possibility of accruing retirement savings, among others. This time is fondly remembered by the whole group of women interviewed. One of them said:

> When I was 20 years old I graduated as a livestock technician and they placed me in the dairy company. That was what I liked, and such was my commitment that I was promoted and promoted until I became the head of production. They rewarded us when we were selected best workers and the truth is that I had many incentives to improve myself. Incredibly, that was when I was better-off economically speaking, because I earned 288.00 pesos and I was able to live with dignity. (Case 37)

It should be added that during these decades, paid domestic work was not an option frequently chosen by women. This era saw the enactment of the "end of domestic workers" in Cuba, in response to the job's perceived connections to the capitalist world, the underdeveloped past and social exploitation. As these concepts gained legitimacy in the public perception, the functions of domestic work itself were increasingly stigmatized, rather than the precarious conditions in which these women lived and worked before 1959.[11] This perception would later bring a different share of problems, as it contributed to the invisibility of this work and the failure to create a legislative framework that would protect people who might opt for employment in domestic labor. These workers were also subjected to harsh criticism, since it was not understood why anyone would "choose" to perform these functions when offered the opportunity to study or do a job involving greater recognition or better pay.

The following account by one of the domestic workers interviewed, whose experience in this job goes back to the year 1956, is a testimony to the above situation:

> I started very young helping my mother, she washed and ironed for people in the street. I also did hairdressing things in my house, I styled women's hair and charged them 50 cents. At the end of the month I almost always collected between 20 and 25 pesos, which represented a great help for my family. When the Revolution triumphed, I enrolled in the courses that began to be organized by the FMC for women and I took a hairdressing course which was what I liked, but I did not complete it, because I had to take a test, I failed and I felt very disappointed. Then I tried other hairdressing programs but I could not complete them, I got tired and did not try any more. Then, I returned to my particular routine of doing hairstyles and doing some domestic chores for others and that's how I stayed from 1959 to 1995. All that time there were many people who criticized me, including my family; but I was not going to do something that I did not like. (Case 39)

It is worth noting that the incorporation of women into the State labor market as in the above case was not a prerequisite for covering their basic needs with the development of a network of basic services (health, education, culture, housing, social security, sports). The existence of a unique and universal social policy made social services and subsidies available to all people regardless of sex, skin color, social background or occupation. These decades were characterized by a high level of equity and homogeneity in society, achieved by the rationed distribution of consumer goods, improvements in urban and rural living conditions and the humanization of rough jobs; strategies were also established to achieve a balance between the population's income and monetary expenditures and narrow differences in wages, and expand the social security system with an emphasis on vulnerable groups such as women, children and the elderly.

"Temporary" Exit from the Labor Market

In this second stage, the work experiences of the women studied were characterized by the disarticulation between the women's aspirations to enter or continue their employment and the social and family pressures to abandon their responsibilities in the public space and devote themselves to full time to caring for family members. For most of the interviewees, the beginning of this period coincided with the birth of the first child. At the beginning of this transition, many enjoyed paid maternity leave, but when the period of these benefits ended, they were faced with the need to leave their jobs temporarily and continue meeting unpaid, reproductive family responsibilities. It is worth noting that families' caregiving arrangements were strongly influenced by the traditional sexual division of labor and also by the impossibility of choosing to hire outside assistance with these services, either from individuals or State institutions (due in large part to the inability of the latter to provide services with the capacity to meet the demand).[12] The story below offers an example of the vulnerability of some of these women due to their families' limited financial possibilities for hiring third-party assistance, combined with the difficulty of accessing formal support networks, namely, free or low-cost State care services. "I had to leave university because of family problems. My mother got sick and I had to work, I had to sacrifice myself and when my mother died I had to take care of my brother. And now that everything seems to take its course, I have to take care of my father, who is already old, has bone problems and is sick with nerves" (Case 31).

The demands of caring for children and parents have had an enormous impact on the women studied their work experiences: of the 14 interviewed, 8 interrupted their work experiences to take care of their children or parents. This situation not only limited or delayed their possibilities for professional growth[13] but in many cases led to their permanent departure from the formal labor market, including its social security benefits. Similarly, some stories exhibited the "cycle of endless care" (Romero, 2009), with some stating that they had not had the possibility of immediately returning to work when their children reached school age or their sick relatives improved or died, due to the appearance of new family demands for care. Such was the case of one of the participants (Case 42) who claimed to have spent 40 years of her life disconnected from work due to raising and caring for her four children. One possible explanation for the similarities in these women's experiences may be the fact that, unintentionally, they all belong to the same time period, which may have led to the appearances of similarities among the research group regarding personal and family situations that defined their role as care providers and the historical-social context within which this took place. For example, five of them became mothers in the late 1980s and early 1990s, years in which very abrupt changes took place in the country with a wide impact on economic and social life.

The disappearance of the Soviet Union, the fall of communist regimes in Central and Eastern Europe, the resurgence of the US blockade and the vulnerability of the Cuban economy led the country to one of the most severe crises in national history, which had an immediate impact on the availability of social services. Not only was there a significant reduction in the quantity and quality of programs designed to support the family in domestic and caregiving tasks; but the gaps of social inequality were accentuated by the loss of the purchasing power of State salaries, which worsened the difficulties of families and especially of women workers.[14] The situation described above led to a sharp decline in female employment during this period: "in absolute figures we have 1.433.114 women working in the civil state sector in 1990, while, according to the National Statistics Office Census, in 1995 the figure had dropped to 1 191 500" (Aguilar, Popowski, & Verdeses, 1996, p. 13).

Re-entry of Domestic Workers in the Labor Market: The Informal Sector

This stage is identified by the re-entry of domestic workers into the world of work outside the home, after a prolonged absence, with 15 years being the average length of inactivity or unemployment after a temporary departure to care for close relatives was 15 years. The change in the family life cycle of these women opened the opportunity for them to regain their salaried status. However, the reinsertion of most of the women was marked by the existence of domestic and care responsibilities that had not completely disappeared; therefore, they needed work options that allowed them a certain time flexibility and, if possible, were close to their places of residence. Since most of the positions offered by State entities do not have open or flexible schedules, the search for alternatives was focused mainly on the informal market.[15] From the narrow universe of possible options, they opted for paid domestic service, an alternative for which they had already trained since they were girls, and perfected in more recent years.

Unlike previous years, the second half of the 1990s and the first decade of the 2000s were characterized by the reappearance and greater visibility of domestic workers in Cuba.[16] The process of social re-stratification that took place, together with the appearance of new economic actors and the weakening of State support mechanisms for the family, had a great impact on the increase in demand for this domestic service. Resident foreigners were not the only potential market; some Cubans now earned income in freely convertible currency or dollars,[17] including private sector employees, cooperative members, employees of the mixed sector and others who were part of new groups and social strata with ascending social mobility, resulting from the transformations carried out in the country's occupational structure and its acceptance of foreign capital. The social impact of the liberalization of the dollar and the establishment of a regime of monetary duality in the country was profound: "In 1993 the exchange rate of the peso against the dollar was 100: 1 and in 1994, in the apogee of the crisis, 130: 1, when the average wage reached only 185 pesos" (BCC, 2001). These circumstances not only promoted women's entry into domestic work for the first time but also created a climate leading others, who had fulfilled these functions before the triumph of the Revolution, to return to this market. Such is the case of Acela Elizalde, who comments on her experience as follows:

> When I was made to retire (because I did not want to do it), I immediately started looking for a job. It was very hard to find a position, since at that time regulations established that I could not earn more than what I had in my old job, and since I used to earn well, the options available were cleaning assistant and security staff. That is why I chose a position looking after a shelter for victims who had lost their homes because of weather events and other issues. That shelter was good and I felt comfortable working there, but after a while the person I replaced claimed his position and I was sent to guard another shelter with very different conditions (...) While I was there, a coworker came to see me and she told me that she needed a person to take care of her mother. She offered me $ 300 pesos and mentioned a few specific considerations ... Then after a while, I had to leave that job which was very unfortunate, because even though that family was good to me and we had an excellent relationship I was affected by transportation problems and it was often after dark when I left work (...) After that job, another woman went to see me at home. She wanted me to take care of her father, staying with him on alternate nights, for the same salary that I was offered in the other house (...) After that experience I had others and others and now, I work for two families. I go twice a week and cook at one house; while in the other, I just have to clean on Saturdays.

If we take into account that only two of the interviewed women began their working life as domestic workers, the transition to this work has significant implications for the majority who did not. They came from jobs linked to their professional profiles in the State economic space, with access to a set of guarantees such as paid vacations, maternity or sick leave, the possibility of accumulating years of work for future retirement and so forth, but they now faced a new, deregulated labor universe, based on the operating principles of private individual-family property, meaning that labor relations were now totally dependent on the characters and values of the actors involved.

In this space, there are no trade union organizations or actors that control the way in which work processes are structured or the rules that ensure decent working conditions. Hiring is governed by the laws of competition within the market, without any mechanism to connect it with the priorities of State planning. The meeting of the parties frequently supposes a prior relationship or shared close acquaintance to introduce them, whether a friend (nine cases), a neighbor (four cases) or a family member (one case). One particular feature of the Cuban context is the absence of a formal system of job advertisements—here, the emphasis is on "formal," as certain classified ad sites (such as "Revolico," "Porlalivre," "La Chopi," etc.) do offer space for advertising job vacancies.

None of the domestic workers in this group had a work contract formalized in writing. Similarly, opportunities for negotiating their terms of work are limited in the face of an absolute need for employment, a fact which speaks to the inequality inherent in this type of labor relations. When initial interviews or preliminary conversations with employers are mentioned, a recurring theme is the absence of opportunities to set appropriate limits in terms of what they were willing to do. Although the interview itself is perceived as a formal process with the purpose of setting out the terms of hire, the majority who have undergone this process also experience it as a space where they are meticulously observed and where the socioeconomic inequalities between domestic workers and their potential employers, especially those related to class and gender, are in full view. In particular, questions directly related to work experience have the effect of highlighting these differences most clearly, by drawing attention to the gaps between the living conditions of employees and the lived experiences of employers, as well as the difference created in the living standards of both parties by the presence or absence of these domestic tasks. Similarly, this occasion demands the presentation of evidence, sometimes using letters of recommendation, as to the ability of these women to adhere to patriarchally imposed norms of femininity, and the degree to which they can function as "role models" of established standards and practices for carrying out household chores.

The above aspects are a reflection on the lack of a legal framework for the working relationship between both parties. The nature of the legal relationship established between one individual and another is not the same as that which exists between an individual and a collective entity (whether State, cooperative, mixed or legalized private); additionally, Cuba has no tradition of the individual as an employer.

In this space, unlike in other countries, there are very few people who work in subsistence conditions. However, not being registered puts them in a situation of total vulnerability when it comes to defending their rights and obtaining labor guarantees. The establishment of appropriate working conditions depends completely on the disposition of the employer and his or her willingness to make resources available to the provider of domestic services. However, this did not constitute a problem for those who participated in this research. They stated that in a general sense, their employment conditions are good and that their employers are attentive to their needs (13 of 14), ensuring not only that they have sufficient quantities of the chemicals used for cleaning but also some electrical appliances to support their work, which are usually the property of the homeowners and commonly used by those who live together in the house. Only one respondent described her working conditions as mediocre, citing occasions when she was forced to complain about the dilapidated state of cleaning equipment (Case 44).

In this group of workers, the working days are usually shorter than in the rest of the spaces studied; 9 of the 14 cases work only 3 or 4 hours each working day, which almost always take place in the morning hours. Another peculiarity is that they usually alternate working days, which gives them the possibility of working in more than one household at a time; for example, one of the interviewees stated that she was performing domestic duties in three different homes.

> I am the sole provider for my house and my three children, the oldest has learning difficulties and the youngest has Down's syndrome. I have to earn money for them, that's why I work in three houses. I know it's a lot of work but it is what it is. Little by little I was able to find more jobs and I have been alternating for some time now. I cannot exchange these three houses for a single one that occupies me the entire week because I need time to take my little boy to his Wednesday activities. (Case 33)

In relation to their activities, the main functions carried out across all groups are linked to cleaning (all) and laundering (13 of 14), while only five mentioned responsibilities associated with the kitchen. One noteworthy aspect of this group is the assignment of duties running of errands and purchasing products for family consumption (nine cases)—an indicator of a greater index of familiarity between employees and employers—and although sometimes a list of required items is provided, most of the only money is left, on the assumption that the employee will see to the rest.

In this space, the majority of the workers are guaranteed food during their work day (12 of 14). Several employers provide their employees with food (nine cases), while others have free access to the contents of the refrigerator (three cases). One woman explains, "We can eat what we want, in moderation of course. They always leave lunch ready and, if not, we can prepare our own snacks" (Case 35). It was found that most of them do not have a specific place to leave their belongings; usually, they use common areas of the house like the closet, kitchen, rooms and so on. They also do not have exclusive restrooms for their use, except two of them who work for foreigners, where special service areas equipped with bathrooms are set aside for employees.

It was observed that only one participant was expected to wear a uniform. In her opinion, this is an essential garment for her place of work and as she explains: "I like to use it, so I save my clothes and I am presentable. In addition, the house requires it; it is a very luxurious house and you must constantly receive visitors" (Case 39). Although they do not follow a specific dress code, most of the rest of the group does not aspire to the use of this garment. Only four of them said that they would like to include it in their outfits, also citing as reasons the protection of their own clothing and the ability to look presentable.

In this space the employer plays a predominant role in the working relationship. There is no control mechanism regulating this operation or protecting those who perform the role of domestic staff. This situation puts employees at a disadvantage if faced of accusations of a breach of duties or in the event of actions that threaten their safety as citizens.

The enjoyment of stipulated basic rights is conditioned similarly to those of the self-employed sector, with the difference that domestic workers have fewer opportunities to seek legal recourse and/or make formal complaints due to their status as informal workers. The legal framework that regulates employment of domestic workers is seen by this group as being removed from their reality, a perspective which fosters their indifference. It is enough for them to know that obtaining a license for this work requires payment of a recurring fee, which they are not willing to do in exchange for retirement benefits (Cases 33, 34, 43 and 44). In the words of one participant: "I heard something about that but I do not know much. They tell me that I have to pay and if I have to give up the little I earn, then, what do I get to keep? After all, the Lord does not forsake me" (Case 34). One remarkable aspect of the above situation is not only domestic workers' lack of knowledge or understanding of the laws that regulate their work but also their lack of interest in learning more,[18] which generates a vicious cycle where the lack of protection limits any possibility of defending their rights.

This group's greatest difficulties with respect to basic workers' rights were related to the enjoyment of paid vacations, since most of the women in the sample (except one) indicated not having this benefit. Similarly, it was found that their holiday periods depended on those of their employers and that they can only take place very sporadically. A common dilemma faced by members of this group concerned the economic problems generated by taking a few days off without being paid, bearing in mind that this is their main source of income. In their own words: "I do not have vacations; when the other employee goes to Oriente, I work every day and it suits me because I earn more" (Case 44), or "I do not take [vacations]; I can ask for them if I want to, but then they do not pay me and that does not suit me" (Case 43).

Regarding periods of protected leave, at the time of the interviews, none of the participants had been in a situation requiring such a period, so their answers were based on their assumptions as to what would happen if they needed one. Of the five cases that answered affirmatively about the possibility of opting for extended periods off work (paid or not), two refer the support they have had from their coworkers, which is not counted as a benefit, but rather as an arrangement between them to be able to address any health or other problems that may arise.

Informal workers are highly unprotected, not only in terms of obtaining protected leave but also regarding the conditions of safety and protection at work. To clarify, the failure to meet adequate safety standards or a disregard for any resulting health problems can be considered a form of violence. Only one of the domestic workers stressed that her employer gave her gloves and bought soft products for her to do her job. The rest insisted that they themselves had to create strategies to protect themselves or complain to their employers any difficulties that might appear. The following examples illustrate this point: "When I see that a product causes me an allergic reaction or is very strong, I ask them to replace it with another one and they do so; but not of their own initiative" (Case 36), or "I had to get the gloves and the mask because although they saw me having breathing difficulties they did not care" (Case 41).

Although most of them deemed the communication with their employers to be positive and reported holding frequent dialogues with their employers, the truth is that very few use these spaces to demand better working conditions. Rather, these moments are spent talking about family, daily life, chores, religion and, in three of the cases, they also have exchanges about private personal problems. It is thought that unlike the relationships established when employed by a foreigner, communication among Cubans is more fluid and diversified regarding the issues addressed.

In answer to the question of whether they feel part of the family they work for, ten of the cases answered affirmatively. It should be noted that many of these employment relationships are preceded by years of friendship or community connection that lead to a certain degree of affinity among the parties. For example, there is the case of one informal worker who lives two doors down from where she works and has this to say about her current employer: "I've been there since I was a girl, we've grown up together, we've gone on vacation together since we were little, our families have always been united since the generation of our grandparents and now they go on vacation and take me with them" (Case 32).

In relation to their perceptions about the advantages of doing this job, it was significant that two of the interviewees did not see the economic factor as an aspect to be considered, despite this being the aspect that mobilized all of the interviewees in the rest of the groups studied. They, unlike the rest of their counterparts, stressed that they do this job because they like it (one case), or because of the flexibility they have due to the schedule or the proximity to their places of residence (one case). Among other positive aspects listed were the attention given to them by their employers (two cases), the absence of close supervision[19] (one case) and the possibilities for acquiring new skills to improve their work (one case). Regarding the disadvantages, they highlighted that it is tedious, stressful and exhausting work (seven cases), the impact of these tasks on their health (two cases), problems with transportation (one case), the limited opportunities to enjoy vacations (one case) and the feeling that they carry out a stupid task (one case).

Notwithstanding the overwhelmingly positive impression expressed by the workers themselves, it cannot be ignored that their vulnerability can become invisible if the assessment of their situation is kept to a superficial evaluation of wages (they can earn up to five times more than a professional) or the flexibility of their schedules. The analysis must go further, even beyond their own assessments. The precariousness they experience leads to a notable level of vulnerability in relation to the enjoyment of their rights and the benefits of social security. As has been observed, without formalization or control in their labor relations, they are exposed to conditions of minimal protection. They cannot access the social security system as workers. They do not enjoy any labor guarantee, and their day-to-day life is marked by the uncertainty of being fired at any time. On the other hand, their work in this period shows features of discontinuity and instability, which is not determined only by their willingness or convenience to change jobs, but has more to do with the decisions of employers and their ability to continue paying for the service.

The precariousness of their condition is also visible in aspects such as (a) the temporary and indefinite character of the demand sustaining the service, (b) the limitations on obtaining social security benefits, (c) the impossibility of controlling whether minimum conditions of protection and security in their posts are met and (d) the lack of opportunities to continue with their cultural and educational development.

Many of these disadvantages or limitations are derived from their status as informal workers; since they operate outside the legal framework, they are not regulated or protected by the State or other organizations, are not registered nor appear in official statistics, cannot access the benefits established by social security nor hope to bring legal action against their employer for any violation against them or their rights.

Bearing these limitations in mind, the ILO at its 104th session (June 2015) recommended that member states facilitate the transition of workers from informal economic units to formal ones, by promoting decent work and inclusive development. Improvements in employment policy are considered the main mechanism for achieving this goal, and have resulted in the transformations that have occurred to date, which are nonetheless insufficient because they mainly apply to the formal sphere. Women are not largely involved in creating the laws governing the more transcendent aspects of the economic, social and political model to which they are subject. These domestic workers' knowledge about these laws is either incomplete or absent; this is one of the reasons why they have not yet had the opportunity or willingness to discuss, analyze and debate them.

In the case of the interviewees, this fact is closely related to the dynamics imposed by this job on those who perform it, which leave them little time to participate in social participation spaces designed to raise awareness and generate discussion and popular consultation on these governing documents. The weakening of policies and unions for many of the people who carry out this work in the informal space has also contributed to this trend. Thinking about the challenges posed by the 2030 Agenda for Sustainable Development, an effective strategy should begin by creating incentives for the integration of these workers, based on aspects that may be of interest and motivation. Similarly, strategies could be implemented such as (a) raising public awareness of the guiding principles behind this policy and their implications for these women's work experiences in terms of labor relations and guarantees, (b) creating specific materials aimed at educating domestic workers since it is known that information is key to participation, (c) participatory consultations directly involving this occupational or social group and (d) the establishment of feedback mechanisms once the preceding strategies have begun to be implemented.

The Challenges of Employment Policy in a Reconfigured Context

The results presented above show some of the changes that have occurred in the drafting of employment policy and their impact on the work experiences and labor relations of the studied sample. In the same way, they show the limitations in the scope of this policy to regulate conditions of informal domestic work. Thus, a specific type of public work, valued essentially as productive and in which men play a leading role, continues to be prioritized.

While current legislation is characterized by new guiding principles grounded firmly within the proposed legal framework, including major changes to the world of work and labor relations, its design must also consider contextual and cultural elements which are left unaddressed despite its good intentions. It was found that the governing documents of this policy, due to way they are drafted, do not promote the narrowing of existing social gaps, especially those of gender. This is due to a clear precedence given to economics over social concerns, assuming the possibility of taking the two spheres separately. This has ultimately led to a disconnect between this policy and those of other areas; for example, some studies show a lack of articulation between education policies and employment policies (Echevarría et al., 2015; Echevarría and Tejuca, 2015), while others point out the gaps between policies centered on the family and those concerning employment (Romero, 2010, 2017). This failure to synchronize policy has had an impact on the experiences of this group of interviewed workers, in aspects such as (1) the lack of consistency between their levels of education and professional specialization and their current job (which implies a waste of the skilled workforce) and (2) the lack of occupational options with flexible hours (not only for them but also for male relatives) that would allow them to reconcile the time destined for paid work in the public space with their own household chores and care responsibilities.[20]

The reality described above relates to the leading role of the market in the configuration of the analyzed labor market and labor relations, set in a reality in which supply and demand behave as follows:

(a) There has been an increase in the demand for this service in recent years due to the complexity of recent socio-demographic and economic processes in Cuba. This causes families, and especially women, to become overburdened with the domestic and care functions, while the labor market becomes increasingly competitive and demanding in general terms.
(b) Demand depends on the resources available to families and their shortcomings or needs associated with this type of service. There is also a close relationship with their ideology and perceptions regarding what it means to hire this type of service.
(c) The supply of this service in the non-State sector of the economy has increased (even though it is more expensive), due to the drastic reduction of State-provided services (which, being subsidized, are more affordable).
(d) Supply and demand are influenced by the actions of a number of variables, and especially by gender, as both are focused on the sexual division of labor, with this work perceived as being done by women, for women. This has led to a number of contradictions in the theory that governs the debate on whether or not increasing the supply of such services can truly lead to women's empowerment; since women's employment in these spaces does not always signify true empowerment, feminist thinkers are divided on this subject.

(e) The social networks in which these women or potential employers participate play a fundamental role in the supply and demand for this type of work. Personal contacts are essential for the establishment of recommendations. It is worth noting that the use of letters of recommendation is becoming more common, especially in the process of obtaining a job with foreign employers.

(f) In the beginning, the ability to demonstrate trustworthiness and references of good character take precedence in the hiring process over the possession of knowledge and skills required for doing the job to the employer's satisfaction. An employee's ability to carry out this job is demonstrated in the practice itself, since very few have specialized degrees that certify training in this work.

(g) Unlike in other countries, the mass media are not widely used for this process, although it should be noted that in recent years there has been an increase in the number of people making use of ad and/or classified spaces to advertise a position or express their interest in offering this service.

It is appropriate to highlight the women's perception of the State as a guarantor of rights and social protection to the detriment of the responsibilities of other actors involved in the labor relations system in which they operate, such as trade unions or the employers themselves. This is a reflection of the characteristics of Cuban social policy over time, a perception which persists in the current context despite the many changes that have taken place in this policy; this is especially true of the belief in the absolute power of the State and excessive centralism that minimizes the prominent role of other actors and fails to consider the diverse needs and aspirations of different territories and groups (Espina, 2008). As such, it is thought that more authentic participation by labor actors involved in politics should be encouraged from the beginning (including those not associated with political and mass organizations), stimulating processes that take into account the existing heterogeneity in terms of career, work experiences and realities, jobs and dreams—aspects that are closely related, as shown in this research, to the particularities of the work being carried out, the socioeconomic space, the type of property on which it is based and the particular characteristics of the hiring entity.

Finally, it should be noted that, in the current context of reforms, despite the stated intentions, the transformations are still more focused on what happens within the State sector than on the idiosyncrasies of other work environments. That is why significant changes have not occurred with respect to the labor practices and relations preceding the current situation; much less in the case of informal workers who are not considered, rendering governing documents effectively "dead letters." The reality is different for those who have obtained their licenses to practice as self-employed; despite the gaps entailed by sub-contracting, many of the changes involved lead to greater guarantees and job stability.

Taking into account the elements raised and considering the scenario of existing inequalities, it is necessary to reassess existing policy, so that it may overcome or narrow the existing gaps, and forge new paths toward the construction of a society in which justice and social equality are guaranteed, with work as the foundational axis of a large part of citizens' rights and welfare.

Conclusions

The above reflections allow us to understand and verify the central role played by the work in the lives of the women interviewed and in the formation of their life trajectories. The results show the presence of non-standard work experiences, and that despite the differences in their stories and circumstances, their paths coincide in many aspects and are marked by gender. Their narratives—and especially the causes that led them to make the decision to temporarily abandon their status as employees or to dedicate themselves to domestic service in the informal space—show how the market is organized on the basis of a system of unequal gender relations, which is reflected by the differences in stability and assignment of value between occupations considered traditionally male or female.

The patriarchy modulates these workers' trajectories inasmuch as it determines their access, maintenance, extension, restriction and loss of social rights, as well as their possibilities for professional development. Although the studied domestic workers have experienced considerable income improvements compared to their previous jobs, the discontinuity of their work experiences and the irregularity that characterizes their non-formalized, uncontrolled labor relations expose them to conditions of minimal protection and few social guarantees. This is due simultaneously to the incidence of other systems of power (class, racial, territorial) that overlap with patriarchy to configure the labor market, affecting the precariousness of working conditions for socially disadvantaged groups. In the case of these women, starting from a certain point of rupture, they were obliged to cut short the work experiences they (or their parents) had dreamed of, exchanging them for a job to which they never aspired but which they needed.

The study of their work experiences as a methodological tool made it possible to follow the record of the work activity of each researched case and its connection with social, family and personal events. Contrary to what could have happened in a cross-sectional analysis, the present longitudinal study allowed us to capture the way in which these workers reached their current status and analyze the impact of historical events and economic, demographic, social and cultural changes on the configurations of their individual and group lives. An analysis of these variations showed a number of similarities in aspects such as:

- The existence of an initial consistency between their field of study and their jobs.
- The link between the degrees studied by the majority and the duties assigned to them according to the principles of the patriarchal culture: nurses (duty to heal and care for the sick), teachers and educators of children's circles (duty to educate and care for infants) and cooks (duty to prepare and serve food), among others.
- The permanence outside the labor market for prolonged periods to focus on the care of others/other relatives, with the birth of the first child being a recurrent reason for leaving the labor market for the first time in the studied stories.
- The choice of paid domestic work as an alternative that allowed them to earn an income while continuing with the assigned/assumed domestic tasks and care after periods of "inactivity."

Their work experiences and current circumstances allow us to visualize the enormous waste of expertise that exists in Cuba, especially among the female labor force, as well as the growing tension between an increasingly competitive labor market and the system of labor security and protection for those who work in the informal market. They are outside the benefits established by the legal framework, which in addition to being biased a priori regulates dynamics that are not in tune with their daily lives as workers. This legal framework is still designed for long, stable career paths framed within the formal socioeconomic space. The recurrence of specific patterns of mobility in their work experiences is revealing, even though their stories may seem so different and their circumstances isolated. The study showed not only how transitions between different occupations and conditions of activity, far from being sporadic episodes, are common features of feminine work experiences but also the impact of family or personal events such as the birth of a child or the illness of a relative on their life stories as well as the changes in the social and economic context.

Finally, it is worth highlighting some aspects related to the social inequalities underlying these realities that are silently reproduced in the stories of these women. It is important to remember that poverty is not just a matter of income; therefore, an analysis related to this phenomenon leads to a multidimensional assessment through which the vulnerability of the studied cases can be observed. Their work experiences and stories reveal the constraints and the strong conditioning situations they face in order to enter, remain and function with equal conditions within the world of public work, the difficulties for their integration and social participation, the obstacles to accessing their rights and having access to the established channels of defense, their low autonomy, the challenges to their self-esteem inherent in the difficulties in achieving their dreams or simple awareness of their own disadvantages, which is the first step toward being able to change their realities.

Notes

1. One of the negative consequences of this procedure was the fall in productivity between 2008 and 2010, years in which, although indicators related to economic growth continue to grow, they do so at much slower rates: GDP at a rate of 2.5% per year, employment at 1.3% and productivity at 1.2% (García, Anaya, & Piñeiro, 2011, p. 7 cited by Echevarría, 2013, p. 137).
2. In Cuba, there is a dual monetary circulation. On one hand, there is the Cuban peso and, on the other, the Cuban convertible peso (a currency similar to the US dollar, although it has been taxed at an additional 10% since November 15, 2004). The Cuban peso is devalued with respect to the Cuban convertible peso at a ratio of 1 to 24.
3. It is worth noting that this situation was much more advantageous in the first decade of the twenty-first century, when experts seemed to agree that Cuba enjoyed a certain "demographic bonus" (since the dependency rates of the inactive with respect to those that do work are particularly low). Although these circumstances have not changed completely, a deterioration in this relationship has been observed, based on the effect of an aging population and, indirectly, on external migration, which usually comprise mostly people of working age (Martin, 2015, p. 87).

4. The author lists the following documents as the synthesis of the axes that make up the new moment of reform: Speeches delivered by Raúl Castro on July 26, 2007, on February 24, 2008, and at the close of the sixth plenary session of the PCC in 2011, PCC 2011, "Guidelines of the Economic and Social Policy of the Party and the Revolution and PCC 2011" Base Document. First National Conference.
5. In Cuba, the employment policy since 1959 was to guarantee employment as a guiding principle; this was later translated into the concept of full employment (with the State in the role of the creator of the main sources of work). In these circumstances, maintaining unemployment and inactivity at minimum levels are expected results. As a result, for more than 50 years, the State generated the main job offers and thereby effectively regulated the labor market. This, together with numerous policies aimed at increasing the participation in the public sphere of vulnerable groups such as women, led to a continuous growth in their participation as employees until the 1990s. However, in the new context these programs have tended to disappear, and from the legal point of view, the General Labor Relations Regulations that established, among other issues, the principles of the country's employment policy have been repealed and replaced by the Regulations of the Labor Code (ANPP, 2014). This regulation, compared to the preceding one, has a higher hierarchical position because it is a decree-law while the previous one is a resolution, and unlike the other, it does not state principles of employment policy; issues related to this principle are addressed more generally (Echevarría et al., 2015).
6. Among the aspects that distinguish this mode of production from the pre-industrial or industrial appear the following: it has a close relationship with the system of patriarchal domination (Delphi, 1982), its prevailing rationality is not always economic/utilitarian (Lautier, 2003, p. 808), and in the labor relations that are established, the family and everyday life can play a definitive role (Benston, 1977; Kofes, 2001).
7. They are areas of action of the objects, means and workforce that are differentiated from each other by the particular way in which they are configured, by a set of internal links: the predominant type of property, the degree of commitment to planning or with the market as a mechanism of regulation, the forms of management and mechanisms and/or prerogatives of the prevailing administration and the working conditions and relationships that exist within it (Campos, 2003).
8. Taking into account the current exchange rate, their income in Cuban pesos would be between 384 CUP and 4800 CUP.
9. This condition continued to grow steadily until the 1990s when it declined, then it recovered and continued to grow (Romero, 2010).

10. Conciliatory strategies include (Romero, 2009, p. 30): (a) the creation of new day cares and Kindergartens; (b) an increase in the number of scholarships for students, in high school, pre-university and higher; (c) the inauguration of camps and Palaces of Pioneers; (d) improvements to vacation plans; (e) an increase in the supply of household electrical appliances that alleviate work at home; (f) the creation of workers' and students' canteens, so that women did not have to return to their homes at lunchtime; (g) the establishment of Care Centers for the Elderly (Homes); (h) the establishment of the "Plan Jaba," a mechanism established to shorten the time of workers queuing for food purchases; (i) the construction of washing machines or dry cleaners; (j) a National Program of Assistance to the elderly and disabled people; (k) a social work program with single mothers who have children with severe disabilities; (l) Maternity Leave for Working Women (1974); (m) paid leave to accompany family members and relatives to medical appointments; (n) Education-Health-FMC (Cuban Women's Federation) Joint Resolution and the creation of children's houses in UBPC (basic units of production), CPA (cooperatives), in sugar mills and in fishing companies; (o) open, flexible schedules in some centers; (p) flexibility in the selection of vacations and special attention given to women with small children so they could leave during weeks of school recess and holiday periods and (q) increase of telecommuting after the appearance and access of workers to new information and telecommunications technologies, which allows spatial flexibility to execute work, among other things.
11. Despite the precarious conditions which contributed to the legitimacy given to this discourse, this job does not constitute a manifestation of slave labor per se, nor of a particular sociopolitical system. Even though it is almost always carried out in conditions of servitude ("this is one of the occupations where the deficit of decent work is greater and situations close to slavery still take place") (De Souza, 2010, p. 35), it has as a starting point an unequal relationship (economic, racial, territorial, gender, generational, etc.), the labor exploitation to which the workers of this sector are subject is sharpened by capitalism and has the peculiarity of being carried out in the private home of the person who contracts the services, which implies limitations to be controlled and inspected; domestic work is a work activity like others, in which a person sells his or her labor in exchange for remuneration in cash and/or in kind. This can be done in conditions of freedom, security and human dignity, that is, it can become a decent job.
12. Given this situation, access to these care services is prioritized for the children of women who have a formal employment relationship (preferably with State institutions) or care-dependent elderly people who do not have any relatives to care for them. While the arguments established to give priority to some cases over others are understandable, these can become counterproductive

factors to the intended reality of equity: first, because mothers who do not have formal employment cannot request this service and therefore they cannot be incorporated and because they cannot be incorporated, they cannot request it; so they are inserted in a vicious circle from which they cannot leave; second, because the policy is designed to give the responsibility of care to the family, since only in cases in which this institution cannot assume this responsibility does it take care of the well-being those who are in situations of dependency.

13. The average number of years out of the labor market among those who left temporarily to care for close relatives was 13 years.
14. Data from the National Institute of Economic Research (INIE) and the State Committee for Labor and Social Security show that in 1990 more than a quarter of the total population and more than a fifth of nuclear families had low incomes (up to 50 pesos) (Zabala, 2010, p. 83).
15. In this space there are more opportunities to find part-time or hourly jobs, even if they do not require their presence every day of the week.
16. Approval of this activity as a possible alternative within self-employment with Decree 141/93.
17. Mainly self-employed people who earned money by renting rooms to tourists or owners of *paladares* (private restaurants), people who received remittances from abroad or worked in the tourism sector, joint ventures or other companies that had this type of stimulation, among others.
18. This fact can have a close relationship with the levels of instruction attained.
19. A sign of the invisibility of power relations on which these relationships are based, which are often masked in the perception of familiarity that emerges from daily interaction and sharing of privacy.
20. It should be noted that although some specialists consider that conciliation policies are family policies of the third generation (Brullet, 2000, and Escobedo, 2000, in Torns, 2005, p. 20), the truth is that they were drafted essentially to promote female employment, rather than the transformation of family dynamics. They are almost always designed based on a patriarchal logic where the public world, paid work and production matter are the most important (Romero, 2014).

Bibliography

Aguilar, C., Popowski, P., & Verdeses, M. (1996). Mujer, Vida cotidiana y Período Especial. *Revista Temas, 5*, 11–17.

Asamblea Nacional del Poder Popular (ANNP). (2014). Ley 116/14 Código del Trabajo. In *Gaceta Oficial Extraordinaria No. 29 del 17 de junio de 2014.*

Banco Central de Cuba (BCC) (2001) Informe Económico. Havana, Cuba: BCC.

Benston, M. (1977). Para una economía política de la liberación femenina. *Revista La liberación de la mujer, Año Cero.*

Blanco, B. (2012). *No me puedo dejar: negociación y resistencia en el empleo doméstico, Tesis de Maestría en Antropología Social.* Chiapas, Mexico: Centro de Investigaciones y Estudios Superiores en Antropología Social.

Blanco, M. (2011). El enfoque del curso de vida: orígenes y desarrollo. *Revista Latinoamericana de Población, 5*(8), 5–31.

Campos, J. C. (2003). *El Sistema de Relaciones Sociales en el Trabajo: Principales categorías y conceptos.* Havana, Cuba: Centro de Investigaciones Psicológicas y Sociológicas.

Castillo, J. J. (1998). *A la búsqueda del trabajo perdido.* Madrid, Spain: Editorial Tecnos.

Delphi, C. (1982). El enemigo principal. *Cuadernos Inacabados, 2–3.*

De Souza, A (2010) Camino del trabajo decente para el personal del servicio doméstico: panorama de la labor de OIT Ginebra, Suiza: ILO.

Echevarría, D. (2013). Procesos de reajustes en Cuba y su impacto en el empleo femenino: entre dos siglos y repetidas desigualdades. In O. Pérez & R. Torres (Eds.), *Miradas a la economía cubana. Entre la eficiencia económica y la equidad social* (pp. 129–146). Havana, Cuba: Editorial Caminos.

Echevarria, D., Díaz, I., & Romero, M. (2015). Política de empleo en Cuba 2008 – 2013: desafíos a la equidad en Artemisa. *Revista CESLA, 18*, 271–294.

Echevarría, D., & Tejuca, M. (2015). Educación y empleo en Cuba 2000–2014: entre ajustes y desajustes. In M. Espina & D. Echevarría (Eds.), *Cuba: los correlatos socioculturales del cambio económico.* Havana, Cuba: Casa Ruth Editorial.

Edith, D. (2014). Código del Trabajo: aplausos… y alerta para nuevas leyes. Retrieved from http://cubaprofunda.org/artmeditar.php?ID=223

Elder, G. (1998). The Life Course as Developmental Theory. *Child Development, 1*, 1–12.

Espina, M. (2008). *Políticas de atención a la pobreza y la desigualdad.* Buenos Aires, Argentina: CLACSO.

Espina, M. (2012). Retos y cambios en la política social. In P. Vidal & O. E. Pérez (Eds.), *Miradas a la economía cubana. El proceso de actualización* (pp. 157–176). Havana, Cuba: Editorial Caminos.

Gaceta Oficial de la República de Cuba. (1978). *Decreto Ley 14/78 sobre el ejercicio de actividades laborales por cuenta propia.* Havana, Cuba: Empresa de Finanzas al día.

Gorban, D. (2012). Empleadas y empleadoras: tensiones de una relación atravesada por la ambigüedad. *Revista española de investigaciones sociológicas (REIS), 140*, 29–48.

ILO (International Labour Office). (2012). *Global Estimate of Forced Labour: Results and Methodology.* Geneva, Switzerland: ILO.

ILO (International Labour Office). (2013). *Domestic Workers Across the World: Global and Regional Statistics and the Extent of Legal Protection*. Geneva, Switzerland: ILO.

Instituto de Estudios e Investigaciones del Trabajo IEIT. (2004). *El empleo en Cuba. Síntesis.* Havana, Cuba: Fondo bibliográfico del centro.

International Labour Organization (ILO) (2010). *Nota 1: Trabajo decente para las trabajadoras domésticas remuneradas del continente*. Retrieved from http://www.oit.org.ar/WDMS/bib/publ/documentos/td_nota_oit_1.pdf

International Labour Organization (ILO) (OIT). (2011). *Convenio 189 sobre El Trabajo Doméstico*. Retrieved from http://www.ilo.org/dyn/normlex/es/f?p=NORMLEXPUB:12100:0::NO::P12100_INSTRUMENT_ID:2551460

Kofes, M. (2001). *Mulher, Mulheres-Identidade, diferença e desigualdade na relação entre patroas e empregadas*. Campinas-SP, Brazil: Ediciones UNICAMP.

Lautier, B. (2003). Las empleadas domésticas latinoamericanas y la sociología del trabajo: algunas observaciones acerca del caso brasileño. *Revista Mexicana de Sociología, 65*(4). Retrieved from http://www.scielo.org.mex/scielo.php?pid-*S0188-25032003000400003*&script-sci_arttext

Martín, J. L. (Ed.). (2000). *Reajuste y Trabajo en los 90*. Havana, Cuba: Centro de Investigaciones Psicológicas y Sociológicas (CIPS).

Martin, J. L. (2015). El toro por los cuernos: La necesaria transformación de las relaciones de trabajo en el país, como asignatura de la actualización del socialismo cubano. In M. Espina & D. Echevarría (Eds.), *Cuba; los correlatos socioeconómicos del cambio económico*. Havana, Cuba: Ciencias Sociales – Ruth Casa Editorial.

Mauro, A., & Yáñez, S. (2005). *Trayectoria laborales y previsión social en Chile en un contexto de flexibilidad. Resultados de una investigación longitudinal.* Santiago de Chile, Chile: Centro de Estudios de la Mujer.

Ministerio de Justicia (MINJUS). (2004). *Constitución de la República de Cuba.* Havana, Cuba: Combinado de Periódicos "Granma".

Ministerio de Justicia (MINJUS). (2011). *Gaceta Oficial No. 028 Extraordinaria Especial.* Havana. Cuba

Ministerio del Trabajo y de Seguridad Social (MINTRAB). (2014). *Informes Estadísticos (2010–2014)*. Havana, Cuba.

Partido Comunista de Cuba (PCC). (2011). *Lineamientos de la política económica y social del Partido y la Revolución*. Retrieved from http://www.granma.cu

Pérez, O. E. (2013). Análisis de la evolución reciente de la economía cubana. In O. E. Pérez & R. Torres (Eds.), *Miradas a la economía cubana. Entre la eficiencia económica y la equidad social* (pp. 15–28). Havana, Cuba: Editorial Caminos.

Romero, M. (2009). Trabajadoras domésticas no remuneradas a tiempo completo. Un estudio de su rol desde la perspectiva de género, Tesis de Maestría en Estudios de Género, Cátedra de la Mujer, Universidad de la Habana. Cuba.

Romero, M. (2010). Mujeres y trabajo doméstico no remunerado. Una reflexión latente en la Sociología del Trabajo Contemporánea, Tesis de Maestría en Sociología, Departamento de Sociología, Universidad de la Habana. Cuba.

Romero, M. (2014). Sobre la importancia de la conciliación con corresponsabilidad social: aspectos conceptuales (I). Retrieved from http://www.semlac.com

Romero, M. (2016). El trabajo doméstico remunerado a domicilio en Cuba. Un estudio de caso en Miramar, Tesis de Doctorado en Ciencias Sociológicas, Departamento de Sociología, Universidad de la Habana. Cuba

Romero, M. (2017). De lo simbólicamente exacto a lo simbólicamente verdadero. Domésticas y Revolución en Cuba: entre cambios y desafíos. In D. López, D. Ortega, L. Martín, M. Romero, & J. A. Monje (Eds.), *Cuba y América Latina: Los desafíos del legado revolucionario* (pp. 185–236). Buenos Aires, Argentina: CLACSO.

Torns, T. (2005). De la imposible conciliación a los permanentes malos arreglos. *Cuaderno de Relaciones Laborales, 23*, 015–033.

Torres, R. (2013). Algunas contradicciones del desarrollo económico cubano contemporáneo. In O. E. Pérez & R. Torres (Eds.), *Miradas a la economía cubana. Entre la eficiencia económica y la equidad social* (pp. 29–40). Havana, Cuba: Editorial Caminos.

Triana, J. (2012). De la actualización del funcionamiento al desarrollo económico. In P. Vidal & O. E. Pérez (Eds.), *Miradas a la economía cubana. El proceso de actualización* (pp. 17–26). Havana, Cuba: Editorial Caminos.

Zabala, M. C. (2010). *Familia y pobreza en Cuba. Estudio de casos.* Havana, Cuba: Publicaciones Acuario.

Zabala, M. C. (2013). Retos de la equidad social en el actual contexto de cambios económicos. In O. E. Pérez & R. Torres (Eds.), *Miradas a la economía cubana. Entre la eficiencia económica y la equidad social* (pp. 161–174). Havana, Cuba: Editorial Caminos.

CHAPTER 8

Conclusion: Final Reflections

María Eugenia Rausky and Mariana Chaves

The motivation to publish this book was to show how those who live in conditions of poverty and social vulnerability approach their work and the difficult task of everyday survival throughout their life courses, and particularly during childhood, youth and adulthood.

As mentioned in the introduction, the studies presented in the preceding chapters were developed during a period which saw a general reduction in the rates of poverty and extreme poverty in our region. The neoliberal government of Mexico and the socialist government of Cuba have remained in power, resulting in very different experiences of inequality for their respective populations, as seen in Chaps. 2 and 7. Argentina and Brazil, on the other hand, have undergone radical changes in government since the writing of this book: following a plethora of measures to extend social rights to vast sectors of society in both countries, the new

M. E. Rausky (✉)
CONICET, Facultad de Humanidades y Ciencias de la Educación,
Universidad Nacional de La Plata, La Plata, Buenos Aires, Argentina
e-mail: erausky@fahce.unlp.edu.ar

M. Chaves (✉)
CONICET, Facultad de Trabajo Social, Universidad Nacional de La Plata,
La Plata, Buenos Aires, Argentina
e-mail: mchaves@fcnym.unlp.edu.ar

M. E. Rausky, M. Chaves (eds.), *Living and Working in Poverty in Latin America*, Governance, Development, and Social Inclusion in Latin America, https://doi.org/10.1007/978-3-030-00901-4_8

governments have introduced sweeping public spending cuts and the reduction or abolition of measures to redistribute wealth. In both countries, there has been an acceleration in the transfer of wealth to the privileged classes and an outflow of resources to international financial entities. This had not yet occurred when the fieldwork for these studies was being carried out, giving us a more favorable context in which to untangle the relationship between poverty and work.

The life course perspective and analysis of work trajectories were used to analyze the subjects' complex relationships from the point of view of the actor (Menendez, 2010) in articulation with work and other dimensions which make up their lives. Some of the chapters are constructed entirely on the basis of interviews, while others add sources and participant observation, and still others (Chaps. 4 and 5) also include statistical data. These biographies are embedded in a time when debates in social science have criticized the uniformity of the life stages, advocating for a shift from a linear consensus to one of diversity, with conceptual and methodological consequences for the life course approach.

The productive effect of inequalities sustained by "a single mode of life course as a parameter" and overall advances in the recognition of cultural diversity and multiculturalism has opened eyes toward the visibility and legitimacy of other trajectories. It is now evident that some hegemonic life course models common to certain sectors of society had been projected to the detriment of others. Along these lines, we have attempted to contribute to the slow advance of the social processing of life course investigation, as life's challenges continue to be faced amidst diversity and inequality. In the context of cultural, technological and economic globalization, the horizons of the imaginable and the possible (Appadurai, 2001) are modified, extended, standardized and reproduced in a combination which, at least according to perception, is increasingly determined by the individual.

Another phenomenon observed by the different researchers was the continuing persistence of social polarization. The opportunities available to populations isolated from other social sectors are limited in both institutional and structural terms, making upward social mobility very difficult. The result is a tendency toward social polarization where the distance between richer and poorer sectors is increased, in spite of social policies of redistribution. Added to this panorama are other ruptures or changes to the linear concept of life courses, such as changes in the family and the formation of intimate relationships which no longer offer the "stability" of times past. Other changing dimensions are those of the entertainment circuit which has diversified along with the fashion, food and pharmaceutical industries, among others, offering constant niches of individuality and possibilities for growth and which paradoxically standardize the sector. It is worth noting that in Latin America where people frequently have a number of occupations and where professional identity is perceived less unambiguously than in other latitudes (Martuccelli, 2007), work trajectories are commonly less linear and more frequently ruptured by economic crises, changes of government and social policies, natural disasters and accidents at work, to name a few of the variables on different scales.

The results showcased in this compilation lead us to a series of final reflections, the objective of which is not only to enrich debate within the social sciences but also to inform policy-making. We believe that the input presented here could be useful in terms of some of the challenges of the 2030 Agenda for Sustainable Development and the corresponding Sustainable Development Goals (SDGs), especially those referring to the reduction of poverty (SDG 1), inequality (SDG 10), the promotion of decent work, the elimination of child labor (SDG 8) and gender equality (SDG 5).

As can be observed in all the cases under study, there is a long way to go despite improvements in global indicators showing reductions in inequality and poverty in the region. The trajectories analyzed show the persistence of a hard nucleus of the population in conditions of poverty, in some cases extreme poverty and/or social vulnerability, beyond the reach of both government social inclusion programs and specific social policies to reduce vulnerability. In countries where there was a historic absence of social intervention to reduce inequality and expand human rights, poverty was found to be a self-perpetuating cycle, with some conditions even worsening during the study period.

The process of cumulative disadvantage is shown in each of the chapters, which trace past, present and future life experiences to reveal how from an early age, conditions and experiences (family, education, work, migration, etc.) become reinforced, with the result of fixing subjects and sectors into subordinate positions in the social structure. Of course, these paths are not linear, there are "ups and downs," gray areas, "better" and "worse" moments; but it is certain that for most of the children, adolescents, youth and adult women interviewed, poverty began in infancy and continued through their life courses.

This compilation seeks to show the need to adjust the sweeping claim that the solution to poverty is "work." In Latin America, the need to develop different work activities for survival is a daily imperative since it is extremely difficult for a poor person to live without work or survive exclusively from the fragments of state payments (which we can read in a non-derogatory way as a right). In contrast to some European countries where state redistribution to the most vulnerable—such as the unemployed, disabled and refugees—could possibly compete with the search for active employment, in our region the ability to cover the most basic needs is severely limited without the different strategies that people invent to make a living. Work, in its multiple forms—whether domestic, rural, urban, care or any type of work—consists of something which guarantees daily survival. Within work, the factor which makes the greatest difference in terms of promoting equality is working conditions. Wages, social security and health cover, union membership, placement within the national system of production and social legitimacy are some of the elements outlined in the preceding chapters which exercise a major influence over social mobility and overcoming inequality.

Work often begins at an early age. As we have insisted, it is not the work in itself, but rather the material and symbolic conditions of the work on a structural, institutional and individual scale which make certain jobs unfavorable and tend to be reproduced further on in the trajectory. The cases studied and dialogue with research on other sectors of poverty showed that while opportunities for self-employment or insertion as employees were available, they involved precarious and informal conditions. In the vast majority of the cases analyzed, there was little social recognition and the work was severely undervalued, sometimes even by the subjects themselves. However, the other side of this gray panorama shows the enormous capacity of these individuals for hard work and their contribution to the process of accumulation as well as the use of resources, strategies, processes of collective organization, family, social and sometimes political networks—all forms of agency that children, young people and adult women use to survive despite the limitations of their positions within the mode of production.

Many of the subjects represented in these pages related their future projects and dreams of a tomorrow that is at least "a little better" than the present. The challenge to finish primary and secondary school for children, adolescents and youth or the opportunity to access training for some youth and adult women is seen as "the opportunity" to access better living conditions by means of a job which guarantees a better relative position. Perhaps the job could be more easily obtained with educational qualifications, but the conversion of education and training capital into economic capital is by no means easy for this sector. The imaginary job is in many cases connected to a traditional image of work with security, stability, regular income, access to health care and other social rights which are at best uneven and often nonexistent.

Gender, work and poverty also form part of most of the chapters of this book. Gender inequalities evolve and solidify from an early age: girls, adolescents and young women accumulate experiences and unfavorable opportunities (including care tasks) assigned to women as part of the social organization of work. The persistence of the double working day—in and outside the home—the difficulty in reconciling work opportunities with family dynamics and the weight of traditional gender stereotypes severely affect the range of labor trajectories possible for women.

Finally, in countries like Cuba and Brazil, racism was found to be a factor which affects trajectories, where in addition to the inequalities of class and gender, individuals suffer discrimination based on the color of their skin. This historically accumulated overlap continues to reproduce social conditions of exploitation and subordination, which makes the issue of Black people's social integration a key dimension in the analysis of inequality, poverty and work. Along with Cuba and Brazil, Mexico and Argentina share what has been termed the "racialization of class relations" (Margulis, 1999) where class is read, named and stigmatized in terms of racial phenotypes. This racialization takes two overlapping forms: on one hand, colonial forms of domination which have remained largely unchanged over time, and on the other hand, the specific and diverse structure of social relations, class and racial discrimination in each country. This phenomenon was described by Anibal Quijano (2014) as the colonialization of power, as something which has always been with us and which takes its most explicit form in the racist treatment of diverse ethnic groups. Even today we still need to remind those who narrate history from the colonial perspective that we inhabited these lands thousands of years before they arrived and that our physical features have never been white.

Finally, in conclusion, this book aims to show that the widespread idea that poverty can be overcome "with work" and/or through "individual effort" is contradicted by the empirical evidence of each chapter. People who live in poverty work and make enormous efforts, both objectively and subjectively; yet in spite of this, their vulnerable conditions remain and are reinforced. This is nothing new, but unfortunately this reality is frequently overlooked in the development of social policies to promote equality. Achieving the SDGs must necessarily involve overcoming historical disadvantage by means of political will and serious investment. Exploitative, low-paid work must be transformed into registered employment with decent wages, social security and child care and be accompanied by fundamental changes in infrastructure and housing policies. Unless significant structural changes are made in our societies, the perpetuation of poverty and inequality for a large sector of the population will continue.

Bibliography

Appadurai, A. (2001). *La modernidad desbordada. Dimensiones culturales de la globalización*. Mexico City, Mexico: Fondo de Cultura Económica.

Margulis, M. (1999). La 'racializacion' de las relaciones de clase. In M. Margulis & M. Urresti (Eds.), *La segregación negada: Cultura y discriminación social*. Buenos Aires, Argentina: Biblos.

Martuccelli, D. (2007). *Cambio de rumbo: La sociedad a escala del individuo*. Santiago de Chile, Chile: LOM Ediciones.

Menendez, E. (2010). *La parte negada de la cultura. Relativismo, diferencias y racismo*. Rosario, Argentina: Prohistoria.

Quijano, A. (2014). *Cuestiones y horizontes: de la dependencia histórico-estructural a la colonialidad/descolonialidad del poder*. City of Buenos Aires, Argentina: CLACSO.

INDEX[1]

[1] Note: Page numbers followed by 'n' refer to notes.

M. E. Rausky, M. Chaves (eds.), *Living and Working in Poverty in Latin America*, Governance, Development, and Social Inclusion in Latin America, https://doi.org/10.1007/978-3-030-00901-4

The manufacturer's authorised representative in the EU is Springer Nature Customer Service Centre GmbH, Europaplatz 3, 69115 Heidelberg, Germany. If you have any concerns regarding our products, please contact ProductSafety@springernature.com

Printed and bound by CPI Group (UK) Ltd, Croydon, CR0 4YY

30/09/2026

02225442-0002